# CONTENTS

# INTRODUCTION

In the tapestry of life, each day is a thread, woven together to create a masterpiece. As women, we often find ourselves in the role of weavers, crafting the intricate patterns of our families, careers, relationships, and dreams. In this beautiful and sometimes chaotic process, it's easy to lose sight of the bigger picture.

But here's the glorious truth: every thread counts, and every day matters.

Welcome to "365 Days of Inspiration: A Devotional for Women." This is not just a book; it's an invitation to embark on a transformative journey—a journey that will illuminate your path, uplift your spirit, and inspire your heart for the next 365 days.
Each dawn brings a fresh canvas, and within the pages of this devotional, you will discover a daily source of light, wisdom, and encouragement. Whether you are a mother nurturing a family, a professional chasing your dreams, a friend seeking connection, or a soul longing for purpose, there is a place for you here.

## The Essence of Inspiration

Inspiration is a flame that ignites the soul, a gentle breeze that fills your sails, and a quiet whisper that says, "You are capable, you are loved, and you are enough." In every sunrise, every smile, and every act of kindness, inspiration dances.
It's found in the laughter of children, the beauty of nature, the wisdom of mentors, and the power of faith. Inspiration is both a gift and a choice—a gift we receive from the Divine and a choice we make each day to embrace its transformative power.

## Let us pray:

Heavenly Father, as we embark on this devotional journey together, we ask for your guidance and presence in every word and reflection. May these pages be a source of inspiration, transformation, and deep connection with you. Bless each woman who reads these words, and may this devotional become a guiding light in their lives. In Jesus Name, we pray. Amen.

# JANUARY

*"In the beginning, God created the world from chaos, and in the midst of darkness, He spoke light into existence. Just as He brought order and brilliance to the formless void, so too can He bring purpose and radiance to our lives. Trust in His divine plan, for in every beginning, there is the potential for a beautiful and transformative story to unfold." - Genesis 1:1-3*

## DAY 01
## Day of New Beginnings

"Therefore, if anyone is in Christ, the new creation has come: The old has gone, the new is here!" - 2 Corinthians 5:17 (NIV)

Dear Sister in Christ Jesus,

Today is a day of new beginnings, a day when the old fades away, and the promise of the new bursts forth like the first rays of dawn. It is a day when the Creator of the universe, the Master Artist, offers you a fresh canvas to paint the masterpiece of your life.

In 2 Corinthians 5:17, we are reminded that in Christ, we are made new. It's a profound transformation that goes beyond the surface, deeper than appearances. It's the renewal of your heart, the rejuvenation of your spirit, and the rebirth of your soul. This transformation is not just a momentary change but a lifelong journey of becoming more like Christ.

Additional Scripture Reference:

*"Forget the former things; do not dwell on the past. See, I am doing a new thing! Now it springs up; do you not perceive it? I am making a way in the wilderness and streams in the wasteland." - Isaiah 43:18-19 (NIV)*

**Action Plan:**

1. Spend time in prayer, asking God to reveal areas of your life that need His renewal.

5

2. Write down any past burdens or regrets on a piece of paper, and symbolically release them to God by tearing up or burning the paper.

3. Reflect on the newness of life in Christ and journal about your hopes and dreams for this fresh beginning.

**Prayer:**

*Heavenly Father, we thank You for the promise of new beginnings in Christ. We surrender our past, our regrets, and our burdens to You today. Renew our hearts, O Lord, and help us walk in the fullness of Your grace. May this day be the start of a remarkable journey filled with faith, hope, and love. In Jesus name, we pray. Amen.*

## DAY 02
# Embracing God's Grace

"But he said to me, 'My grace is sufficient for you, for my power is made perfect in weakness.' Therefore, I will boast all the more gladly about my weaknesses, so that Christ's power may rest on me." - 2 Corinthians 12:9 (NIV)

God's grace is like an ocean, vast and deep, overflowing with love and mercy. It is a gift freely given to us, not because of our merits, but because of His boundless compassion. Embracing God's grace is acknowledging that we are imperfect, but in our imperfection, we find His strength and sufficiency.

**Action Steps:**

1. Reflect on Your Weaknesses: Take time to identify areas in your life where you feel inadequate or weak. Surrender these weaknesses to God and trust in His sufficiency.

2. Practice Self-Compassion: Just as God extends grace to you, learn to extend grace to yourself. Release the burden of perfectionism and accept that you are loved as you are.

3. Share Your Story: Don't be afraid to share your testimonies of God's grace with others. Your vulnerability can inspire and encourage those who are struggling.

**Prayer:**

## DAY 03

## Finding Strength In Weakness

In 2 Corinthians 12, Paul quotes Jesus who said, "My grace is sufficient for you, for my power is made perfect in weakness." God is perfect in every way, giving Him the power to make up for any weaknesses we have. And we have a lot.

In the beautifully penned words of Ephesians 2:8, we are reminded of a profound truth—a truth that has the power to reshape our perspective on weakness. It says, "For by grace you have been saved through faith, and that not of yourselves; it is the gift of God." This scripture teaches us that our salvation, our very connection to the Divine, is a gift freely given, not earned through our strength or merit.

*It is in acknowledging our weakness that we discover the incredible strength of God's grace. Our human nature often seeks to hide our vulnerabilities, to appear strong and self-sufficient. However, it is precisely in our moments of weakness that God's grace shines most brilliantly.*

**Action Plan:**

1. Embrace Vulnerability: Take a moment to reflect on areas of your life where you have felt weak or vulnerable. Don't shy away from these feelings; instead, acknowledge them as opportunities for God's grace to abound.

2. Seek God's Strength: When faced with challenges or difficulties, turn to God in prayer. Ask Him for His strength to carry you through, trusting that His grace is sufficient.

3. Encourage Others: Share your experiences of finding strength in weakness with someone you trust. Encourage them to also seek God's grace in their times of need.

**Prayer:**

*Heavenly Father, we thank You for the gift of Your grace, which strengthens us in our moments of weakness. Help us embrace vulnerability as an opportunity to experience Your power and love. May we trust in Your sufficiency and lean on Your grace in every aspect of our lives. In Jesus name, we pray. Amen.*

## DAY 04
## The Power Of Forgiveness

"For if you forgive other people when they sin against you, your heavenly Father will also forgive you. But if you do not forgive others their sins, your Father will not forgive your sins." - Matthew 6:14-15 (NIV)

Forgiveness is a profound act of love and liberation, a divine gift that not only transforms the lives of others but also our own hearts. In Matthew 6:14-15, we are given a powerful reminder of the significance of forgiveness in our spiritual journey.

Additional Scripture Reference:

*"Bear with each other and forgive one another if any of you has a grievance against someone. Forgive as the Lord forgave you." - Colossians 3:13 (NIV)*

**Action Plan:**

1. Reflect on Forgiveness: Take time to reflect on any unresolved conflicts or grudges in your life. Pray for the strength to forgive those who have wronged you.

2. Seek Reconciliation: If it's safe and possible, consider reaching out to the person you need to forgive or seek forgiveness from. Communication can be a powerful step toward healing.

3. Practice Self-Forgiveness: Remember that forgiveness extends to yourself as well. Let go of self-blame and guilt, knowing that God's grace covers your shortcomings.

**Prayer:**

*Heavenly Father, we thank You for the profound gift of forgiveness. Help us to forgive others as You have forgiven us, releasing the burdens that weigh down our hearts. May Your grace flow through us, bringing healing and reconciliation to our lives. In Jesus name, we pray. Amen.*

## DAY 05
## Cultivating Inner Peace

"Do not be anxious about anything, but in every situation, by prayer and petition, with thanksgiving, and present your request to God. And the peace of God, which transcends all understanding, will guide your heart and your mind in Christ Jesus." - Philippians 4:6-7 ( NIV)

Philippians 4:6-7 invites us into a profound journey of cultivating inner peace. It encourages us not to be anxious about anything but, instead, to bring our concerns to God through prayer, petition, and thanksgiving. As we do, a remarkable transformation occurs—God's peace, which transcends human comprehension, becomes our guard and refuge.

Additional Scripture Reference:

*"You will keep in perfect peace those whose minds are steadfast because they trust in you." - Isaiah 26:3 (NIV)*

**Action Plan:**

1. Create a Peaceful Space: Designate a quiet place where you can spend time in prayer and reflection. This space can become your sanctuary of peace.

2. Practice Gratitude: Each day, take a moment to thank God for His blessings, both big and small. Cultivating a thankful heart paves the way for inner peace.

3. Pray Specifically: When faced with anxieties or worries, present them to God in prayer, naming them specifically. Trust that He hears and cares about your concerns.

**Prayer:**

*Heavenly Father, we come before You with hearts burdened by the cares of this world. We thank You for the promise of Your peace, which transcends all understanding. Help us to cultivate inner peace by entrusting our anxieties to You through prayer and thanksgiving. Guard our hearts and minds in Christ Jesus, and may Your peace be our constant companion. In Jesus name, we pray. Amen.*

# DAY 06
# Unleashing Your Potential

"For I know the plans I have for you, declare the Lord, plans for welfare not of evil, give you a future and a hope." - Jeremiah 29:11 (ESV)

Within each one of us lies a wellspring of untapped potential, waiting to be unleashed. In Jeremiah 29:11, God's promise to us is revealed: He knows the plans He has for us, plans filled with hope and a future. This promise is an affirmation that our Creator has uniquely designed us for purpose, significance, and impact.

*Consider this promise as a gentle whisper to your heart: You have potential beyond measure, and your life has a divine purpose. Embrace it with courage and confidence.*

Additional Scripture Reference:

"For we are his workmanship, created in Christ Jesus for good works, which God prepared beforehand, that we should walk in them." - Ephesians 2:10 (ESV)

**Action Plan:**

1. Self-Reflection: Spend time in quiet reflection, seeking to understand your passions, talents, and dreams. What stirs your heart? What talents do you possess?

2. Seek God's Guidance: In prayer, ask God to reveal His plans and purpose for your life. Listen for His still, small voice, and be open to His leading.

3. Set Goals: Based on your reflection and prayer, set achievable goals that align with your potential and God's purpose for you.

**Prayer:**

*Heavenly Father, we thank You for the promise of a future filled with hope and purpose. Help us to recognize the potential within us, which is a gift from You. Guide us, Lord, in unleashing our potential for Your glory and the well-being of others. May we walk confidently in the plans You have prepared for us. In Jesus name, we pray. Amen.*

## DAY 07

## Courage In Times Of Fear

"Fear not for I am with you; be not dismayed, for I am your God; I will strengthen you, I will help, I will uphold you with my righteous hand." - Isaiah 41:10 (ESV)

Fear is a powerful and pervasive emotion that can often grip our hearts and minds. It can make us feel small, vulnerable, and powerless. But in the midst of fear, there is a profound promise from our Heavenly Father—one that assures us of His unwavering presence and steadfast support.

*Isaiah 41:10 reminds us not to be afraid, for God is with us. It's a declaration that resonates with the deepest parts of our being. In moments of fear, it's as if the Almighty Himself reaches out and says, "You are not alone. I am here with you."*

Additional Scripture Reference:

"When I am afraid, I put my trust in you." - Psalm 56:3 (ESV)

**Action Plan:**

1. Identify Your Fears: Take time to reflect on your fears and anxieties. Write them down and acknowledge them.

2. Prayer and Surrender: In prayer, present your fears to God. Surrender them to His care and trust that He is in control.

3. Meditate on Scripture: Choose a verse or passage that speaks to courage and trust, like Psalm 56:3. Memorise it and meditate on it daily.

**Prayer:**

*Heavenly Father, we come before You with our fears and anxieties, knowing that in Your presence, fear has no place. Strengthen us, Lord, in times of fear, and help us to trust in Your unfailing love and protection. Uphold us with Your righteous right hand, and grant us the courage to face our fears with faith. In Jesus name, we pray. Amen.*

## DAY 08
## Nurturing A Grateful Heart

"Give thanks in all circumstances; for this is the will of God in Christ Jesus for you."
1 Thessalonians 5:18 ( ESN)

Gratitude is more than a fleeting feeling of contentment; it's a deliberate choice to recognize and appreciate the blessings, both big and small, that grace our lives. It's an acknowledgment that every day, regardless of the circumstances, holds moments of beauty and grace that are worthy of our thanks.

**Action Plan:**

1. Daily Gratitude Journal: Begin each day by jotting down at least three things you are thankful for. This practice can help you cultivate a habit of gratitude.

2. Express Your Thanks: Take time to express your gratitude to those who have impacted your life positively. A simple "thank you" can brighten someone's day.

3. Pray with Gratitude: During your daily prayers, include a segment where you express your gratitude to God for His blessings, love, and faithfulness.

**Prayer:**

Heavenly Father, we thank You for the precious gift of gratitude. Help us nurture thankful hearts, even in challenging circumstances. Teach us to see the beauty in the everyday, to appreciate Your blessings, and to express our thanks to You and to those around us. May gratitude be a guiding light in our lives, drawing us closer to Your will and Your presence. In Jesus name, we pray. Amen.

DAY 09

## Trusting God's Timing

"Wait for the Lord; be strong, and let your heart take courage; wait for the Lord."
Psalm 27:14 (ESN)

In the tapestry of life, patience is often the thread that weaves together our hopes and dreams. It can be challenging to understand why certain things take longer than expected or why we encounter delays and setbacks. Yet, in the midst of uncertainty, we find a profound reassurance in Psalm 27:14—to wait for the Lord.

*Waiting is not merely an exercise in passing time; it's an opportunity to cultivate trust. It's an invitation to surrender our timelines and expectations to the One who knows the beginning from the end. When we wait for the Lord, we acknowledge that His timing is perfect, and His plans are filled with wisdom and love.*

**Action Plan:**

1. Surrender Control: In prayer, surrender your desire for control and your own timelines to God. Trust that His timing is for your ultimate good.

2. Seek God's Guidance: Seek God's wisdom in your decisions and actions. Ask Him for discernment to know when to act and when to wait.

3. Practice Patience: In moments of frustration or impatience, remind yourself of Psalm 27:14. Take a deep breath and allow God's peace to fill your heart.

**Prayer:**

*Heavenly Father, we thank You for the reminder to wait for You in Psalm 27:14. Help us to trust Your timing, even when we cannot see the full picture. Grant us patience and courage as we wait, knowing that Your plans are perfect and Your love is unfailing. May our hearts find rest in Your sovereign hands. In Jesus name, we pray. Amen.*

## DAY 10
## God's Unconditional Love

"For I am convinced that neither death nor life, neither angels nor demons, neither the present nor the future, nor any powers, neither height nor depth, nor anything else in all creation, will be able to separate us from the love that is in Christ Jesus our Lord."
Romans 8:38-39 (NIV)

In the vast expanse of our experience, there is no force more profound, more enduring, and more transformative than the love of God. It is a love that transcends all barriers and defies all logic. In Romans 8:38-39, we find a resounding declaration that nothing, absolutely nothing, can separate us from this extraordinary love.

*Consider the depths of God's love as an ocean without bounds. It reaches to the highest peaks of our joys and the lowest valleys of our sorrows. It embraces us in moments of triumph and comforts us in times of despair. This love is constant, unchanging, and unwavering.*

## Action Plan:

1. Reflect on God's Love: Take time each day to meditate on Romans 8:38-39. Let these verses remind you of the unshakable love that surrounds you.

2. Practice Self-Love: Recognize that God's love for you is unconditional. Practice self-compassion and self-acceptance, knowing that you are loved just as you are.

3. Extend Love to Others: Emulate God's love by showing kindness and compassion to those around you. Be a vessel of His love to others in both your words and actions.

**Prayer:**

*Heavenly Father, we thank You for the boundless and unconditional love You have lavished upon us. In moments of doubt and insecurity, remind us of Romans 8:38-39, that nothing can separate us from Your love. Help us to live in the assurance of Your love, to extend it to others, and to carry it as a beacon of hope in this world. In Jesus name, we pray. Amen.*

## DAY 11
## Pursuing True Joy

Psalm 16:11 invites us to embark on a different kind of pursuit—an eternal pursuit of true joy. It says, "You make known to me the path of life; in your presence there is fullness of joy; at your right hand are pleasures forevermore" (ESV). This verse reminds us that true joy is not found in the external, but in our relationship with God.

*True joy is not a fleeting emotion; it's a state of being that transcends circumstances. It's an inner contentment that comes from knowing our Creator and walking in His presence. In God's presence, we discover a joy that is deep, abiding, and unshakable.*

**Action Plan:**

1. Prioritise Time with God: Set aside dedicated moments each day for prayer, meditation, and reading Scripture. Seek to deepen your relationship with God and experience His presence.

2. Practice Gratitude: Cultivate a habit of gratitude by daily reflecting on the blessings in your life. A thankful heart opens the door to joy.

3. Serve Others: Engage in acts of kindness and service to those in need. There is immense joy in giving and helping others.

**Prayer:**

*Heavenly Father, we come before You with a longing for true joy. We thank You for revealing that in Your presence, there is fullness of joy. Help us prioritise our relationship with You, cultivate gratitude, serve others, and savour the beauty of each moment. May our trust in Your plan fill our hearts with the abiding joy that comes from knowing You. In Jesus name, we pray. Amen.*

## DAY 12
## A Human Heart Of Humility

"Humble yourselves in the presence of the Lord, He will exalt you." - James 4:10 (NASB)

In a world that often celebrates self-promotion and self-reliance, the concept of humility can seem counterintuitive. Yet, James 4:10 invites us to embrace the transformative power of humility, a virtue that not only deepens our relationship with God but also enriches our interactions with others.

*Humility is not about thinking less of yourself; it's about thinking of yourself less. It is the recognition that our worth and identity are rooted in Christ, not in worldly achievements or accolades. A heart of humility acknowledges our dependence on God and the need for His guidance and grace in our lives.*

**Action Plan:**

1. Self-Reflection: Set aside time for self-reflection. Examine your attitudes and actions to identify areas where pride may be hindering your growth in humility.

2. Practice Active Listening: In your interactions with others, practice active listening. Seek to understand their perspectives before expressing your own.

3. Serve Others: Look for opportunities to serve without seeking recognition. Acts of kindness and service are powerful expressions of humility.

**Prayer:**

*Heavenly Father, we come before You with humble hearts, recognizing our need for Your grace and guidance. Teach us the beauty of humility, help us to think of ourselves less and others more. May our actions and words reflect the gentle strength of humility, and may You exalt us in Your perfect way and timing. In Jesus name, we pray. Amen.*

## DAY 13
## Walking In Faith, Not By Sight

"For we walk by faith not by sight."- 2 Corinthians 5:7 (ESN)

Life often presents us with a paradox—a tension between what we see with our physical eyes and what we believe in our hearts. In 2 Corinthians 5:7, we are reminded of the profound truth that as followers of Christ, we are called to walk by faith, not by sight.

*Walking by faith is not the absence of doubt or fear but the decision to press on despite them. It's the confidence that God is with you every step of the way, guiding you through the storms and valleys of life. It's the conviction that His promises are true and that His love is unwavering.*

**Action Plan:**

1. Daily Devotion: Begin each day with prayer and Scripture reading to strengthen your faith. Focus on passages that remind you of God's faithfulness and love.

2. Challenge Doubts: When doubts and fears arise, confront them with the truth of God's Word. Meditate on verses that speak to His promises and sovereignty.

3. Step Out in Faith: Identify an area in your life where you need to step out in faith. It could be a decision, a dream, or an opportunity. Trust that God is guiding you.

**Prayer:**

*Heavenly Father, we thank You for the call to walk by faith, not by sight. Help us to trust in Your unfailing love and promises, even when our circumstances seem uncertain. Increase our faith, Lord, and give us the courage to step out in faith, believing that You are with us every step of the way. In Jesus name, we pray. Amen.*

DAY 14

## Finding Comfort In Suffering

"For I consider the suffering of this present time are not worth comparing with the glory that is to be revealed to us." - Romans 8:18 (ESN)

In this verse, the apostle Paul encourages us to consider the sufferings of this present time in light of the glory that will be revealed to us. It's a reminder that our sufferings, while real and often painful, are temporary when compared to the eternal glory that awaits us in Christ. This perspective shifts our focus from the immediate pain to the ultimate hope.

*Finding comfort in suffering means recognizing that God is with us in our pain. It means trusting that He can work through our trials to bring about something beautiful and redemptive. It's an invitation to anchor our hope in His promises, knowing that He will bring us through the storms of life.*

**Action Plan:**

1. Seek God's Presence: In moments of suffering, turn to God in prayer. Seek His comfort, knowing that He is near to the brokenhearted (Psalm 34:18).

2. Focus on Eternal Perspective: Reflect on the truth that your suffering is temporary. Meditate on passages that speak of God's promises and the hope of eternity.

3. Daily Hope: Each day, commit to finding at least one thing to be thankful for, even in the midst of suffering. Maintain a journal of gratitude to remind yourself of God's faithfulness.

**Prayer:**

*Heavenly Father, we come before You in our times of suffering, seeking comfort and hope. Help us to trust in Your eternal perspective and to find solace in the promise of glory that awaits us. May Your presence be our refuge, and may we draw strength from Your unwavering love. In Jesus name, we pray. Amen.*

## DAY 15
## Surrendering Control To God

"Trust in the Lord with all your heart, and do not learn in your own understanding, in all your ears acknowledge Him, and He will make straight your paths." - Proverbs 3:5-6 (ESN)

In a world that often encourages self-sufficiency and control, the concept of surrender can be challenging. Yet, in Proverbs 3:5-6, we find a profound invitation—to trust in the Lord with all our hearts and to relinquish the need to rely solely on our own understanding. It's an invitation to surrender control to God, a journey that leads to deeper faith, peace, and alignment with His divine plan.

*Surrendering control means acknowledging our limitations and recognizing that God's wisdom far surpasses our own. It's an act of humility and trust that opens the door to God's guidance and intervention in our lives. In surrender, we release the burdens of trying to orchestrate every aspect of our existence and invite God to take the lead.*

**Action Plan:**

1. Seek God's Will: In prayer, ask God for His guidance and wisdom in decision-making. Seek His will above your own desires.

2. Let Go of Worry: When worries and anxieties arise, consciously release them to God. Trust that He is in control and that His plans are for your good.

3. Study Scripture: Explore passages in the Bible that speak to surrender and trust in God's providence. Meditate on these verses regularly.

**Prayer:**

Heavenly Father, we come before You with hearts willing to surrender control. We trust in Your wisdom, your love, and your plan for our lives. Help us to let go of our own understanding and to acknowledge You in all our ways. Guide us, Lord, and make our paths straight. In Jesus name, we pray. Amen.

## DAY 16
## Living In A Life Of Generosity

"Each one must give has he has decided in his, not reluctantly or under compulsion, for God loves a cheerful giver." - 2 Corinthians 9:7 (ESV)

Generosity is a virtue that radiates the very heart of God. It's a disposition of selflessness, a willingness to give freely, and a recognition that all we have ultimately belongs to our Heavenly Father. In 2 Corinthians 9:7, we are reminded of the essence of true generosity—a cheerful and willing heart.

*Generosity is not driven by compulsion or obligation; it flows from a heart transformed by gratitude and love. It's a response to the boundless generosity of our Heavenly Father, who gave His Son for our salvation. When we give with a cheerful heart, we emulate the very nature of God, who delights in giving good gifts to His children.*

**Action Plan:**

1. Reflect on God's Generosity: Begin by meditating on God's generosity in your own life. Consider the ways He has blessed you and express gratitude in your prayers.

2. Pray for a Generous Heart: Ask God to cultivate a heart of generosity within you. Pray for opportunities to give and serve others.

3. Identify Areas of Giving: Reflect on the areas in which you can be more generous—whether it's with your time, resources, or talents. Set specific goals for giving.

**Prayer:**

*Heavenly Father, we thank You for the generosity You have shown us through the gift of Your Son, Jesus Christ. Teach us to live lives of generosity, giving freely and cheerfully to* others. Cultivate in us a heart that overflows with compassion and love for those in need. May our generosity be a reflection of Your boundless grace. In Jesus name, we pray. Amen.

## DAY 17
## Overcoming Life's Obstacles

"I can do all things through Christ who strengthens me." - Philippians 4:13

This verse is a beacon of hope, a declaration that we are not alone in our struggles. It's an assurance that we are connected to a wellspring of divine power that enables us to press on, even when we feel weak or inadequate. It's an invitation to partner with God, drawing on His limitless strength to overcome whatever obstacles stand in our way.

*Overcoming life's obstacles doesn't mean the absence of difficulties; it means facing them with a spirit of courage and determination, knowing that we are strengthened by the One who has conquered all. It's about shifting our focus from our limitations to Christ's unlimited power.*

**Action Plan:**

1. Meditate on God's Word: Spend time daily meditating on Scripture, especially verses that remind you of God's strength. Let His Word renew your mind and perspective.

2. Prayer for Strength: In your prayers, ask God for His strength to face specific obstacles in your life. Seek His guidance and empowerment.

3. Break Challenges into Steps: When faced with a daunting obstacle, break it into smaller, manageable steps. Focus on one step at a time, trusting God for each.

**Prayer:**

*Heavenly Father, we thank You for the promise of Philippians 4:13—that through Christ, we can do all things. Strengthen us, Lord, in times of difficulty and uncertainty. Help us to face life's obstacles with courage, knowing that Your empowering strength is with us. May Your name be glorified as we overcome challenges and grow in faith. In Jesus name, we pray. Amen.*

## Cultivating Patience

"And let us not throw weary of doing good, for in due season we will reap, if we do not give up." - Galatians 6:9 (ESV)

Patience is a virtue that often feels elusive in our fast-paced world. In the face of challenges, delays, and setbacks, we may find ourselves growing weary and discouraged. However, Galatians 6:9 offers a profound reminder—a call to cultivate patience, to persevere in doing good, and to trust that in due season, we will reap a harvest of blessings if we do not give up.

*Cultivating patience is an act of faith, a willingness to trust in God's timing and to continue sowing seeds of kindness and goodness, even when we cannot see immediate results. It's an acknowledgment that God's plans often unfold gradually and that the fullness of His blessings may require seasons of waiting.*

**Action Plan:**

1. Daily Reflection: Begin each day with a moment of reflection. Consider areas in your life where patience is needed and ask God for His guidance.

2. Practice Patience: In your interactions with others, consciously practice patience. Seek to understand their perspectives and be slow to anger or frustration.

3. Set Goals: Identify specific areas where you struggle with patience. Set achievable goals for improvement in those areas.

**Prayer:**

*Heavenly Father, we come before You with a desire to cultivate patience in our lives. Teach us to trust in Your timing, to persevere in doing good, and to wait with hope for the harvest of blessings You have prepared. May we not grow weary, knowing that in due season, we will reap a bountiful harvest. In Jesus name, we pray. Amen.*

DAY 19
## Encouraging Others

"Therefore encourage one another and build one another up, just as you are doing." - 1 Thessalonians 5:11 (ESV)

Encouraging others is a reflection of the love that God has poured into our hearts. It's an extension of His grace and compassion to those around us. When we encourage, we offer a ray of hope to those who may be walking through difficult seasons. It's a simple yet profound way of demonstrating God's love in action.

*1 Thessalonians 5:11 calls us not only to encourage but also to build up one another. This involves investing in the growth and well-being of those around us. It's about nurturing the potential in others, fostering their self-esteem, and helping them reach their full God-given potential.*

**Action Plan:**

1. Daily Affirmation: Begin each day by affirming your intention to encourage and build up others. Ask God to guide your words and actions.

2. Active Listening: Practice active listening when others speak. Seek to understand their thoughts and feelings before offering encouragement.

3. Prayer for Encouragement: In your daily prayers, ask God to use you as a source of encouragement in the lives of those you encounter.

**Prayer:**

*Heavenly Father, we thank You for the gift of encouragement. Teach us to be channels of Your love and grace, that we may uplift and build up one another. May our words and actions reflect Your kindness and compassion. Use us, Lord, to be sources of hope and strength to those in need. In Jesus name, we pray. Amen.*

## DAY 20
## Resting In God's Promises

"Let us hold fast the confession of our hope without wavering, for He who promised is Faithful." - Hebrews 10:23 (ESV)

God's promises, scattered throughout the pages of Scripture, are declarations of His character and His intentions toward His children. They assure us of His unchanging love, His steadfast presence, and His divine plan for our lives. When we rest in His promises, we find solace in the knowledge that His Word is true and His faithfulness is unwavering.

*Resting in God's promises is not passive; it's an active choice to trust in His Word, even when circumstances may suggest otherwise. It's a declaration that we believe in His faithfulness, even in the face of doubt or adversity. It's an invitation to anchor our hope in His unwavering character.*

**Action Plan:**

1. Daily Scripture Reading: Begin each day by reading and meditating on a promise from God's Word. Let His promises be a source of strength and encouragement.

2. Declare God's Promises: Speak God's promises over your life, especially during challenging moments. Declare His faithfulness and trust in His Word.

3. Prayer for Faith: In your daily prayers, ask God to deepen your faith in His promises and to help you rest in His unwavering character.

**Prayer:**

*Heavenly Father, we thank You for the richness of Your promises. Teach us to rest in Your Word, to hold fast to the confession of our hope, and to trust in Your unwavering faithfulness. May Your promises be a source of strength and hope in every season of our lives. In Jesus name, we pray. Amen.*

## DAY 21
## The Beauty Of Contentment

"But godliness with contentment is great gain."
1 Timothy 6:6 (ESV)

In a world that often encourages us to chase after more—more possessions, more success, more recognition—1 Timothy 6:6 reminds us of the profound beauty and wisdom found in contentment. It declares that godliness coupled with contentment is of great gain. The beauty of contentment lies in the deep peace and fulfilment it brings to our hearts.

*Contentment is the antidote to the restlessness that often plagues our culture. It's a declaration that true wealth is not measured by possessions but by the richness of a life lived in God's presence. It's an acknowledgment that joy is not found in the pursuit of more but in gratitude for what we already have.*

**Action Plan:**

1. Contentment Journal: Maintain a journal where you record moments of contentment and joy. Reflect on what led to those moments and how you can cultivate them.

2. Simplify Your Life: Evaluate your lifestyle and identify areas where you can simplify. Often, less clutter and complexity lead to greater contentment.

3. Prayer for Contentment: In your daily prayers, ask God to cultivate contentment in your heart. Surrender any desires for more and trust in His sufficiency.

**Prayer:**

*Heavenly Father, we thank You for the beauty of contentment. Teach us to find our satisfaction in You and to trust in Your provision for our lives. May godliness and contentment be the hallmarks of our hearts, and may we find great gain in the peace that surpasses understanding. In Jesus name, we pray. Amen.*

## DAY 22

## Embracing God's Peace

"Peace I leave with you, my peace I give to you. Not as the world gives do I give to you. Let not your heart be troubled, neither let it be afraid."
John 14:27 (ESV)

God's peace is unlike any other form of peace known to humanity. It is not dependent on external circumstances or the absence of conflict; rather, it emanates from the very presence of God in our lives. It is a deep, abiding sense of well-being that resides within the soul, a peace that calms our fears and dispels our anxieties.

*Embracing God's peace is a declaration of trust. It signifies that we place our confidence not in our own strength or the world's promises but in the unchanging nature of our Heavenly Father. It is an acknowledgment that we can rest in His loving care, knowing that He is the source of true peace.*

**Action Plan:**

1. Daily Quiet Time: Set aside time each day for prayer and meditation on God's Word. Seek His presence and allow His peace to fill your heart.

2. Breathing Exercises: In moments of stress, practice deep breathing exercises. As you inhale and exhale, imagine receiving God's peace.

3. Forgiveness: Extend forgiveness to others, as harbouring resentment can rob you of God's peace. Let go of grudges and trust God to bring healing.

**Prayer:**

*Heavenly Father, we thank You for the gift of Your peace. In a world filled with turmoil, may Your peace be our refuge and our strength. Teach us to embrace the peace that only You can give, and let it guard our hearts and minds. May we not be troubled or afraid, for Your peace is our anchor. In Jesus name, we pray. Amen.*

## DAY 23
## Serving With Love

"For you were called to freedom, brothers. Only do not use your freedom as an opportunity for the flesh, but through Love serve one another." Galatians 5:13 (ESV)

The call to serve with love stands as a profound testament to the essence of the Christian life. Galatians 5:13 reminds us that our freedom in Christ is not meant for self-indulgence but for selfless service. Serving with love is the highest expression of our faith and a reflection of the love of Christ dwelling within us.

*Serving with love is a beautiful paradox—it's both an act of humility and an elevation of the human spirit. It involves willingly setting aside our own desires and agenda to meet the needs of others. It's about extending a helping hand, offering a listening ear, and showing kindness, not because we have to, but because we genuinely care.*

**Action Plan:**

1. Pray for a Servant's Heart: Begin each day with a prayer, asking God to cultivate a servant's heart within you.
   Pray for opportunities to serve with love.

2. Identify Needs: Be observant of the needs around you—in your family, community, or church. Seek ways to meet those needs with love.

3. Random Acts of Kindness: Incorporate random acts of kindness into your daily life. These small gestures can have a significant impact on others.

**Prayer:**

*Heavenly Father, we thank You for the privilege of serving with love. Teach us to follow the example of Your Son, Jesus Christ, who came to serve. May our hearts be filled with Your love, and may we extend that love to those around us. Use us, Lord, as instruments of Your grace and kindness. In Jesus name, we pray. Amen.*

## DAY 24
## Building Strong Relationships

"Iron sharpens iron, and one man sharpens another. " - Proverbs 27:17 (ESV)

One of the most precious treasures in life is the gift of relationships—deep, meaningful connections with others that bring joy, support, and growth. Proverbs 27:17 paints a vivid picture of this truth by likening our relationships to the way iron sharpens iron. Building strong relationships is a beautiful tapestry woven with threads of love, trust, and mutual edification.

*The essence of strong relationships lies in the mutual sharpening of one another. Just as iron blades become sharper when they interact, so too do we become better versions of ourselves through our interactions with others. God has designed us to be relational beings, and our connections with fellow believers are a vital aspect of our Christian journey.*

**Action Plan:**

1. Prioritise Communication: Invest time in open and honest communication with your loved ones. Share your thoughts, feelings, and experiences with them.

2. Conflict Resolution: Learn healthy ways to address conflicts and disagreements within your relationships. Seek reconciliation and forgiveness when needed.

3. Quality Time: Set aside intentional quality time with your loved ones. These moments foster deeper connections and create lasting memories.

**Prayer:**

*Heavenly Father, we thank You for the gift of relationships. Teach us to build strong and meaningful connections with others. May our interactions be marked by love, trust, and mutual edification. Help us to reflect Your love in our relationships and to strengthen one another in our faith journey. In Jesus name, we pray. Amen.*

## DAY 25
## Seeking Wisdom From God

"If any of you lacks wisdom, let him ask God, who gives generously to all without reproach, and it will be given to him." - James 1:5 (ESV)

Wisdom is not merely the accumulation of knowledge or the mastery of facts; it is the discernment to apply knowledge rightly. It's the ability to see life's complexities through the lens of God's truth and to make choices that honour Him. Seeking wisdom from God is an acknowledgment that our own understanding is limited, and that true wisdom flows from Him who is all-knowing.

*Seeking wisdom from God is also an act of humility. It recognizes that we need His guidance and that we are willing to submit our plans and desires to His higher purposes. It is a prayerful request for His wisdom to permeate every aspect of our lives—our relationships, decisions, and responses to the challenges we encounter.*

**Action Plan:**

1. Daily Prayer for Wisdom: Begin each day with a prayer, asking God for wisdom to navigate the challenges and decisions you may face.

2. Study God's Word: Regularly engage with the Bible, seeking wisdom and insight from its pages. Meditate on passages that offer wisdom.

3. Seek Counsel: Don't hesitate to seek wise counsel from trusted mentors or friends when facing important decisions.

**Prayer:**

*Heavenly Father, we come before You with a humble heart, recognizing our need for Your wisdom. We thank You for Your promise to generously give wisdom to those who seek it. We ask for Your guidance in every aspect of our lives. May Your wisdom be a light to our path and a source of discernment in all our decisions. In Jesus name, we pray. Amen.*

## DAY 26
## Discovering Your Purpose

"For we are in His workmanship, created in Christ Jesus for good works, which God prepared for beforehand, that we should work in them." - Ephesians 2:10 (ESV)

Discovering your purpose is akin to uncovering a hidden treasure—a journey of self-discovery that unveils the unique gifts, talents, and passions that God has placed within you. It's about aligning your life with God's plan, so that you can live out the purpose for which you were created.

*Our purpose is not solely about what we do but also about who we become in Christ.*
*It involves becoming more like Him, embodying His love, and making a positive*
*impact in the lives of others. When we discover our purpose, we find fulfilment and a*
*deep sense of meaning in our existence.*

**Action Plan:**

1. Prayerful Reflection: Spend time in prayerful reflection, seeking God's guidance in discovering your purpose. Ask Him to reveal His plan for your life.

2. Gifts and Passions: Identify your gifts and passions. What activities bring you joy and fulfilment? How can you use these for God's glory?

3. Service: Look for opportunities to serve others and make a positive impact. Often, purpose is revealed in acts of selfless service.

**Prayer:**

*Heavenly Father, we thank You for creating us with purpose and intention. We seek Your guidance in discovering our unique calling and how we can use our gifts and talents for Your glory. Open our hearts to Your leading, and grant us the wisdom to align our lives with Your divine plan. In Jesus name, we pray. Amen.*

## DAY 27
## The Gift Of Salvation

"For the wages of sin is death, but the free gift of God is eternal life in Christ Jesus
our Lord."
Romans 6:23 (ESV)

At the heart of our faith lies a gift beyond measure—the gift of salvation. Romans 6:23 succinctly captures the essence of this divine offering. It reminds us that, by nature, we stand condemned by the consequences of sin, but through God's boundless grace, we are granted the free gift of eternal life in Christ Jesus. This gift is not earned or deserved; it is an unmerited favour from a loving God.

*The gift of salvation is, perhaps, the most profound expression of God's love for humanity. It is a rescue mission initiated by a God who desires to redeem and restore His creation. This gift is not just a ticket to heaven; it is an invitation to a transformed life—a life lived in intimate relationship with our Heavenly Father.*

**Action Plan:**

1. Personal Reflection: Take time to reflect on the gift of salvation in your own life. How has it transformed you? Express gratitude to God for His grace.

2. Share the Gospel: Share the message of salvation with others. Be a bearer of this good news to friends, family, and those who have yet to hear.

3. Live in Freedom: Recognize that you are no longer bound by the power of sin. Live in the freedom and victory that Christ's sacrifice has secured for you.

**Prayer:**

*Heavenly Father, we stand in awe of Your gift of salvation. It is a grace beyond comprehension, a love beyond measure. Thank You for rescuing us from the bondage of sin and offering us eternal life in Christ Jesus. May we never take this gift for granted but live in gratitude and share it with others. In Jesus name, we pray. Amen.*

## DAY 28
## Finding Hope In Hard Times

"May the God of hope fill you with all joy and peace in believing, so that by the power of the Holy Spirit you may abound in hope." - Romans 15:13 (ESV)

In the midst of life's storms and trials, finding hope can sometimes feel like searching for a flickering light in the darkest night. Yet, Romans 15:13 reminds us that we serve a God of hope—a God who not only offers hope but also fills us with joy and peace as we believe in Him. This hope is not wishful thinking;

it's a confident expectation that God's promises will be fulfilled, even in the hardest of times.

*Finding hope in hard times is also a choice to believe that God can bring beauty out of brokenness. It's the understanding that He can use our trials to refine our character, deepen our faith, and fulfil His purposes. It's an affirmation that, even when we cannot see the way forward, God is working behind the scenes to bring about His good plan.*

**Action Plain:**

1. Daily Devotion: Commit to a daily time of devotion, reading Scripture, and meditating on passages that offer hope and encouragement.

2. Prayer for Hope: Spend time in prayer, asking God to fill you with hope and to help you trust in His promises, even in hard times.

3. Join a Support Group: Consider joining a support group or community of believers who can offer encouragement and prayer during challenging seasons.

**Prayer:**

*Heavenly Father, we thank You for being the God of hope. In times of difficulty, we trust in Your promises and look to You as our source of strength and courage. Fill us with joy and peace as we believe in You, and may Your Holy Spirit abound in us with hope. In Jesus name, we pray. Amen.*

## DAY 29
## God's Faithfulness In Trials

"The steadfast love of the Lord never ceases; His mercies never come to an end; they are new every morning; great is your faithfulness.
Lamentations 3:22-23 (ESV)

In the midst of life's trials and tribulations, the unchanging truth of God's faithfulness shines as a beacon of hope. Lamentations 3:22-23 reminds us that no matter how challenging our circumstances may be, the steadfast love and mercies of the Lord never cease. They are new every morning, a testament to His unwavering faithfulness.

*God's faithfulness is not contingent on our circumstances or our own faithfulness. It is an outpouring of His character—a character marked by love, grace, and unwavering commitment to His children. It is a promise that He will never leave us nor forsake us, no matter how difficult the path may become.*

**Action Plan:**

1. Reflect on God's Faithfulness: Take time to reflect on moments in your life when God has shown His faithfulness in trials. Journal these experiences as a source of encouragement.

2. Meditate on Scripture: Meditate on passages that speak of God's faithfulness. Allow His Word to fill your heart with confidence in His unwavering love.

3. Thanksgiving: In times of trial, offer prayers of thanksgiving for God's faithfulness. Thank Him for His presence and His promises.

**Prayer:**

*Heavenly Father, we thank You for Your unchanging faithfulness. In the midst of life's trials, we find comfort and hope in Your steadfast love. Help us to trust in Your faithfulness, even when circumstances seem overwhelming. We know that Your mercies are new every morning, and we rest in Your unwavering commitment to us. In Jesus name, we pray. Amen.*

# DAY 30
## Strengthening Your Prayer Life

"Do not be anxious about anything, but by everything in prayer and supplication with thanksgiving are your requests to be made known to God." - Philippians 4:6 (ESV)

Prayer is the lifeline of our relationship with God—a sacred conversation between the created and the Creator. Philippians 4:6 calls us to a life of prayer, urging us not to be anxious but to bring our requests, concerns, and gratitude before our Heavenly Father. Strengthening your prayer life is an invitation to deepen your connection with God and experience His peace in every circumstance.

*Prayer is more than a religious ritual; it's a powerful means of communion with the Almighty. It's a channel through which we pour out our hearts, share our burdens, and receive God's guidance and comfort. Strengthening your prayer life means approaching God with authenticity, vulnerability, and a heart full of gratitude.*

**Action Plan:**

1. Establish a Prayer Routine: Set aside specific times each day for prayer. Create a routine that allows you to connect with God consistently.

2. Pray with Purpose: Be intentional in your prayers. Pray for your needs, the needs of others, and for God's will to be done.

3. Pray for Others: Intercede for others in your prayers. Lift up the needs and concerns of your loved ones and those who may be hurting.

**Prayer:**

*Heavenly Father, we come before You with hearts full of gratitude for the gift of prayer. Teach us to strengthen our prayer lives, to come to You with authenticity and vulnerability. May we find peace in laying our burdens at Your feet and joy in expressing our gratitude for Your faithfulness. In Jesus name, we pray. Amen.*

## DAY 31
## Trusting In God's Provision

"Look at the birds of the air: they neither sow nor reap nor gather into barns, and yet your Heavenly Father feeds them. Are you not of more value than them?" - Matthew 6:27 (ESV)

We are always driven by worry about tomorrow's provisions, Matthew 6:26 calls us to a profound truth—trust in God's provision. This verse invites us to look at the birds of the air, creatures that neither sow nor reap, yet are cared for by our Heavenly Father. It reminds us that if God provides for the birds, how much more will He provide for us, His beloved children.

*Trusting God's provision is an act of faith, a surrendering of our anxieties and fears about the future into His loving hands. It's recognizing that God is our ultimate Provider, and He knows our needs even before we ask. It's an assurance that He is not only aware of our circumstances but deeply concerned about our well-being.*

**Action Plan:**

1. Contentment in Christ: Seek contentment in your relationship with Christ rather than in material possessions. Find joy in His presence.

2. Generosity: Practice generosity in your own life. Share what you have with others, recognizing that God's blessings are meant to be shared.

3. Faith in Action: Step out in faith, knowing that God is your Provider. Pursue opportunities or challenges with confidence in His faithfulness.

**Prayer:**

*Heavenly Father, we thank You for being our Provider. Help us to trust in Your provision, even when circumstances seem uncertain. May we find peace in Your care, knowing that You are aware of our needs and will supply them according to Your riches in glory. In Jesus name, we pray. Amen.*

# FEBRUARY

*2 Corinthians 1:3-4*
*Blessed be the God and Father of our Lord Jesus Christ, the Father of mercies and*
*God of all comfort, who comforts us in all our affliction, so that we may be able to*
*comfort those who are in any affliction, with the comfort with which we ourselves*
*are comforted by God.*

## DAY 01

## Finding Comfort in God's Word

"Your word is a lamp to my feet and a light to my path." - Psalm 119:105 (ESV)

Dear Sister in Christ Jesus,

In this new month, I come to you with God's word filled with divine protection, wisdom and understanding of His word, and fulfilment in all areas of life. May you excel in all ramifications of your life. In Jesus name, Amen.

*Finding comfort in God's Word is like finding a refuge in the midst of life's storms. It's turning to Scripture when our hearts are heavy with burdens, when we face uncertainty, or when we long for solace. In God's Word, we discover timeless promises, eternal truths, and the comforting presence of our Heavenly Father.*

**Action Plan:**

1. Daily Reading: Commit to daily reading of Scripture, even if it's just a short passage. Start with the Psalms, a book filled with comfort and hope.

2. Meditation: Take time to meditate on verses that bring comfort and encouragement. Reflect on how they apply to your life.

3. Journaling: Keep a journal of your reflections and prayers as you read God's Word. Write down verses that resonate with you.

**Prayer:**

## DAY 02

## Cultivating A Heart Of Thankfulness

"And let the peace of Christ Jesus rule in your hearts, to which indeed you were called in one body. And be thankful." - Colossians 3:15 (ESV)

God's grace has brought us to another beautiful day in this month. As we all know that we live in the bustle and hustle of life, it's easy to overlook the beauty of a thankful heart. Colossians 3:15 reminds us of the transformative power of gratitude. It encourages us not only to be thankful but to let the peace of Christ rule in our hearts. Cultivating a heart of thankfulness is an invitation to a life characterised by joy, contentment, and a deep sense of God's presence.

*A heart of thankfulness is like a fertile soil in which the seeds of joy and peace can flourish. It's an acknowledgment that every good and perfect gift comes from the Father above. When we cultivate thankfulness, we shift our focus from what we lack to what we have, from our problems to God's provision.*

**Action Plan:**

1. Thanksgiving in Prayer: Incorporate thanksgiving into your daily prayers. Thank God for specific blessings and for His love and faithfulness.

2. Express Gratitude: Take time to express your gratitude to others. Write a note or send a message to someone you appreciate.

3. Memorise Scripture: Commit Bible verses about thankfulness to memory. They serve as reminders of God's call to gratitude.

**Prayer:**

Heavenly Father, we thank You for the gift of thankfulness. Help us to cultivate hearts that overflow with gratitude, even in the midst of life's challenges. May Your peace rule in our hearts as we choose to be thankful. In Jesus name, we pray. Amen.

# DAY 03
## Persevering Through Challenges

"Blessed is the man who remains steadfast under trial, for when he has stood the test, he will receive the crown of life, which God has promised to those who love Him." - James 1:12 (ESV)

Life is a journey filled with ups and downs, joys and sorrows, victories and trials. It's in the midst of these trials that the essence of our faith is revealed. James 1:12 reminds us that those who persevere through challenges are blessed. It's an encouragement to remain steadfast under trial, knowing that through perseverance, we will receive the crown of life promised by our faithful God.

*Perseverance is not a sign of weakness but a testament to our strength in Christ. It's a choice to stand firm in the face of adversity, to trust that God's grace is sufficient, and that His strength is made perfect in our weakness (2 Corinthians 12:9).*

**Action Plan:**

1. Prayer for Strength: Begin each day with a prayer for God's strength to persevere through challenges.

2. Scripture Study: Study the lives of biblical figures who faced trials and overcame them through faith. Draw inspiration from their stories.

3. Encouragement: Seek encouragement from fellow believers. Share your challenges with trusted friends who can pray with you and offer support.

**Prayer:**

*Heavenly Father, we thank You for the promise of blessings to those who persevere through trials. Grant us the strength and faith to remain steadfast in the face of challenges. Help us to trust in Your goodness and love, knowing that You are with us every step of the way. In Jesus name, we pray. Amen.*

# DAY 04
## The Blessing Of Unity

"Behold, how good and pleasant it is when brothers dwell in unity." - Psalm 133:1 (ESV)

Unity is a precious gift from God—a gift that brings beauty, harmony, and blessings into our lives. Psalm 133:1 paints a vivid picture of the goodness and pleasantness of unity among believers. It's a reminder that when we come together in love and harmony, we create an environment where God's blessings flow abundantly.

*The blessing of unity is like a fragrant oil that anoints our relationships and interactions. It's a soothing balm that heals wounds and restores brokenness. When we dwell in unity, we experience a taste of heaven on earth, for it is in unity that the love of Christ shines brightly.*

**Action Plan:**

1. Prayer for Unity: Begin each day with a prayer for unity among believers, both in your local church and worldwide.

2. Forgiveness: Practice forgiveness and reconciliation in your relationships. Let go of past hurts and seek unity with those you may have disagreements with.

3. Study God's Word: Study passages in the Bible that emphasise the importance of unity and love among believers. Let His Word guide your actions and attitudes.

**Prayer:**

*Heavenly Father, we thank You for the precious gift of unity among believers. Help us to dwell in unity, to love one another as You have loved us, and to be a shining example of Your love to the world. May Your blessings flow abundantly as we come together in unity for Your glory. In Jesus name, we pray. Amen.*

## DAY 05
## Experiencing God's Rest

"Come to me, all who labour and are heavy laden, and I will give you rest." - Matthew 11:28 (ESV)

We often find ourselves weary, carrying heavy burdens of responsibilities, worries, and stress. It is in this weariness that the invitation from our Saviour in Matthew 11:28 shines brightly—a promise of rest for our souls. Experiencing God's rest is an opportunity to find solace, renewal, and deep peace in His presence.

*Experiencing God's rest is an act of surrender. It's acknowledging our limitations and entrusting our cares to the One who is greater than all. It's taking a pause from our busyness to sit at the feet of Jesus, to listen to His voice, and to find refreshment for our weary souls.*

**Action Plan:**

1. Daily Quiet Time: Set aside a specific time each day for quiet reflection and prayer. Use this time to come to Jesus and lay down your burdens.

2. Sabbath Rest: Observe a weekly Sabbath as a day of rest and worship. Use it to recharge physically and spiritually.

3. Practice Mindfulness: Cultivate mindfulness by being present in the moment. Let go of worries about the future and focus on God's presence today.

**Prayer:**

Heavenly Father, we thank You for the promise of rest in Your presence. As we come to You with our burdens, we trust in Your promise to give rest to our souls. Help us to find solace, renewal, and deep peace in You. In Jesus name, we pray. Amen.

## DAY 06
## Living As A Light In The World

"You are the light of the world, a city set on a hill cannot be hidden." - Matthew 5:14
(ESV)

Living as a light in the world means embracing our role as ambassadors of God's love and grace. It's a recognition that we are called to be different, to stand out as beacons of hope and righteousness. Just as a city on a hill is impossible to conceal, our lives should bear witness to the transforming power of Christ.

*Living as a light in the world also involves reflecting the character of Christ. It's about displaying qualities such as love, kindness, forgiveness, and compassion in a world that often lacks these virtues. Our lives should draw people closer to Jesus, the ultimate source of light and life.*

**Action Plan:**

1. Daily Prayer: Begin each day with a prayer asking God to use you as a light in the world and to help you reflect His character.

2. Scripture Study: Study passages in the Bible that emphasise the role of believers as lights in the world.

3. Random Acts of Kindness: Intentionally perform acts of kindness and love for those around you, even to strangers.

**Prayer:**

*Heavenly Father, we thank You for calling us to be lights in the world. Help us to shine brightly, to reflect Your character, and to draw others closer to You. May our lives be a testimony to Your love and grace. In Jesus name, we pray. Amen.*

## DAY 07
## Embracing God's Guidance

"In all your ways acknowledge Him, and He will make straight your paths." - Proverbs 3:6 (ESV)

Life is often a journey filled with choices, decisions, and crossroads. In the midst of this complexity, Proverbs 3:6 offers us a profound truth—an invitation to embrace God's guidance in every aspect of our lives. When we acknowledge Him in all our ways, we open ourselves to His wisdom, direction, and the assurance that He will make our paths straight.

*Embracing God's guidance is also an act of trust. It's believing that His ways are higher than our ways, and His thoughts are higher than our thoughts (Isaiah 55:9). It's acknowledging that God's guidance is for our good, even when we may not fully understand His plans.*

**Action Plan:**

1. Daily Prayer: Begin each day with a prayer, asking God for His guidance in all your decisions and choices.

2. Seek Wisdom: Read and meditate on passages in the Bible that offer wisdom and guidance. Proverbs is a great starting point.

3. Consult Wise Counsel: Seek advice from trusted mentors, friends, or spiritual leaders when facing significant decisions.

**Prayer:**

*Dear Lord, we thank You for the promise of Your guidance in our lives. Help us to trust Your wisdom and to acknowledge You in all our ways. May Your guidance make our paths straight and lead us closer to Your perfect plan. In Jesus name, we pray. Amen.*

## DAY 08
## The Power Of A Praying Heart

"Pray without ceasing." ' 1 Thessalonians 5:17 (ESV)

Prayer is not merely a religious ritual but a direct line of communication with our Heavenly Father—a source of power, comfort, and transformation. In 1 Thessalonians 5:17, we are encouraged to pray without ceasing, which is an invitation to cultivate the power of a praying heart—a heart that is continually turned toward God in conversation, supplication, and communion.

*The power of a praying heart lies in its ability to connect with the Creator of the universe, the One who knows our hearts intimately and listens to every word we utter. It's an understanding that prayer is not limited by time or place but is a constant conversation with our loving Father.*

**Action Plan:**

1. Establish a Prayer Routine: Set aside dedicated time each day for prayer and communion with God.

2. Pray for Specific Needs: Create a list of specific prayer requests for yourself, your family, and your community.

3. Practice Gratitude: Incorporate thanksgiving into your prayers, acknowledging God's blessings and goodness.

**Prayer:**

*Heavenly Father, we thank You for the gift of prayer and the power it holds. Help us to cultivate praying hearts that seek Your presence continually. May our prayers be a source of strength, comfort, and transformation in our lives and the lives of those we pray for. In Jesus name, we pray. Amen.*

## DAY 09
## Finding Strength In Community

"And let us consider how to stir up one another, to love and good work, not neglecting to meet together, as is the habit of some, but encouraging one another, and all the more as you see the day drawing near." Hebrews 10:24-25 (ESV)

We were never meant to journey through life alone. In Hebrews 10:24-25, we are reminded of the profound strength and encouragement that can be found in community. The fellowship of believers is a gift from God—a place where we can stir up love, inspire good works, and draw strength from one another.

*Finding strength in community is not about perfect people coming together but about imperfect individuals who love and serve a perfect God. It's about embracing our differences, forgiving one another, and growing in Christ together. In community, we become a reflection of Christ's love to the world.*

**Action Plan:**

1. Join a Small Group: Seek out a small group or Bible study within your church or community where you can connect with other believers.

2. Be Vulnerable: Open your heart to others and share your joys and struggles. Let others do the same with you.

3. Pray for Your Community: Lift up your community in prayer, asking God to strengthen relationships and inspire acts of love and service.

**Prayer:**

*Heavenly Father, we thank You for the gift of community and the strength it provides. Help us to cherish and nurture the bonds we share with our fellow believers. May our gatherings be times of encouragement, love, and mutual support. In Jesus name, we pray. Amen.*

## DAY 10
## Trusting God's Character

"Your kingdom is an everlasting kingdom, and your dominion endures throughout all generations. [The LORD is faithful in all His Words and kind in all His works.]" - Psalm 145:13 (ESV)

Trusting God's character is the foundation of our faith—a rock on which we stand when life's storms rage. Psalm 145:13 reminds us of the unwavering nature of God's character. He is faithful in all His words, and His kindness extends to all His works. In this truth, we find a source of unshakable trust and confidence.

*Trusting character is not blind faith; it's faith rooted in His Word and His actions throughout history. It's an acknowledgment that His kindness, mercy, and love extend to all generations. We can look back on His faithfulness in the past and trust that He will be faithful in our present and future.*

**Action Plan:**

1. Study His Word: Dive into the Bible to discover more about God's character through the stories of His interactions with people.

2. Journal Your Trust: Keep a journal of moments when you have experienced God's faithfulness and kindness in your life.

3. Share Your Trust: Share your trust in God's character with others, encouraging them to trust Him too.

**Prayer:**

*Heavenly Father, we thank You for the unchanging nature of Your character. Help us to trust in Your faithfulness and kindness, knowing that You are who You say You are. May our trust in Your character be a source of peace, confidence, and unwavering faith. In Jesus name, we pray. Amen.*

## DAY 11
## A Heart Of Compassion

"Put on them, as God's chosen ones, Holy and beloved, compassionate hearts, kindness, humility, meekness, and patience." - Colossians 3:12 (ESV)

A heart of compassion is a reflection of God's love in our lives. Colossians 3:12 calls us to clothe ourselves with compassionate hearts, for compassion is not merely an emotion but a way of living—a choice to extend kindness, love, and understanding to others, especially in their times of need.

*Compassion is not reserved for those who deserve it but is extended to all, just as God's grace is freely given to us. It's a choice to show kindness even when it's difficult, to offer a listening ear when someone needs to be heard, and to provide help when it's within our means.*

**Action Plan:**

1. Acts of Kindness: Seek out opportunities to perform acts of kindness for those in need, whether through service, gifts, or words of encouragement.

2. Listen Actively: Practice active listening when someone shares their struggles or concerns, offering empathy and support.

3. Forgive and Let Go: Release any grudges or resentments you may hold, choosing instead to extend forgiveness and compassion.

**Prayer:**

*Heavenly Father, we thank You for Your compassion and mercy toward us. Help us to put on compassionate hearts, reflecting Your love in our interactions with others. May our lives be a testimony to Your kindness and grace. In Jesus name, we pray. Amen.*

## DAY 12

# Living With Integrity

"Whosoever walks in integrity walks securely, but he who makes his ways crooked will be found out." - Proverbs 10:9 (ESV)

Integrity is a rare gem in a world often marked by deception and compromise. Proverbs 10:9 reminds us of the profound importance of living with integrity. When we walk in integrity, we walk securely, standing on a firm foundation of honesty, truthfulness, and moral uprightness.

*Living with integrity means aligning our actions with our values and principles, regardless of the circumstances. It's choosing to do what is right even when no one is watching, because we recognize that our character is shaped by the choices we make in secret.*

**Action Plan:**

1. Self-Reflection: Take time each day for self-reflection, examining your actions, words, and motivations for any signs of compromise.

2. Accountability: Seek an accountability partner or group with whom you can share your commitment to living with integrity.

3. Daily Decision: Before making decisions, ask yourself if your choice aligns with your values and principles.

**Prayer:**

*Heavenly Father, we thank You for the gift of integrity and the security it brings to our lives. Help us to walk in integrity, even when faced with challenges and temptations. May our actions and words reflect Your truth and righteousness. In Jesus name, we pray. Amen.*

## DAY 13
## Overcoming Fear With Faith

"For I, the Lord your God, hold your right hand; it is I who say to you, 'fear not, I am the one who helps you." - Isaiah 41:13 (ESV)

Fear can be a powerful and paralysing force in our lives, but faith in God's promises can conquer even the most profound fears. Isaiah 41:13 reminds us that our Heavenly Father not only commands us to "fear not" but also offers His unwavering support, saying, "I am the one who helps you."

*Overcoming fear with faith is an acknowledgment that our God is greater than any circumstance or challenge we may face. It's trusting in His sovereignty and His promise to be with us always, even in the darkest of times.*

**Action Plan:**

1. Prayer of Surrender: Whenever fear arises, offer a prayer of surrender to God, acknowledging your dependence on Him.

2. Faith Declarations: Speak faith-filled affirmations and declarations based on God's promises to combat fear.

3. Encourage Others: Share your journey of overcoming fear with faith with others who may be struggling, offering them hope and support.

**Prayer:**

*Heavenly Father, we thank You for being our refuge and our help in times of fear. Help us to overcome fear with unwavering faith in Your promises. May our trust in You be a source of courage and peace. In Jesus' name, we pray. Amen.*

## DAY 14
## Walking In God's Love

*"Beloved, let's love one another, love is from God, and whoever loves has been born of God knows God." - 1 John 4:7 (ESV)*

Walking in God's love is a transformational journey that reflects the very essence of our Heavenly Father. In 1 John 4:7, we are called "beloved" and urged to love one another, for love is not just a feeling or an emotion but the very nature of God Himself.

*God's love is not limited by our imperfections or the flaws of those around us. It's a love that extends to all, regardless of their circumstances, actions, or backgrounds. In walking in God's love, we become vessels of His grace, sharing His love with the world.*

**Action Plan:**

1. Act of Kindness: Purposefully perform a random act of kindness for someone, whether a friend, family member, or stranger.

2. Forgiveness: Forgive someone who has wronged you, releasing any bitterness or resentment in your heart.

3. Prayer for Love: In your daily prayers, ask God to fill your heart with His love and help you walk in it.

**Prayer:**

*Heavenly Father, we thank You for Your boundless love that fills our hearts and overflows to those around us. Help us to walk in Your love, showing kindness, forgiveness, and compassion to others. May our lives be a reflection of Your love in this world. In Jesus' name, we pray. Amen.*

## DAY 15
## Surrendering Your Worries

"Casting your anxieties on Him, because He cares for you." - 1 Peter 5:7 (ESV)

Life can often feel like a stormy sea, tossing us with worries and anxieties. In these moments, 1 Peter 5:7 offers a profound truth: we can cast all our anxieties on God because He cares for us. Surrendering your worries means trusting in God's loving care and releasing the burdens that weigh on your heart.

*Additional Scripture Reference:*

*"Cast your cares on the Lord and he will sustain you; he will never let the righteous be shaken." -Psalm 55:22*

Worry often stems from a lack of trust, as if we believe we must navigate life's challenges on our own. But in surrendering your worries, you acknowledge that you have a Heavenly Father who loves you deeply and is intimately involved in every aspect of your life.

**Action Plan:**

1. Daily Prayer: Dedicate time each day to pray about your worries, laying them before God and asking for His peace and guidance.

2. Scripture Meditation: Memorise and meditate on verses that speak to God's care and faithfulness.

3. Trust Exercise: Practice letting go of one worry each day, consciously releasing it into God's hands.

**Prayer:**

Heavenly Father, we thank You for caring for us and inviting us to cast our anxieties on You. Help us to surrender our worries, trusting in Your loving care and wisdom. May Your peace guard our hearts and minds as we release our burdens to You. In Jesus name, we pray. Amen.

## DAY 16
## The Joy of Salvation

"Restore to me the joy of your salvation, and uphold me with a willing spirit." - Psalm 51:12 (ESV)

The joy of salvation is a profound and life-altering experience. It's not merely a momentary feeling but a deep and abiding wellspring of happiness that flows from knowing we are redeemed, forgiven, and reconciled with our Heavenly Father. In Psalm 51:12, David's heartfelt plea to God for the restoration of this joy serves as a beautiful reminder of the depth of joy found in salvation.

*Additional Scripture Reference:*

*"Ephesians 2:8-10: 8 For by grace you have been saved through faith. And this is not your own doing; it is the gift of God, not a result of works, so that no one may boast. 10 For we are his workmanship, created in Christ Jesus for good works, which God prepared beforehand, that we should walk in them."*

This joy is not meant to be hoarded but shared. It's a joy that overflows, leading us to worship, thanksgiving, and service. When we experience the joy of salvation, it becomes a wellspring of hope, even in the midst of trials and tribulations.

**Action Plan:**

1. Daily Reflection: Spend time each day reflecting on the gift of salvation and what it means in your life.

2. Share Your Testimony: Share your story of salvation with someone who may need to hear it, whether a friend, family member, or coworker.

3. Thanksgiving Journal: Keep a journal of things you're thankful for as a reminder of the joy of salvation in your life.

**Prayer:**

*Heavenly Father, we thank You for the immeasurable gift of salvation and the joy it brings. Restore to us the joy of Your salvation, that it may overflow in our lives and touch the lives of those around us. May we live with gratitude, purpose, and a heart full of joy, serving You faithfully. In Jesus name, we pray. Amen.*

## DAY 17
## Encountering God in Nature

*"The heavens declare the glory of God, and the sky above proclaims his handiwork." - Psalm 19:1 (ESV)*

When we immerse ourselves in nature, we can experience a profound sense of awe and wonder. The intricate design of a flower, the vastness of a starry sky, or the gentle rustle of leaves in the wind can all serve as reminders of God's presence and His loving care for every detail of His creation.

*Nature also teaches us valuable spiritual lessons. Just as seasons change, so do the seasons of our lives. Just as a tree remains rooted in the storm, we can remain rooted in our faith in God. Just as a river flows, we can allow God's love to flow through us to others.*

## Action Plan:

1. Nature Walks: Schedule regular walks or hikes in natural settings to immerse yourself in God's creation.

2. Contemplative Silence: Spend time in silent meditation, allowing the sights and sounds of nature to draw you closer to God.

3. Creation Care: Commit to taking care of the environment as an expression of your gratitude for God's creation.

## Prayer:

*Heavenly Father, we thank You for the beauty and wonder of Your creation. Help us to encounter You in the midst of nature, recognizing Your handiwork and drawing near to You. May our time in nature be a source of spiritual refreshment and a reminder of Your glory. In Jesus name, we pray. Amen.*

## DAY 18

## Finding Peace Amidst Chaos

"You keep in Him in perfect peace whose mind is stayed on you because He trusts in you." - Isaiah 26:3 (ESV)

In the midst of life's chaos and uncertainties, finding peace can feel like trying to grasp a handful of wind. Yet, Isaiah 26:3 reminds us that perfect peace is not only attainable but promised to those whose minds are steadfastly fixed on the Lord, trusting in His unwavering presence and sovereignty.

*Additional Scripture Reference:*

*John 14:27 – "Peace I leave with you; my peace I give to you. Not as the world gives do I give to you. Let not your hearts be troubled, neither let them be afraid." 2 Thessalonians 3:16 – "Now may the Lord of peace himself give you peace at all times in every way.*

Finding peace amidst chaos begins with a conscious choice to redirect your thoughts and focus. It's recognizing that God is in control, even when circumstances seem overwhelming. Trusting Him allows you to let go of anxiety and rest in His peace.

**Action Plan:**

1. Daily Quiet Time: Set aside a quiet time each day for prayer, meditation, and reading Scripture to centre your thoughts on God.

2. Breath Prayer: Develop a simple breath prayer, such as "God, grant me peace," to repeat in moments of stress.

3. Gratitude Journal: Keep a journal of things you're thankful for to shift your focus toward God's blessings.

**Prayer:**

*Heavenly Father, we thank You for the promise of perfect peace when our minds are fixed on You. In the midst of life's chaos, help us to trust in Your unfailing presence and sovereignty. May Your peace guard our hearts and minds. In Jesus name, we pray. Amen.*

## DAY 19
## Restoring Broken Relationships

"Bearing with one another and, if one has a complaint against another, forgiving each other; as the Lord has forgiven you, so you also must forgive." - Colossians 3:13 (ESV)

Restoring broken relationships is an act of love and grace. It's acknowledging that, just as we have received forgiveness from our Heavenly Father, we are called to extend forgiveness to others. It's a willingness to let go of grievances, hurts, and grudges in pursuit of healing and reconciliation.

*Additional Scripture Reference:*

*2 Corinthians 5:18-20*

*"He has restored our relationship with him through Christ, and has given us this ministry of restoring relationships."*

Restoring broken relationships often requires humility, vulnerability, and patience. It may involve honest conversations, active listening, and a commitment to understanding one another's perspectives. It's a process that acknowledges that both parties are flawed and in need of grace.

**Action Plan:**

1. Prayer for Healing: Dedicate time in prayer for the restoration of broken relationships, asking God for wisdom, guidance, and a heart of forgiveness.

2. Initiate Reconciliation: Take the first step towards reconciliation by reaching out with love and a desire for resolution.

3. Boundaries: Establish healthy boundaries to protect yourself and the relationship as you work towards restoration.

**Prayer:**

*Heavenly Father, we thank You for Your model of forgiveness and reconciliation. Help us to bear with one another and to extend forgiveness, just as You have forgiven us. Grant us the wisdom and courage to restore broken relationships, and may Your love be the foundation of our efforts. In Jesus name, we pray. Amen.*

## DAY 20
## Embracing Your Identity in Christ

"I have been crucified with Christ. It is no longer I who live, but Christ who lives in me. And the life I now live in the flesh I live by faith in the Son of God, who loved me and gave himself for me." - Galatians 2:20 (ESV)

Embracing your identity in Christ is a transformative journey of self-discovery. Galatians 2:20 reminds us that, as believers, our lives are no longer defined by our own desires, successes, or failures. Instead, our true identity is found in the One who gave Himself for us - Jesus Christ.

*Embracing your identity in Christ is a daily choice. It's a decision to align your thoughts, actions, and desires with God's truth. It's a journey of becoming who you were created to be - a beloved child of God, empowered by the Holy Spirit to live a life of purpose and impact.*

## Action Plan:

1. Scripture Study: Dive into the Bible to discover what it says about your identity in Christ. Start with passages like Ephesians 2:10, Romans 8:37, and 1 Peter 2:9.

2. Identity Declarations: Create personal declarations based on biblical truths about your identity and speak them over your life daily.

3. Community: Surround yourself with a supportive Christian community that encourages and reminds you of your identity in Christ.

## Prayer:

*Heavenly Father, we thank You for the incredible gift of identity in Christ. Help us to fully embrace who we are in You and to live in the freedom and purpose You've provided. May Your truth shape our thoughts, actions, and attitudes. In Jesus name, we pray. Amen.*

## DAY 21
### Cultivating a Heart of Advocacy

Proverbs 31:8-9 (NIV) - "Speak up for those who cannot speak for themselves, for the rights of all who are destitute. Speak up and judge fairly; defend the rights of the poor and needy."

Cultivating a heart of advocacy is a divine calling. As women of faith, we are entrusted with the power to be voices for the voiceless. Inspired by Proverbs 31, our hearts are awakened to champion justice, compassion, and equality.

**Action Plan:**

1. Educate yourself about issues of injustice and inequality.

2. Actively support organisations and initiatives promoting positive change.

3. Speak out with love, grace, and courage for those in need.

**Prayer:**

*Heavenly Father, ignite our hearts with a passion for advocacy. May we be vessels of Your justice and love, defending the vulnerable and making a difference in Your name. Amen.*

## DAY 22
## The Gift of Eternal Life

"For God so loved the world, that he gave his only Son, that whoever believes in him should not perish but have eternal life." - John 3:16 (ESV)

The gift of eternal life is a treasure beyond measure, a promise that transcends the boundaries of time and space. John 3:16 encapsulates the essence of God's boundless love and sacrifice - the gift of His Son, Jesus Christ, so that we might have eternal life.

*Eternal life is not just about living forever; it's about living in perfect communion with our Creator, the source of all love and joy. It's an invitation to a relationship with God that begins here on earth and continues into eternity.*

**Action Plan:**

1. Reflect on John 3:16: Spend time meditating on the depth of God's love and the gift of eternal life.

2. Share the Good News: Take opportunities to share the message of eternal life with those who may not know it.

3. Live with Hope: Let the assurance of eternal life shape your perspective on life's challenges and uncertainties.

**Prayer:**

*Heavenly Father, we are in awe of Your love and the gift of eternal life through Your Son, Jesus Christ. Thank You for this precious gift that assures us of Your eternal presence and love. Help us to share this Good News with others and to live with the hope it brings. In Jesus name, we pray. Amen.*

## DAY 23
## Trusting God's Plan

"For I know the plans I have for you, declares the Lord, plans for welfare and not for evil, to give you a future and a hope." - Jeremiah 29:11 (ESV)

Trusting God's plan is an act of faith that invites us to surrender our desires, fears, and uncertainties into the hands of our loving and sovereign Creator. Jeremiah 29:11 reassures us that God's plans for us are filled with goodness, hope, and a future that far exceeds our wildest dreams.

*Trusting God's plan means releasing our grip on control and placing it firmly in His capable hands. It's an acknowledgment that He knows what is best for us, even when we can't fully comprehend it.*

**Action Plan:**

1. Prayer of Surrender: Spend time in prayer, surrendering your plans and desires to God, and asking for His guidance.

2. Daily Scripture Reading: Read and meditate on verses that remind you of God's trustworthy plan, like Proverbs 3:5-6.

3. Encourage Others: Share stories of how God's plan has unfolded in your life to encourage others to trust in Him.

**Prayer:**

*Heavenly Father, we thank You for the assurance of Your good and hopeful plan for our lives. Help us to trust in Your wisdom and timing, even when we don't understand. Grant us the faith to surrender our plans to Yours and to follow Your path with confidence and hope. In Jesus name, we pray. Amen.*

## DAY 24

# Living a Life of Compassion

"Be kind to one another, tenderhearted, forgiving one another, as God in Christ forgave you." - Ephesians 4:32 (ESV)

Living a life of compassion is a reflection of God's heart in our own. Ephesians 4:32 calls us to be kind, tenderhearted, and forgiving, mirroring the very nature of our Heavenly Father who forgave us through Christ.

*Living a life of compassion means seeing the world through God's eyes. It's recognizing the worth and dignity of every person, regardless of their circumstances or background. It's being quick to forgive, slow to judge, and eager to extend grace.*

## Action Plan:

1. Daily Compassion Prayer: Begin each day with a prayer, asking God to fill your heart with compassion and to show you opportunities to be kind.

2. Random Acts of Kindness: Purposefully perform small acts of kindness for friends, family, and strangers.

3. Listen with Empathy: Practice active listening, seeking to understand others' perspectives and feelings.

## Prayer:

Heavenly Father, we thank You for Your boundless compassion and forgiveness towards us. Teach us to be kind, tenderhearted, and forgiving just as You are. Fill our hearts with Your love and help us be vessels of Your compassion to a hurting world. In Jesus name, we pray. Amen.

## DAY 25
## The Blessing of God's Guidance

"I will instruct you and teach you in the way you should go; I will counsel you with my eye upon you." - Psalm 32:8 (ESV)

The blessing of God's guidance is a precious gift that brings direction, wisdom, and comfort to our lives. In Psalm 32:8, God promises to instruct, teach, and counsel us with His loving gaze upon us. This assurance is a source of great hope and confidence.

*Living in the blessing of God's guidance involves active participation. It means seeking His wisdom through prayer and His Word, listening to the still, small voice of the Holy Spirit, and trusting His leading even when the path is unclear.*

**Action Plan:**

1. Seek Godly Counsel: Consult with trusted mentors or friends who can provide godly wisdom and perspective.

2. Wait on God: Sometimes, God's guidance comes in His timing. Practice patience as you wait for His direction.

3. Step in Faith: When you sense God's leading, take steps of faith, trusting that He is guiding you.

**Prayer:**

Heavenly Father, we are grateful for Your promise to guide and counsel us. Teach us to seek Your wisdom and to trust Your leading in every aspect of our lives. May Your guidance be a light in our path and a source of hope on our journey. In Jesus name, we pray. Amen.

## DAY 26
## Persevering with Hope

"Rejoice in hope, be patient in tribulation, be constant in prayer." - Romans 12:12
(ESV)

Persevering with hope is a call to endure life's challenges with a spirit that remains unbroken, a heart that continues to hope, and a faith that stands unwavering. Romans 12:12 beautifully encapsulates this journey of perseverance, reminding us to rejoice in hope, remain patient in tribulation, and be steadfast in prayer.

*Perseverance doesn't mean simply enduring; it means pressing on with purpose and determination. It's about finding strength in the midst of adversity, knowing that God is working all things together for good.*

**Action Plan:**

1. Daily Gratitude: Begin each day by thanking God for His promises and the hope you have in Him.

2. Scripture Meditation: Memorise and meditate on verses that speak of hope and perseverance, such as Romans 5:3-5.

3. Support System: Seek encouragement and prayer from your Christian community during times of tribulation.

**Prayer:**

*Heavenly Father, we thank You for the hope we have in Christ. In times of tribulation, help us to stand firm, knowing that Your promises are true. Teach us to persevere with patience, rejoicing in the hope that does not disappoint. May our prayers be a constant connection to You. In Jesus name, we pray. Amen.*

## DAY 27
## Rejoicing in God's Goodness

"Oh, taste and see that the Lord is good! Blessed is the man who takes refuge in him!"
- Psalm 34:8 (ESV)

Rejoicing in God's goodness is an invitation to savour the abundant blessings He pours into our lives. In Psalm 34:8, we are encouraged to "taste and see" that the Lord is good, and in doing so, we find ourselves in a state of blessedness.

*Rejoicing in God's goodness involves cultivating a heart of gratitude, a spirit of worship, and a lifestyle of praise. It's a deliberate choice to focus on His blessings rather than our burdens and to find joy in His presence.*

**Action Plan:**

1. Praise and Worship: Dedicate time to worship God for His goodness, using songs or simply your own words.

2. Share His Goodness: Look for opportunities to share God's goodness with others through acts of kindness.

3. Pray for a Grateful Heart: Ask God to cultivate in you a heart that constantly rejoices in His goodness.

**Prayer:**

*Heavenly Father, we thank You for Your abundant goodness that surrounds us daily. Help us to truly taste and see that You are good, and may our hearts overflow with gratitude and praise. Use us as vessels of Your goodness to bless those around us. In Jesus name, we pray. Amen.*

## DAY 28
## Embracing Forgiveness

"Bearing with one another and, if one has a complaint against another, forgiving each other; as the Lord has forgiven you, so you also must forgive." - Colossians 3:13 (ESV)

Embracing forgiveness is a profound act of love and obedience to our Heavenly Father. In Colossians 3:13, we are reminded of the imperative to bear with one another and forgive, just as the Lord forgave us. This call to forgiveness is not only a command but also an invitation to experience freedom and healing.

*Embracing forgiveness requires a heart willing to let go of grudges, offences, and the desire for revenge. It's about releasing the burden of unforgiveness and trusting God to be the ultimate judge. When we forgive, we free ourselves from the prison of anger and find the strength to move forward.*

**Action Plan:**

1. Heart Examination: Regularly assess your heart for any unforgiveness or bitterness and bring it before God in prayer.

2. Speak Forgiveness: If someone has hurt you, have an open and honest conversation, extending forgiveness where necessary.

3. Study Forgiveness: Study passages on forgiveness in the Bible to deepen your understanding and practice of forgiveness.

**Prayer:**

*Heavenly Father, we thank You for the forgiveness we have received through Christ. Help us to embrace forgiveness as an act of obedience and love. Give us the grace to release grudges and bitterness, and may our hearts be instruments of Your reconciliation and peace. In Jesus name, we pray. Amen.*

# DAY 29
# Trusting God's Sovereignty

"The Lord has established his throne in the heavens, and his kingdom rules over all."
- Psalm 103:19 (ESV)

Trusting God's sovereignty is an anchor for our souls in the tumultuous sea of life. Psalm 103:19 reminds us that the Lord has established His throne in the heavens, and His kingdom reigns over all things. This truth invites us to surrender control and find peace in the assurance that God is in charge.

*Trusting God's sovereignty requires a surrendering of our will to His. It's acknowledging that His plans are higher than ours and that His wisdom surpasses our understanding. It's finding peace in knowing that even when life is uncertain, God's purposes are unwavering.*

**Action Plan:**

1. Surrender Daily: Start each day with a prayer of surrender, acknowledging God's sovereignty over your life.

2. Study God's Word: Explore Scriptures that highlight God's sovereignty, such as Romans 8:28 and Isaiah 55:8-9.

3. Practice Patience: When faced with uncertainty, wait on God's timing and trust His plan.

## Prayer:

*Heavenly Father, we thank You for Your sovereign rule over all things. Help us to trust in Your wisdom, goodness, and perfect plans. Grant us the grace to surrender our will to Yours and find peace in Your sovereignty. In Jesus name, we pray. Amen.*

# MARCH

*"By faith Moses, when he was born, was hidden for three months by his parents, because they saw that the child was beautiful, and they were not afraid of the king's edict" (Heb. 11:23).*

## DAY 01
### A Heart of Worship

"God is spirit, and those who worship him must worship in spirit and truth." - John 4:24 (ESV)

Dear sister in Christ Jesus,

With the grace of our Lord Jesus Christ, I welcome you to the month of March, a month filled with divine fruitfulness and abundance, may God's protection never depart from you and your family, In Jesus name. We pray. Amen.

Worship is like a symphony of the soul, where every note and melody is an expression of our love for the Creator. It's more than just singing songs; it's a lifestyle of surrender, gratitude, and awe. When we worship in spirit and truth, we draw near to God's heart, offering Him the praise and honour He deserves.

*Additional Scripture Reference:*

*(John 4:14) The outflow of worship is in John 7:38, "Whoever believes in me, as the Scripture has said, 'Out of his heart will flow rivers of living water.'" Like water, the worship of God always returns to its Source who is the Father. He flows in and out of us by the waters of the Holy Spirit.*

**Action Plan:**

1. Daily Praise: Begin each day with a song or prayer of worship, expressing your love and adoration for God.

2. Practice Gratitude: Keep a gratitude journal, noting the blessings and answered prayers you're thankful for.

3. Share Your Worship: Invite others to join you in worship, whether through music, prayer, or studying God's Word.

**Prayer:**

*Heavenly Father, we come before You with hearts of worship, recognizing Your greatness and majesty. Teach us to worship You in spirit and truth, drawing near to Your heart. May our lives be a constant expression of love and gratitude to You. In Jesus name, we pray. Amen.*

## DAY 02
## The Beauty of God's Creation

"And God saw everything that he had made, and behold, it was very good." - Genesis 1:31 (ESV)

The beauty of God's creation is a masterpiece that surrounds us every day. In Genesis 1:31, we are reminded that God looked upon His creation and declared it to be "very good." This proclamation invites us to see the world through the eyes of the Creator, appreciating the wonder and splendour that He has fashioned.

*Additional Scripture Reference:*

*Ecclesiastes 3:11 (NIV)*

*"He has made everything beautiful in its time. He has also set eternity in the human heart; yet no one can fathom what God has done from beginning to end." This Bible verse reminds us that God's timing is sometimes so vastly different from our concept of time.*

**Action Plan:**

1. Daily Observation: Take a moment each day to observe and appreciate a specific aspect of God's creation.

2. Environmental Stewardship: Make intentional choices to reduce waste, conserve resources, and care for the environment.

3. Creation Walks: Go for walks or hikes in nature to connect with God's creation and pray or meditate on His goodness.

**Prayer:**

*Heavenly Father, we thank You for the breathtaking beauty of Your creation. Open our eyes to see and appreciate the wonders around us. Help us to be good stewards of this gift, caring for the Earth and all living creatures. May our hearts overflow with gratitude for Your creative hand. In Jesus name, we pray. Amen.*

## DAY 03
## Finding Strength in Adversity

"So we do not lose heart. Though our outer self is wasting away, our inner self is being renewed day by day. For this light momentary affliction is preparing for us an eternal weight of glory beyond all comparison, as we look not to the things that are seen but to the things that are unseen. For the things that are seen are transient, but the things that are unseen are eternal." - 2 Corinthians 4:16-18 (ESV)

Dear sister in Christ Jesus,

Adversity is like a refining fire. It tests our faith, endurance, and character. It's during these challenging moments that we discover the depth of our trust in God. As we endure, our faith grows stronger, and our perspective shifts from the temporary to the eternal.

*Finding strength in adversity requires a deliberate choice to fix our gaze on Christ. It's about finding hope in the midst of despair, peace in the midst of turmoil, and strength in the midst of weakness. In adversity, we discover that God's grace is sufficient, and His power is made perfect in our weakness (2 Corinthians 12:9).*

**Action Plan:**

1. Scripture Study: Dive into passages like Psalm 46, Isaiah 41:10, and Romans 8:28 for encouragement.

2. Prayer and Community: Seek support through prayer and Christian community during difficult times.

3. Serve Others: Look for opportunities to help others facing adversity, as it can bring healing and strength.

**Prayer:**

*Heavenly Father, we thank You for the strength and resilience You provide in times of adversity. Help us to trust in Your promises, knowing that our present troubles are temporary compared to the eternal glory You have prepared for us. Renew our inner selves day by day as we lean on Your grave. In Jesus name, we pray. Amen.*

## DAY 04
### Building A Life Of Faith

"And without faith, it is impossible to please him, for whoever would draw near to God must believe that he exists and that he rewards those who seek him." - Hebrews 11:6 (ESV)

Building a life of faith is like constructing a solid foundation for a house. Hebrews 11:6 reminds us that faith is not only essential but pleasing to God. It's the unwavering belief in God's existence and the assurance that He rewards those who earnestly seek Him.

*Building a life of faith requires intentionality. It's a continuous process of seeking God, studying His Word, and allowing His Spirit to transform our hearts. Faith grows when we put our trust in God's hands and surrender our fears and doubts to Him.*

**Action Plan:**

1. Daily Devotion: Commit to a daily time of prayer and Bible study to deepen your faith.

2. Step Out in Faith: Identify an area in your life where you need to trust God more and take a step of faith.

3. Prayer Partners: Seek out a prayer partner or small group for mutual support and growth in faith.

**Prayer:**

*Heavenly Father, we thank You for the gift of faith. Help us to build our lives upon the solid foundation of trust in You. Strengthen our belief in Your existence and Your promises. May our faith please You and draw us closer to Your heart. In Jesus name, we pray. Amen.*

## DAY 05

"Teach me your way, O LORD, that I may walk in your truth; unite my heart to fear your name." - Psalm 86:11 (ESV)

Walking in God's truth is a journey of aligning our lives with His perfect will and wisdom. In Psalm 86:11, the psalmist implores the Lord to teach him His way, recognizing that this is the path to walking in truth. It's an acknowledgment that God's way is the ultimate guide for our lives.

*Walking in God's truth requires a heart fully surrendered to Him. It's not just about knowing the truth but living it out daily. It's a commitment to seek His guidance, study His Word, and allow His Spirit to transform our thoughts, attitudes, and actions.*

**Action Plan:**

1. Daily Bible Study: Set aside time each day for studying God's Word and meditating on His truth.

2. Prayer for Discernment: Pray for wisdom and discernment to recognize and follow God's truth in all circumstances.

3. Truth Journal: Keep a journal where you record insights, lessons, and ways you've applied God's truth in your life.

**Prayer:**

*Heavenly Father, we humbly ask You to teach us Your way and lead us in Your truth. Unite our hearts to fear Your name and walk in obedience to Your Word. May Your truth be a lamp to our feet and a light to our path. In Jesus name, we pray. Amen.*

## DAY 06
### Trusting God's Guidance in Decisions

"The heart of man plans his way, the LORD establishes his steps." - Proverbs 16:9 (ESV)

Trusting God's guidance in decisions is an essential aspect of our journey with Him. Proverbs 16:9 reminds us that while we may make our plans, it is the Lord who ultimately establishes our steps. This verse invites us to surrender our plans to God, acknowledging His sovereignty and wisdom.

*Making decisions, big or small, can often feel like navigating through a maze. But when we trust in God's guidance, we walk in the assurance that His ways are higher than our ways (Isaiah 55:9). He sees the bigger picture, and His guidance is always aligned with His perfect will.*

**Action Plan:**

1. Seek God's Wisdom: Spend time in prayer seeking God's guidance for specific decisions you are facing.

2. Consult Scripture: Look for biblical principles that apply to your decision-making process.

3. Listen in Silence: Spend time in silent reflection, allowing God to speak to your heart.

**Prayer:**

*Heavenly Father, we acknowledge Your wisdom and sovereignty. Help us to trust Your guidance in every decision we face, big or small. May our plans align with Your perfect will, and may Your steps be established in our lives. We surrender our desires to You. In Jesus name, we pray. Amen.*

## DAY 07
### Cultivating Joy In Everyday life

"This is the day that the LORD has made; let us rejoice and be glad in it." - Psalm 118:24 (ESV)

Let me say this to you that cultivating joy in everyday life is a beautiful journey of embracing the gift of each day that the Lord has made. Psalm 118:24 reminds us that each day is a precious opportunity to rejoice and be glad. It's an invitation to find joy not only in the extraordinary moments but in the ordinary, mundane aspects of life.

*Cultivating joy in everyday life requires intentionality. It means choosing to focus on the blessings rather than the burdens, the beauty rather than the brokenness, and the love rather than the lack. It's a decision to live with an attitude of gratitude, knowing that God is the source of our joy.*

**Action Plan:**

1. Gratitude Journal: Start a journal to record daily blessings and moments of joy.

2. Mindfulness: Practice being fully present in each moment, savouring the simple joys of life.

3. Joyful Worship: Spend time in worship and prayer, rejoicing in the Lord's presence.

**Prayer:**

*Heavenly Father, we thank You for the gift of each day. Help us to cultivate joy in our hearts, finding delight in Your presence and the beauty of everyday life. May our lives be a reflection of Your goodness and love. In Jesus name, we pray. Amen.*

## DAY 08
## God's Comfort in Times of Grief

"The LORD is near to the brokenhearted and saves the crushed in spirit." - Psalm 34:18 (ESV)

Always remember one thing that in our journey through life, we all encounter moments of profound grief and loss. During these times, Psalm 34:18 serves as a comforting reminder that the Lord is near to the brokenhearted and saves those crushed in spirit.

*Grief is a universal experience, and it can feel isolating and overwhelming. Yet, in the midst of our deepest sorrows, God's presence is a source of profound comfort. He draws near to us, extending His arms of compassion and understanding. He knows our pain intimately and is with us in our darkest moments.*

**Action Plan:**

1. Prayer and Reflection: Spend time in prayer, pouring out your grief to God and seeking His comfort.

2. Scripture Meditation: Meditate on passages that offer comfort and hope, such as Psalm 23.

3. Support Group: Seek a support group or counsellor to help you process your grief.

**Prayer:**

*Heavenly Father, we come before You with heavy hearts, seeking Your comfort in our times of grief. Draw near to us and heal our broken spirits. May Your presence be our refuge and strength during these challenging times. In Jesus name, we pray. Amen.*

## DAY 09
## Surrendering Anxiety To God

"Do not be anxious about anything, but in everything by prayer and supplication with thanksgiving let your requests be made known to God. And the peace of God, which surpasses all understanding, will guard your hearts and your minds in Christ Jesus."
- Philippians 4:6-7 (ESV)

Anxiety can often feel like an unwelcome companion on our journey through life. It creeps into our hearts, casting a shadow of worry over our thoughts and stealing our peace. However, Philippians 4:6-7 offers us a powerful remedy for anxiety—surrendering it to God in prayer.

*Additional Scripture Reference:*

*The Bible says in 1 John 4:18, "Where God's love is, there is no fear, because God's perfect love drives out fear" (NCV). How do you learn to live in God's love so that you can live free of fear? Every day, you have to surrender your heart to God.*

Surrendering anxiety to God is an ongoing process. It means taking our worries one by one, day by day, and handing them over to Him. It's choosing faith over fear, trust over doubt, and prayer over panic.

**Action Plan:**

1. Daily Prayer Time: Set aside a specific time each day to bring your anxieties to God in prayer.

2. Breathing Exercises: Practice deep breathing exercises to calm your mind and body during anxious moments.

3. Seek Support: Don't hesitate to seek support from a trusted friend or counsellor when anxiety feels overwhelming.

**Prayer:**

*Heavenly Father, we come before You with our anxieties and worries. Help us to release them to You in prayer, trusting in Your love and wisdom. May Your peace guard our hearts and minds, even in the midst of life's storms. In Jesus name, we pray. Amen.*

## DAY 10
## The Power Of God's Word

"For the word of God is living and active, sharper than any two-edged sword, piercing to the division of soul and of spirit, of joints and of marrow, and discerning the thoughts and intentions of the heart." - Hebrews 4:12 (ESV)

I want you to understand that the Word of God is not just a collection of ancient texts; it is a living and active force in our lives. Hebrews 4:12 paints a vivid picture of its power, likening it to a sharp, two-edged sword that pierces to the very core of our being. It has the capacity to discern the thoughts and intentions of our hearts.

God's Word is more than ink on paper; it is the revelation of God's character, His love, and His plan for our lives. When we engage with Scripture, we invite transformation. It has the power to convict us, guide us, comfort us, and give us wisdom. It is through the Word that we come to know God intimately.

*Additional Scripture Reference:*

*1 Thessalonians 2:13*

*And we also thank God constantly for this, that when you received the word of God, which you heard from us, you accepted it not as the word of men but as what it really is, the word of God, which is at work in you believers.*

## Action Plan:

1. Daily Reading: Set aside time each day to read a portion of Scripture.

2. Scripture Memorization: Choose key verses to memorise and carry with you throughout the day.

3. Bible Study: Join or start a Bible study group to delve deeper into the Word.

4. Application: Reflect on how each passage applies to your life and seek to live it out.

## Prayer:

*Heavenly Father, we thank You for the living and active Word that guides, comforts, and transforms us. Help us to engage with Your Word daily, seeking to know You more deeply and allowing it to shape our lives. May it be a lamp to our feet and a light to our path. In Jesus name, we pray. Amen.*

*As you delve into the power of God's Word, may you experience its transformative impact on your life. May it pierce through the depths of your heart, renewing your mind, and drawing you closer to the heart of God.*

## DAY 11
## Embracing God's Promises

"By which he has granted to us his precious and very great promises, so that through them you may become partakers of the divine nature, having escaped from the corruption that is in the world because of sinful desire." - 2 Peter 1:4 (ESV)

God's promises are like a priceless treasure chest filled with gifts waiting to be unwrapped. 2 Peter 1:4 reminds us that through these promises, we are not only recipients of God's blessings but also partakers of His divine nature.

God's promises are the firm and unwavering commitments of a faithful and loving Father. They offer us hope, assurance, and a reason to press on, even when life's challenges seem insurmountable. These promises are the very essence of His character, revealing His unchanging love and faithfulness.

Embracing God's promises involves not merely knowing them but making them an integral part of our lives. It's a conscious decision to trust that God will fulfil what He has spoken, even when circumstances suggest otherwise.

**Action Plan:**

1. Promise Journal: Create a journal where you record God's promises as you encounter them in Scripture.

2. Meditation: Spend time meditating on a different promise each day, reflecting on how it applies to your life.

3. Confession: Speak God's promises aloud as declarations of faith.

**Prayer:**

*Heavenly Father, we thank You for the precious and very great promises You have given us. Help us to embrace them fully, knowing that Your word is trustworthy and true. May these promises be our source of hope and strength in every season of life. In Jesus name, we pray. Amen.*

## DAY 12
### The Blessing Of A Grateful Heart

"Enter his gates with thanksgiving, and his courts with praise! Give thanks to him; bless his name!" - Psalm 100:4 (ESV)

Gratitude is a powerful force that has the ability to transform our lives. Psalm 100:4 encourages us to enter God's presence with thanksgiving and praise. It's a reminder that a heart filled with gratitude is a heart that draws near to God's loving embrace.

A grateful heart is not dependent on circumstances but rooted in the recognition of God's goodness, faithfulness, and love. It's an acknowledgment that every breath we take, every blessing we receive, is a gift from our Heavenly Father. Gratitude shifts our focus from what we lack to what we have, from complaints to praise.

*Additional Scripture Reference:*

*1 Thessalonians 5:16-18*

*Rejoice always, pray continually, give thanks in all circumstances; for this is God's will for you in Christ Jesus.*

**Action Plan:**

1. Daily Gratitude Journal: Start each day by writing down at least three things you are thankful for.

2. Prayer of Thanksgiving: Dedicate a portion of your prayer time to thank God for His blessings.

3. Random Acts of Kindness: Show your gratitude by blessing others with acts of kindness.

**Prayer**

*Heavenly Father, we thank You for the blessing of a grateful heart. Help us to cultivate an attitude of gratitude, recognizing Your goodness in every aspect of our lives. May our praise and thanksgiving draw us closer to Your presence. In Jesus name, we pray. Amen.*

## DAY13
## Finding Peace in God's Presence

"I have set the Lord always before me; because he is at my right hand, I shall not be shaken." - Psalm 16:8 (ESV)

In the reality of life, finding true peace can sometimes feel elusive. But Psalm 16:8 offers us a profound insight into the source of enduring peace: setting the Lord always before us.

In God's presence, we find refuge from life's storms. It's a shelter where fear, worry, and anxiety are replaced with tranquillity, trust, and confidence. God's presence is not bound by location or circumstance; it's with us in the joyous celebrations and the darkest valleys.

Peace in God's presence is not dependent on our circumstances; it's anchored in the unchanging nature of our Heavenly Father. When we abide in Him, we remain unshaken by the challenges that life may bring.

**Action Plan:**

1. Daily Surrender: Begin each day by consciously inviting God's presence into your life.

2. Meditation: Spend time meditating on a specific attribute of God's character or a comforting Bible verse.

3. Silent Retreat: Set aside time for a silent retreat to deepen your awareness of God's presence.

**Prayer:**

Heavenly Father, we thank You for the gift of Your presence, where true peace is found. Help us to set You always before us, to trust in Your unwavering love and care. May Your presence be our refuge and our source of lasting peace. In Jesus' name, we pray. Amen.

## DAY 14
### Trusting God's Healing

"But he was pierced for our transgressions; he was crushed for our iniquities; upon him was the chastisement that brought us peace, and with his wounds, we are healed." - Isaiah 53:5 (ESV)

The Bible says in, Matt. 28:18,19. That power was given to you as part of your inheritance in Christ Jesus. You have entered into this position of authority because you are in Him.

The word (Power and authority) has already been given to you, the power to heal and authority to cast out demons and take control of your life.

Isaiah 53:5 reminds us again of a profound truth - God is our healer. The wounds of Christ, borne on the cross, carry not only the weight of our sins but also the promise of healing. In Him, we find restoration, renewal, and hope.

Life often brings us physical, emotional, and spiritual wounds. These wounds can leave us broken and hurting, searching for relief and restoration. But God's healing power is not limited by the depth of our wounds or the complexity of our pain.

**Action Plan:**

1. Daily Prayer for Healing: Dedicate time each day to pray for your own healing or for the healing of others.

2. Seek Medical Help: If you have physical health concerns, trust God's healing alongside seeking medical advice.

3. Forgiveness: Release any unforgiveness or bitterness that may hinder your healing process.

**Prayer:**

*Heavenly Father, we come before You, trusting in Your healing power. We bring our wounds and brokenness to You, knowing that You are the ultimate healer. Grant us the faith to trust Your perfect timing and the patience to wait on Your healing touch. In Jesus name, we pray. Amen.*

## DAY 15
### Living With Purpose

"And whatever you do, in word or deed, do everything in the name of the Lord Jesus, giving thanks to God the Father through him." - Colossians 3:17 (ESV)

Living with purpose is a calling that resonates deep within our souls. It's the recognition that every word we speak, every action we take, can be infused with meaning when done in the name of the Lord Jesus.

Colossians 3:17 encourages us to live with a profound awareness of God's presence in our daily lives. It's an invitation to align our thoughts, words, and deeds with His will and to honour Him in everything we do. When we do this, even the simplest tasks become acts of worship.

Our purpose is to reflect God's love, grace, and truth to the world around us. It's to be the hands and feet of Jesus, bringing His light into the darkness. When we live with this purpose, our lives take on a new and profound meaning.

**Action Plan:**

1. Prayerful Reflection: Regularly reflect on your daily activities and how they align with God's purpose.

2. Service: Seek opportunities to serve others in your community, church, or through charitable organisations.

3. Scripture Study: Study the Bible to better understand God's will and how you can live in alignment with it.

**Prayer:**

Heavenly Father, we thank You for the purpose You have given us in Christ. Help us to live each day with a deep sense of purpose, honouring You in all we do. May our lives be a reflection of Your love and grace to the world. In Jesus name, we pray. Amen.

## DAY 16
### Strengthening Your Faith

"So faith comes from hearing, and hearing through the word of Christ." - Romans 10:17 (ESV)

Faith is the cornerstone of our relationship with God. It's the unwavering trust and confidence in His promises, even when circumstances seem uncertain. Romans 10:17 reminds us that faith comes through hearing the word of Christ, and this truth can profoundly impact our daily lives.

Strengthening your faith involves immersing yourself in God's Word, prayer, and a deepening understanding of His character. It's about nurturing a trust in Him that can withstand life's trials and uncertainties.

Prayer, too, is vital for faith's growth. Through prayer, you develop a personal relationship with God, pouring out your heart to Him, and listening for His guidance and comfort. In this communion with the Almighty, your faith deepens as you experience His presence and guidance.

**Action Plan:**

1. Daily Scripture Reading: Set aside time each day to read and reflect on the Bible.

2. Scripture Journaling: Keep a journal to record insights, prayers, and the ways God is working in your life.

3. Join a Bible Study Group: Seek fellowship with other believers to study and discuss the Scriptures together.

**Prayer:**

*Heavenly Father, we thank You for the gift of faith and the means to strengthen it through Your Word and prayer. Help us to daily draw nearer to You, growing in faith and trust in Your promises. May our lives be a testament to Your unfailing love and grace. In Jesus name, we pray. Amen.*

## DAY 17
### Rest In God's Love

"So we have come to know and to believe the love that God has for us. God is love, and anyone who abides in love abides in God, and God abides in them." - 1 John 4:16 (NRSV)

Resting in God's love means finding solace and security in the arms of the One who created us. It's releasing our burdens, fears, and anxieties into His loving care, knowing that His love never fails. When we abide in His love, we experience a peace that transcends circumstances.

This deep sense of love also calls us to love one another as God has loved us. It's an outpouring of His love in our lives, touching those around us with the same love we have received. Resting in God's love empowers us to navigate life's challenges with grace and compassion.

**Action Plan:**

1. Daily Reflection: Spend time each day reflecting on God's love and how it has touched your life.

2. Acts of Love: Purposefully show love and kindness to those you encounter, demonstrating God's love in action.

3. Meditative Prayer: Engage in meditative prayer practices that allow you to rest in God's love and receive His peace.

**Prayer:**

*Heavenly Father, we thank You for the immeasurable love You have for us. Help us to fully grasp the depth of Your love and to rest in it, finding peace and solace in Your presence. May Your love flow through us, touching the lives of those we encounter. In Jesus' name, we pray. Amen.*

## DAY 18
### The Blessing Of Friendship

"A man of many companions may come to ruin, but there is a friend who sticks closer than a brother." - Proverbs 18:24 (ESV)

Friendship is a precious gift from God that enriches our lives in countless ways. Proverbs 18:24 reminds us that true friends are rare treasures, those who stand by us through thick and thin, offering support, love, and companionship.

Friendship is a reflection of God's love for us. It's a bond formed not just by shared interests, but by shared experiences, laughter, and tears. In friends, we find comfort, encouragement, and a shoulder to lean on during life's storms.

**Action Plan:**

1. Nurture Existing Friendships: Make an effort to spend quality time with your friends, whether through calls, texts, or face-to-face meetings.

2. Be a Good Friend: Actively listen, offer your support, and be present for your friends in their times of need.

3. Seek Authentic Connections: Be open to forming new friendships based on shared values and interests.

**Prayer:**

*Heavenly Father, we thank You for the gift of friendship, for friends who stick closer than family. Help us cherish and nurture these relationships, and may our friendships be a reflection of Your love. May we be good friends to others, showing them Your love and grace. In Jesus name, we pray. Amen.*

## DAY 19
## Rejoicing In Salvation

"Behold, God is my salvation; I will trust, and will not be afraid; for the Lord God is my strength and my song, and he has become my salvation." - Isaiah 12:2 (ESV)

Salvation is not just a theological concept but a profound experience that should fill our hearts with unending joy. Isaiah 12:2 reminds us that God Himself is our salvation, our source of trust, strength, and unending joy.

Our salvation brings freedom from the bondage of sin and the promise of eternal life with God. It's a reason to rejoice even in the midst of life's challenges. We can trust in God's unfailing love, knowing that He is our strength and our song.

**Action Plan:**

1. Share the Good News: Share your salvation story with others, sharing the joy and hope it brings.

2. Study Scripture: Dive deeper into God's Word to understand the depth of His salvation plan.

3. Prayer of Thanksgiving: Dedicate time in your prayer life to thank God for your salvation.

**Prayer:**

*Heavenly Father, we rejoice in the salvation You have provided through Your Son, Jesus Christ. May this profound gift fill us with unending joy and gratitude. Help us share the good news of salvation with others, that they too may experience the joy of knowing You. In Jesus name, we pray. Amen.*

## DAY 20
### Embracing God's Mercy

"But God, being rich in mercy, because of the great love with which he loved us, even when we were dead in our trespasses, made us alive together with Christ—by grace you have been saved." - Ephesians 2:4-5 (ESV)

God's mercy is a gift beyond measure, a reflection of His boundless love for us. In Ephesians 2:4-5, we're reminded of His abundant mercy that reaches out to us even when we were lost in sin, offering us life and salvation through Christ.

God's mercy is not based on our worthiness but on His character. It's His loving nature that extends a hand of forgiveness and grace when we least deserve it. When we embrace God's mercy, it transforms our lives. We are no longer bound by guilt and shame, for His mercy offers us a fresh start.

**Action Plan:**

1. Forgiveness: Extend the same mercy to others that God has shown to you by forgiving those who have wronged you.

2. Acts of Kindness: Practice acts of mercy and kindness towards those in need, reflecting God's love.

3. Study God's Word: Explore Scriptures that highlight God's mercy, deepening your understanding of this precious gift.

**Prayer:**

*Heavenly Father, we are humbled by Your abundant mercy. Thank You for loving us despite our shortcomings. Help us embrace Your mercy fully and extend it to others. May our lives be a testimony to Your love and grace. In Jesus name, we pray. Amen.*

## DAY 21
## Trusting God's Protection

"He will cover you with his feathers, and under his wings you will find refuge; his faithfulness will be your shield and rampart." - Psalm 91:4 (NIV)

In the often tumultuous journey of life, we find solace and security in the promise of God's protection. Psalm 91:4 beautifully illustrates this truth by comparing God's care to a mother bird sheltering her chicks under her wings.

When we trust in God's protection, we acknowledge that He is our ultimate refuge. His faithfulness stands as an unwavering shield, guarding us against life's storms. Just as a mother bird watches over her young, our Heavenly Father watches over us, shielding us from harm.

**Action Plan:**

1. Daily Prayer: Begin each day by entrusting yourself and your loved ones to God's protective care.

2. Meditate on Psalm 91: Spend time reflecting on the verses in Psalm 91, allowing God's promises to deepen your trust.

3. Encourage Others: Share the comfort of God's protective love with those who are anxious or in need.

**Prayer:**

*Heavenly Father, we find refuge in Your loving care. Thank You for being our shield and fortress. May our trust in Your protection grow stronger each day, and may we share the assurance of Your love with others. In Jesus name, we pray. Amen.*

## DAY 22
## The Power Of Prayer

"The prayer of a righteous person has great power as it is working." - James 5:16
(ESV)

Prayer is not merely a routine, but a profound connection to our Heavenly Father. In James 5:16, we are reminded of the incredible power contained within the prayers of the righteous. It's a power that transcends human understanding, bringing healing, comfort, and transformation.

When we pray, we enter into a sacred conversation with God, sharing our joys, sorrows, and hopes. Our prayers are not in vain; they are the means by which we access God's wisdom, guidance, and miraculous intervention.

**Action Plan:**

1. Dedicated Prayer Time: Set aside a specific time each day for focused prayer, nurturing your relationship with God.

2. Pray with Others: Join a prayer group or partner with friends to intercede for one another and witness the power of collective prayer.

3. Pray Boldly: Don't hesitate to bring your deepest concerns before God, trusting in His ability to answer according to His perfect will.

**Prayer:**

*Heavenly Father, we are in awe of the privilege of prayer. May our hearts be steadfast in seeking Your face, and may our prayers be a source of strength, healing, and transformation. In Jesus name, we pray. Amen.*

## DAY 23
## Cultivating A Heart Of Generosity

"Give, and it will be given to you. A good measure, pressed down, shaken together and running over, will be poured into your lap. For with the measure you use, it will be measured to you." - Luke 6:38 (NIV)

Generosity is a reflection of God's heart, and when we cultivate a heart of generosity, we mirror His love to the world. Luke 6:38 reminds us of the beautiful principle that when we give freely, we receive abundantly.

Generosity is not limited to material possessions; it extends to our time, talents, and compassion. It's about selflessly giving without expecting anything in return. When we embrace this lifestyle, we open the door to blessings overflowing, not just in material wealth, but in spiritual richness and fulfilment.

**Action Plan:**

1. Daily Acts of Kindness: Purposefully perform small acts of kindness each day, whether it's helping someone in need or offering a kind word.

2. Give Cheerfully: When you give, do so with a cheerful heart, knowing that your generosity is sowing seeds of joy.

3. Support Charitable Causes: Contribute to charities or causes that align with your values, extending your generosity beyond your immediate circle.

**Prayer:**

*Heavenly Father, thank You for Your generosity in giving us the gift of salvation. Teach us to cultivate generous hearts, willing to share Your love and blessings with others. May our lives be a testament to Your boundless grace. In Jesus name, we pray. Amen.*

## DAY 24
### Persevering In Faith

"Therefore, since we are surrounded by so great a cloud of witnesses, let us also lay aside every weight, and sin which clings so closely, and let us run with endurance the race that is set before us, looking to Jesus, the founder and perfecter of our faith, who for the joy that was set before him endured the cross, despising the shame, and is seated at the right hand of the throne of God." - Hebrews 12:1-2 (ESV)

Life often presents us with challenges, obstacles, and moments of doubt. Yet, in the midst of these trials, we are called to persevere in faith. Hebrews 12:1-2 beautifully illustrates this journey of faith as a race, one that requires endurance, courage, and unwavering trust in our Saviour, Jesus Christ.

Our faith is not a sprint but a marathon, and it's not meant to be easy. Just as runners train and discipline themselves, we too must lay aside the weights of doubt, fear, and sin that hinder our progress. With our eyes fixed on Jesus, who endured the ultimate suffering for our sake, we can find the strength to persevere.

**Action Plan:**

1. Daily Devotion: Dedicate time each day to study God's Word, seeking encouragement and guidance.

2. Prayer and Worship: Cultivate a habit of fervent prayer and worship to draw nearer to God.

3. Seek Accountability: Find an accountability partner or join a small group for mutual support in your faith journey.

**Prayer:**

*Heavenly Father, grant us the strength to persevere in our faith journey, just as Your Son, Jesus, endured the cross for our sake. May we lay aside every weight that hinders us and run with endurance, looking to Him as our source of strength and hope. In Jesus name, we pray. Amen.*

## DAY 25
### Navigating Life's challenges

"Even though I walk through the valley of the shadow of death, I will fear no evil, for you are with me; your rod and your staff, they comfort me." - Psalm 23:4 (ESV)

Life is a journey filled with both mountaintop joys and valley-like challenges. In those moments when the path ahead seems shadowed and daunting, we can find solace and courage in the words of Psalm 23:4.

The imagery of walking through the valley of the shadow of death resonates with our experiences of trials, suffering, and uncertainty. Yet, as daughters of

God, we have a Shepherd who walks beside us, providing comfort and guidance. He is our source of unwavering strength and hope.

**Action Plan:**

1. Scripture Memorization: Commit Psalm 23:4 to memory, allowing it to be a source of comfort and assurance during difficult times.

2. Community Support: Lean on your faith community for prayer and encouragement during life's challenges.

3. Journaling: Keep a gratitude journal to record moments of God's provision and comfort.

**Prayer:**

*Heavenly Father, we thank You for being our Shepherd, guiding us through life's challenges. Grant us the courage to fear no evil, knowing that Your presence comforts us. May we trust in Your unfailing love and walk boldly through the valleys, for You are with us. In Jesus name, we pray. Amen.*

## DAY 26
## The Gift Of God's Peace

"Peace I leave with you; my peace I give to you. Not as the world gives do I give to you. Let not your hearts be troubled, neither let them be afraid." - John 14:27 (ESV)

In a world often marked by chaos, stress, and uncertainty, the gift of God's peace is a treasure beyond measure. The words of Jesus in John 14:27 assure us that His peace is not fleeting or dependent on external circumstances. It's a peace that surpasses all understanding and offers solace to our restless hearts.

This divine peace isn't just the absence of turmoil; it's the presence of a calm assurance that God is in control. It's the kind of peace that stills the storms within us, even when the storms around us rage.

**Action Plan:**

1. Daily Meditation: Spend quiet moments meditating on John 14:27 and let the truth of God's peace fill your heart.

2. Breathing Exercises: Practice deep breathing and mindfulness to centre your thoughts on God's peace during moments of anxiety.

3. Scripture Exploration: Explore other Bible verses about God's peace (e.g., Philippians 4:6-7, Isaiah 26:3) to deepen your understanding.

**Prayer:**

*Heavenly Father, we thank You for the precious gift of Your peace. In a world filled with turmoil, Your peace is a refuge for our souls. Help us to hold onto this gift, knowing that it is rooted in Your presence and love. Let not our hearts be troubled, but let them be filled with Your perfect peace. In Jesus name, we pray. Amen.*

## DAY 27
### Embracing God's Forgiveness

"If we confess our sins, he is faithful and just to forgive us our sins and to cleanse us from all unrighteousness." - 1 John 1:9 (ESV)

God's forgiveness is a profound and liberating gift. It's the assurance that no matter our past mistakes, our sins can be washed away through repentance and confession. In 1 John 1:9, we are reminded of God's faithfulness and justice in forgiving our sins and cleansing us from all unrighteousness.

Embracing God's forgiveness means releasing the burdens of guilt, shame, and regret. It's acknowledging our need for His mercy and receiving the freedom that comes from being forgiven by our Heavenly Father. When we confess our sins and turn to Him, we find not condemnation but open arms waiting to welcome us back into His love.

**Action Plan:**

1. Daily Self-Examination: Take time each day to reflect on your actions and thoughts, confessing any sins to God.

2. Practice Forgiveness: Extend the forgiveness you receive from God to others in your life who may have wronged you.

3. Study God's Forgiveness: Dive into Scripture to explore other verses about God's forgiveness (e.g., Psalm 103:12, Micah 7:18-19).

**Prayer:**

*Heavenly Father, we come before You with grateful hearts for the gift of Your forgiveness. Thank You for being faithful and just to forgive our sins when we confess them. Help us to embrace this forgiveness fully, releasing the weight of our past mistakes. May we also extend forgiveness to others as You have forgiven us. In Jesus name, we pray. Amen.*

## DAY 28
## Trusting God's Guidance In Career

"Trust in the Lord with all your heart and lean not on your own understanding; in all your ways submit to him, and he will make your paths straight." - Proverbs 3:5-6 (NIV)

Navigating our careers can be one of life's most significant challenges. We face choices, decisions, and uncertainties about our professional journeys. In these moments, Proverbs 3:5-6 offers us profound wisdom and comfort. It reminds us to trust in the Lord with all our hearts, acknowledging that His understanding surpasses our own.

Trusting God's guidance in your career means seeking His direction in your choices, big or small. It involves surrendering your plans to Him, knowing that His purpose for your life includes your professional path. When you submit to Him, He promises to make your paths straight, guiding you toward the opportunities and decisions that align with His divine plan.

**Action Plan:**

1. Daily Prayer for Guidance: Begin and end each day with a prayer, seeking God's wisdom and guidance in your career.

2. Seek Wise Counsel: Connect with a mentor or trusted friend for career advice, ensuring it aligns with your faith and values.

3. Step Out in Faith: When faced with a career decision, make a choice, trusting that God is leading you, even if you don't have all the answers.

**Prayer:**

## DAY 29
### Living With Gratitude

"So then, just as you received Christ Jesus as Lord, continue to live your lives in him, rooted and built up in him, strengthened in the faith as you were taught, and overflowing with thankfulness." - Colossians 2:6-7 (NIV)

Gratitude is a powerful force that can transform our lives. In Colossians 2:6-7, we are reminded to live our lives in Christ, deeply rooted in Him, and overflowing with thankfulness. What a beautiful way to approach each day!

Living with gratitude means recognizing God's blessings, both big and small, and responding with a heart full of thanks. It's about shifting our focus from what we lack to what we have, from life's challenges to its opportunities. Gratitude is a choice—a choice to see the goodness of God in every aspect of our lives.

**Action Plan:**

1. Daily Gratitude Journal: Set aside time each day to write down at least three things you're thankful for. Cultivate a habit of counting your blessings.

2. Express Thankfulness: Don't keep your gratitude to yourself. Tell God, and tell others, how thankful you are for them and the blessings in your life.

3. Pray with Thanksgiving: In your prayers, focus on gratitude before presenting your requests to God.

**Prayer:**

## DAY 30
## Resting In God's Provision

"So do not worry, saying, 'What shall we eat?' or 'What shall we drink?' or 'What shall we wear?' For the pagans run after all these things, and your heavenly Father knows that you need them. But seek first his kingdom and his righteousness, and all these things will be given to you as well." - Matthew 6:31-33 (NIV)

In a world filled with constant worries about provision, Jesus' words in Matthew 6:31-33 bring solace and reassurance. He reminds us not to fret over material needs, for our Heavenly Father knows them all. Instead, He invites us to focus on something greater—His kingdom and righteousness.

Resting in God's provision means surrendering our anxieties about food, drink, clothing, and other earthly concerns to the One who holds the universe in His hands. It's an act of faith that acknowledges God as our loving Provider, the One who cares for our every need.

**Action Plan:**

1. Daily Surrender: Start and end your day by surrendering your worries to God. Trust Him to provide for you and your loved ones.

2. Seek His Kingdom: Dedicate time to seek God's presence through prayer, Scripture, and acts of service. Make His priorities your own.

3. Generosity: Practice giving to others in need. Sharing God's provision with those less fortunate is an act of faith.

**Prayer:**

*Gracious Father, we thank You for being our Provider. Help us to rest in Your unfailing care, knowing that You are aware of our needs. May we seek Your kingdom above all else, trusting that You will supply us with all we require. In Jesus name, we pray. Amen.*

## Be Strong In The LORD

Ephesians 6:10 (NIV)
"Finally, be strong in the Lord and in his mighty power."

In the journey of life, we often find ourselves facing challenges that test the limits of our strength and resilience. The Apostle Paul's words in Ephesians 6:10 serve as a timeless reminder that our true strength lies not in ourselves but in the boundless power of our Lord.

Life's trials can be overwhelming, but as women of faith, we are called to draw strength from a wellspring that knows no bounds. Just as a tree finds its roots deep in the soil to withstand storms, we must anchor ourselves in the Lord's might. This strength is not about physical prowess but the inner fortitude that comes from unwavering faith and trust in our Heavenly Father.

*Additional Scripture References:*

*Isaiah 41:10 (NIV): "So do not fear, for I am with you; do not be dismayed, for I am your God. I will strengthen you and help you; I will uphold you with my righteous right hand."*

*Philippians 4:13 (NIV): "I can do all this through him who gives me strength."*

**Action Plan:**

1.  Prayer and Meditation: Dedicate time daily to pray and meditate on Ephesians 6:10 and the additional scriptures. Seek guidance and strength from the Lord.

2.  Community Support: Connect with fellow sisters in faith for encouragement and mutual support in your journey of being strong in the Lord.

3.  Acts of Kindness: Channel the strength you receive from the Lord into acts of kindness and love toward others, reflecting His grace.

**Prayer:**

*Heavenly Father, We humbly come before You, seeking the strength that can only be found in Your mighty power. As women of faith, help us anchor our souls in You, knowing that in our weakness, Your strength is made perfect. Grant us the courage to face life's challenges with unwavering trust in Your guidance and provision. May we be beacons of Your love and grace in this world.*
*In Jesus name, we pray. Amen.*

*May you find renewed strength in the Lord every day, dear sister. Stay strong, and let His power guide you through life's journey.*

# APRIL

*Psalm 34:18 (NIV)*
*"The Lord is close to the brokenhearted and saves those who are crushed in spirit."*
*This verse reminds us that in our moments of pain, grief, and despair, the Lord is not distant but near. His presence offers solace and redemption to those who feel shattered in spirit. It's a beautiful testament to the compassion and love that God extends to His children during their most challenging moments.*

## DAY 01
## Surrendering To God's Will

"Therefore, I urge you, brothers and sisters, in view of God's mercy, to offer your bodies as a living sacrifice, holy and pleasing to God—this is your true and proper worship. Do not conform to the pattern of this world, but be transformed by the renewing of your mind. Then you will be able to test and approve what God's will is—his good, pleasing and perfect will." - Romans 12:1-2 (NIV)

The journey of faith often leads us to the profound realisation that our own plans and desires must yield to God's perfect will. Surrendering to God's will is not a sign of weakness but a demonstration of faith and trust. In Romans 12:1-2, we are encouraged to offer our lives as living sacrifices, allowing God to shape us according to His divine purpose.

**Action Plan:**

1. Daily Dedication: Begin each day with a prayer of surrender, offering your thoughts, words, and actions to God.

2. Discernment in Decisions: Seek God's guidance in every aspect of your life, big or small, and trust His leading.

3. Fruitful Living: Live in a way that reflects God's love and transforms the world around you.

**Prayer:**

*Heavenly Father, we humbly present ourselves as living sacrifices, ready to do Your will. Grant us the strength to resist conformity to this world and the wisdom to discern Your perfect plan for our lives. May our surrender be an act of worship and a testimony to Your faithfulness. In Jesus name, we pray. Amen.*

## DAY 02
## The Blessing Of God's Presence

"The Lord replied, 'My Presence will go with you, and I will give you rest.'" - Exodus
33:14 (NIV)

One of the most precious gifts God offers us is the assurance of His presence.
In Exodus 33:14, the Lord promises Moses, "My Presence will go with you, and
I will give you rest." This promise isn't exclusive to Moses; it's for all of us who
seek God's companionship.

God's presence is not merely a comforting thought; it's a reality that brings
rest, peace, and strength to our souls. It's in His presence that we find refuge
from life's storms, guidance in times of uncertainty, and comfort in moments
of despair.

**Action Plan:**

1. Daily Practice of His Presence: Start your day by acknowledging God's
   presence with you. Invite Him into every moment.

2. Quiet Reflection: Spend time in quiet reflection, listening for God's
   gentle voice and seeking His guidance.

3. Worship and Gratitude: Express your love and gratitude to God through
   worship, prayer, and thanksgiving.

**Prayer:**

*Heavenly Father, we thank You for the incredible blessing of Your presence in our lives. May
we be ever mindful of Your nearness, finding rest and refuge in You. Help us to seek Your
face daily and share Your love with the world around us. In Jesus name, we pray. Amen.*

## DAY 03
## Rejoicing In God's Faithfulness

"Great is his faithfulness; his mercies begin afresh each morning." - Lamentations
3:23 (NLT)

In a world that often feels unpredictable, there's one constant we can always rely on: God's faithfulness. Lamentations 3:23 reminds us of this beautiful truth, declaring, "Great is his faithfulness; his mercies begin afresh each morning." This verse encapsulates the unwavering nature of God's love and grace.

God's faithfulness is a source of great comfort and joy. It means that His promises endure, His love never wavers, and His mercies are renewed every day. We can rejoice because no matter what challenges we face, God remains steadfast.

**Action Plan:**

1. Daily Remembrance: Start each day by reflecting on God's faithfulness. Remind yourself of His past acts of love and provision in your life.

2. Gratitude Journal: Maintain a gratitude journal to record God's faithfulness and the blessings He bestows daily.

3. Prayer of Thanksgiving: Dedicate time in prayer to thank God for His faithfulness and faithfulness to you.

**Prayer:**

*Heavenly Father, we rejoice in Your faithfulness, knowing that Your love and mercies are new every morning. Help us to trust in Your promises and share the joy of Your faithfulness with others. In Jesus name, we pray. Amen.*

## DAY 04
### Embracing God's Comfort

"Praise be to the God and Father of our Lord Jesus Christ, the Father of compassion and the God of all comfort, who comforts us in all our troubles, so that we can comfort those in any trouble with the comfort we ourselves receive from God." - 2 Corinthians 1:3-4 (NIV)

Life can be filled with moments of hardship, pain, and sorrow. During these challenging times, we often yearn for comfort and solace. Thankfully, as daughters of the Almighty, we have access to a wellspring of divine comfort. 2 Corinthians 1:3-4 reminds us of this, declaring that God is the "Father of compassion and the God of all comfort."

God's comfort is not merely a warm embrace during our trials, but a source of strength that equips us to face life's difficulties. It is through His comfort that we can find peace in the midst of turmoil, healing in times of brokenness, and hope in moments of despair.

**Action Plan:**

1. Seek His Presence: Spend time in prayer and meditation, inviting God's comforting presence into your life.

2. Extend Comfort: As you experience God's comfort, share it with others who are hurting, becoming a vessel of His compassion.

3. Hold Fast to His Promises: Memorise and meditate on comforting Bible verses to lean on during trying times.

**Prayer:**

Heavenly Father, we thank You for being our source of comfort in times of trouble. Help us to fully embrace Your comforting presence and to share it with those who need it. May we find strength in You and extend Your love to others. In Jesus name, we pray. Amen.

As you embrace God's comfort, may you discover renewed strength, and may His love flow through you to comfort others, transforming lives through His grace.

## DAY 05
## Trusting God's Guidance In Relationships

"Do not be wise in your own eyes; fear the Lord and shun evil. This will bring health to your body and nourishment to your bones." - Proverbs 3:7-8 (NIV)

Relationships are an essential part of our lives, but they can also be complex and challenging. We often seek guidance on how to navigate them, and Proverbs 3:7-8 offers a profound insight: "Do not be wise in your own eyes; fear the Lord and shun evil. This will bring health to your body and nourishment to your bones."

Trusting God's guidance in relationships begins with humility—a recognition that our wisdom is limited, but His is boundless. When we fear the Lord and turn away from evil, we open the door to His divine wisdom, which can heal and nourish our relationships.

**Action Plan:**

1. Listen Actively: In your interactions, practice active listening, seeking to understand before being understood.

2. Forgive and Seek Forgiveness: Embrace the power of forgiveness in relationships, letting go of grudges, and being willing to apologise when needed.

3. Boundaries: Set healthy boundaries that protect your well-being and the well-being of others.

**Prayer:**

*Heavenly Father, we acknowledge that Your wisdom surpasses our own. Grant us the humility to seek Your guidance in our relationships. Help us to listen, forgive, and set healthy boundaries as we walk in Your ways. In Jesus name, we pray. Amen.*

*Trusting God's guidance in relationships is a path to healthier, more fulfilling connections. May His wisdom guide your interactions and bring blessings to your life and the lives of those around you.*

## DAY 06
### Persevering With Patience

*"May the God who gives endurance and encouragement give you the same attitude of mind toward each other that Christ Jesus had." - Romans 15:5 (NIV)*

Life often presents us with trials and challenges that require patience and endurance. The Bible reminds us in Romans 15:5 that God, who gives us both endurance and encouragement, desires us to adopt the same attitude of patience that Jesus exemplified.

Patience is more than just waiting; it's an attitude of trust and endurance amid difficulties. Christ's life was marked by unwavering patience in the face of adversity, and we are called to emulate His example. In times of struggle, our patience not only helps us persevere but also becomes a testimony of our faith.

**Action Plan:**

1. Prayer for Patience: Begin your day with a prayer for patience, asking God to help you respond to challenges with grace.

2. Meditation on Scripture: Reflect on passages in the Bible that highlight patience, like Psalm 37:7 or James 5:7-8.

3. Count Your Blessings: When facing difficulties, take a moment to count your blessings and remind yourself of God's faithfulness.

**Prayer:**

*Heavenly Father, grant us the endurance and patience to face life's challenges with the grace that Christ displayed. May our attitudes reflect His love and trust in Your perfect plan. In Jesus' name, we pray. Amen.*

*As we persevere with patience, we align ourselves with God's plan and become beacons of His love in a world often marked by haste and impatience. Trust that His enduring love will sustain you through every trial.*

## DAY 07
## Nurturing Family Bond

"Children are a heritage from the Lord, offspring a reward from him." - Psalm 127:3
(NIV)

In a world that often pulls us in countless directions, nurturing our family bonds is a precious endeavour guided by the wisdom of Psalm 127:3. This verse reminds us that children are a gift from the Lord, a heritage to be treasured and cultivated.

Our families are a vital part of God's plan for our lives. They provide love, support, and a foundation for our faith. Psalm 127:3 encourages us to cherish our children and recognize them as a divine blessing. By nurturing these bonds, we not only honour God's gift but also create a legacy of love and faithfulness.

**Action Plan:**

1. Quality Time: Dedicate intentional quality time with your family, free from distractions, to build stronger connections.

2. Spiritual Growth: Encourage spiritual growth within your family through prayer, Bible study, and attending church together.

3. Acts of Love: Show love through acts of service, forgiveness, and support, creating an atmosphere of grace and acceptance.

**Prayer:**

*Heavenly Father, we thank You for the gift of family. Help us nurture these bonds, recognizing the incredible blessing they are. May our families be places of love, faith, and support, reflecting Your divine plan. In Jesus name, we pray. Amen.*

*By nurturing family bonds, we create a haven of love and faith where each member can grow and flourish. Trust that God's guidance will strengthen these connections, allowing His love to shine through your family.*

## DAY 08
## Living As God's Ambassador

"We are therefore Christ's ambassadors, as though God were making his appeal through us." - 2 Corinthians 5:20 (NIV)

As followers of Jesus, we are called to be His ambassadors on this Earth, representing His love, grace, and truth to the world around us. The verse from 2 Corinthians 5:20 reminds us of this high and noble calling.

To be an ambassador of Christ means that we are His messengers, His representatives. We carry the responsibility of showing the world who He is by how we live, speak, and love. It's a calling that goes beyond our individual lives; it's about being part of something much bigger—the expansion of God's kingdom on Earth.

## Action Plan:

1. Reflect Christ's Character: In every situation, ask yourself, "What would Jesus do?" Strive to emulate His love, compassion, and integrity.

2. Share the Gospel: Be intentional about sharing the good news of Jesus with others. You don't need to be a theologian; your personal testimony and the transformative power of Jesus in your life are compelling.

3. Pray for Wisdom: Ask God for wisdom and discernment in your interactions. Pray for the people you encounter daily.

## Prayer:

*Heavenly Father, we thank You for the incredible privilege of being Your ambassadors. Help us to reflect Your character, share Your message, and serve others with love and grace. May our lives be a testimony to Your goodness. In Jesus name, we pray. Amen.*

*Living as God's ambassadors is a profound calling that carries both responsibility and great joy. Embrace this role, knowing that you are part of God's plan to bring His love and redemption to the world.*

# DAY 09
## The Power God's Love

Romans 8:37-39 (NIV)
"No, in all these things we are more than conquerors through him who loved us. For I am convinced that neither death nor life, neither angels nor demons, neither the present nor the future, nor any powers, neither height nor depth, nor anything else in all creation, will be able to separate us from the love of God that is in Christ Jesus our Lord."

In these verses from Romans, we are reminded of the unwavering love of God. It's a love so profound that it defies every challenge and transcends every circumstance. God's love is a mighty force that empowers us to overcome any obstacle that life throws our way. It's a love that knows no bounds and stands firm against all odds, assuring us of His eternal presence.

**Action Plan:**

1. Reflect Daily: Begin each day by reflecting on God's love. Meditate on the scripture, Romans 8:37-39, to reinforce the depth of His love for you.

2. Love Others: Embrace the transformative power of God's love by sharing it with others. Perform acts of kindness and compassion to radiate His love to those around you.

3. Prayer and Surrender: Dedicate time to prayer, allowing you to surrender your worries and anxieties to God's love. Trust that His love will guide you through any challenges.

**Prayer:**

*Dear Heavenly Father,*
*We thank you for the immeasurable love you have bestowed upon us. Help us to fully grasp the depth of your love, to live as conquerors, and to share that love with others. In times of doubt or hardship, remind us that nothing can separate us from your love. Guide us, protect us, and fill us with your everlasting love.*
*In Jesus name, we pray. Amen.*

## DAY 10
### Finding Peace In Solitude

Psalm 46:10 (NIV)
"Be still, and know that I am God; I will be exalted among the nations, I will be exalted in the earth."

In the hustle and bustle of life, it's easy to get lost in the noise and chaos. Psalm 46:10 reminds us to embrace moments of solitude, to be still, and to reconnect with our Creator. It's in these tranquil moments that we find profound peace and rediscover our purpose. In solitude, we can hear God's gentle whispers, feel His presence, and gain clarity amidst life's challenges.

**Action Plan:**

1. Daily Quiet Time: Dedicate a portion of your day to quiet reflection and prayer. Find a peaceful space where you can commune with God without distractions.

2. Nature Retreats: Spend time in nature, whether it's a walk in the park or a weekend camping trip. Nature's serenity can amplify the sense of peace in solitude.

3. Digital Detox: Regularly disconnect from technology and social media to create space for solitude. Use this time for introspection and spiritual growth.

**Prayer:**

*Dear Heavenly Father,*
*We thank you for the gift of solitude, where we can find solace in your presence. In the stillness, we hear your voice, and in the quiet, we feel your love. Grant us the wisdom to prioritise moments of solitude in our daily lives. May we find deep peace in these moments and carry that tranquillity into the world, exalting your name among the nations.*
*In Jesus name, we pray. Amen.*

## DAY 11
## Resting In God's Strength

Isaiah 30:15 (NIV)
"This is what the Sovereign Lord, the Holy One of Israel, says: 'In repentance and rest is your salvation, in quietness and trust is your strength, but you would have none of it.'"

In a world filled with hustle and constant demands, finding rest can feel like an elusive dream. Yet, Isaiah 30:15 reminds us that true strength comes from resting in God's presence. It's in moments of quietness, trust, and repentance that we discover His unwavering support. Resting in His strength doesn't signify weakness but rather the acknowledgment that we are dependent on a higher power.

**Action Plan:**

1. Daily Quiet Time: Set aside a sacred time each day for prayer, meditation, and reading of scripture. Use this time to seek God's presence and reflect on His strength.

2. Let Go of Control: Surrender the need to control every aspect of your life. Trust that God's plan is far greater than your own, and find peace in His guidance.

3. Practice Self-Care: Prioritise self-care to rejuvenate both physically and spiritually. Rest is not laziness; it's essential for maintaining the strength to fulfil your purpose.

**Prayer:**

*Heavenly Father,*
*We come before you seeking the strength that can only come from resting in your presence. Teach us to let go of our worries and to trust in your perfect plan. In moments of quietness, may we find renewed strength, and in times of repentance, may we experience your unending grace. Guide us, Lord, as we journey through life, relying on your unwavering strength.*
*In Jesus name, we pray. Amen.*

## DAY 12
## Embracing God's Purpose For Your Life

Jeremiah 1:5 (NIV)
"Before I formed you in the womb, I knew you, before you were born, I set you apart; I appointed you as a prophet to the nations."

Jeremiah 1:5 serves as a powerful reminder that each of us has a unique and divine purpose. Before we were even conceived, God knew us and had a plan for our lives. Embracing His purpose is a journey of discovering our true selves, talents, and passions, aligning them with His will. It's a journey that fills our lives with meaning, fulfilment, and a profound sense of God's guidance.

**Action Plan:**

1. Seek His Guidance: Begin each day with prayer, seeking God's guidance for your life. Ask Him to reveal His purpose and give you the wisdom to follow it.

2. Self-Reflection: Spend time reflecting on your strengths, passions, and life experiences. Identify how they might align with God's purpose for you.

3. Persevere Through Challenges: Know that the path to fulfilling your purpose may not always be easy. Lean on God's strength during challenges, trusting that He is with you every step of the way.

**Prayer:**

*Dear Heavenly Father,*
*We are grateful for the assurance that you have a unique purpose for each of us. Help us to seek and embrace that purpose with open hearts and unwavering faith. Guide us in using our gifts and passions to serve others and bring glory to your name. May we find fulfilment and joy in living out the purpose you have ordained for us.*
*In Jesus name, we pray. Amen.*

## DAY 13
### Trusting God's provision In finance

Philippians 4:19 (NIV)
"And my God will meet all your needs according to the riches of his glory in Christ Jesus."

In a world often consumed by financial worries, Philippians 4:19 brings a comforting promise: God will provide for all our needs. Trusting God's provision in finances is about recognizing that He is the ultimate source of abundance. It's acknowledging that our value is not solely defined by our bank account but by our relationship with Him. When we place our trust in His provision, we release the grip of fear and stress that often accompanies financial struggles.

**Action Plan:**

1. Stewardship: Take time to assess your financial situation regularly. Create a budget that aligns with your values and includes a portion for giving. Prioritise responsible stewardship.

2. Seek Wisdom: When facing financial decisions, seek godly wisdom through prayer and seeking advice from trusted mentors or financial experts.

3. Faithful Tithing: Make tithing a regular practice. Dedicate a portion of your income to support your local church and charitable causes. Trust that God will multiply your faithfulness.

**Prayer:**

*Heavenly Father,*
*We come before you with our financial worries and concerns. Help us to trust in your promise of provision and release the burden of financial stress. Grant us the wisdom to manage our finances responsibly and the generosity to share our blessings with others. May we find peace in knowing that you are our ultimate provider, and in you, we lack nothing.*
*In Jesus name, we pray. Amen.*

## DAY 14
## Rejoicing In God's Creation

Psalm 148:5 (NIV)
"Let them praise the name of the Lord, for at his command they were created."

Psalm 148:5 calls us to celebrate the grandeur of God's creation. Every aspect of the natural world, from the towering mountains to the smallest of creatures, reflects the handiwork of our Creator. Rejoicing in God's creation is an opportunity to connect with the divine artist behind it all, to recognize His majesty in the world around us. It's about finding wonder in the intricate design of a flower, the power of a storm, and the grace of a bird in flight. In this appreciation, we find a deep sense of peace and connection with the One who spoke the universe into existence.

**Action Plan:**

1. Daily Nature Time: Set aside time each day to immerse yourself in nature, whether it's a walk in the park, a hike in the woods, or simply sitting in your garden. Observe the beauty of creation and thank God for it.

2. Practice Gratitude: Make gratitude a habit. Keep a journal and jot down things from nature that you're grateful for each day. This will cultivate a thankful heart.

3. Environmental Stewardship: Take steps to care for God's creation. Reduce your ecological footprint, recycle, conserve energy, and support eco-friendly initiatives.

**Prayer:**

*Dear Heavenly Father,*
*We thank you for the breathtaking beauty and wonder of your creation. Help us to open our eyes and hearts to the world around us, to find joy in the smallest details of nature. May our gratitude for your handiwork deepen our faith and our commitment to care for this precious gift. Let us always rejoice in the marvel of your creation.*
*In Jesus name, we pray. Amen.*

## DAY 15
## The Blessing Of Christian Community

Acts 2:42 (NIV)
"They devoted themselves to the apostles' teaching and to fellowship, to the breaking of bread and to prayer."

Acts 2:42 paints a vivid picture of the early Christian community's devotion to one another. They shared not only in worship but in every aspect of their lives. The blessing of Christian community lies in its power to provide support, encouragement, and spiritual growth. It's a place where we find kindred spirits who help us navigate life's challenges and celebrate its joys. In community, we strengthen our faith, learn from one another, and find a sense of belonging that is essential for our spiritual journey.

**Action Plan:**

1. Regular Church Attendance: Make attending church services a priority. Engage in worship, listen to teachings, and actively participate in your local Christian community.

2. Join Small Groups: Seek out or start small groups within your church. These gatherings provide an intimate setting for fellowship, Bible study, and prayer.

3. Be Vulnerable: Open up to fellow believers about your struggles and joys. Authenticity in Christian community strengthens bonds and allows for mutual support.

**Prayer:**

Heavenly Father,
We thank you for the gift of Christian community. Help us to appreciate the blessings that come from walking this journey of faith together. Guide us to be active and engaged members of our church, to seek out fellowship, and to serve one another with love. May our bonds grow stronger as we learn, pray, and share life's ups and downs within this community of believers.
In Jesus name, we pray. Amen.

## DAY 16
### Cultivating A Heart Of Kindness

Ephesians 4:32 (NIV)
"Be kind and compassionate to one another, forgiving each other, just as in Christ God forgave you."

Ephesians 4:32 serves as a powerful reminder of the transformative power of kindness. Cultivating a heart of kindness means extending love and compassion to others, just as God has shown us His forgiveness and grace. It's about actively choosing to respond with empathy and gentleness, even in the face of adversity. Kindness creates a ripple effect of positivity, healing wounds, and nurturing deeper connections with those around us. In practicing kindness, we mirror Christ's love and become beacons of His light in the world.

**Action Plan:**

1. Daily Acts of Kindness: Make a conscious effort to perform small acts of kindness every day. Hold the door for someone, offer a listening ear, or send an encouraging message.

2. Practice Forgiveness: Embrace forgiveness as a cornerstone of kindness. Let go of grudges and resentments, understanding that forgiveness frees both the giver and receiver.

3. Empathy and Understanding: Take time to truly understand others' perspectives and feelings. Practice active listening and seek to empathise with their struggles.

**Prayer:**

*Heavenly Father,*
*We come before you seeking the strength to cultivate a heart of kindness. Teach us to be kind and compassionate, just as you are to us. Help us to extend forgiveness and grace, mirroring your love in our interactions with others. May our actions and words be a testament to your boundless kindness, spreading light and hope in a world that often needs it most. In Jesus name, we pray. Amen.*

## DAY 17

## Living As A Salt And Light

Matthew 5:13-16 (NIV)
"You are the salt of the earth. But if the salt loses its saltiness, how can it be made salty again? It is no longer good for anything, except to be thrown out and trampled underfoot. You are the light of the world. A town built on a hill cannot be hidden. Neither do people light a lamp and put it under a bowl. Instead, they put it on its stand, and it gives light to everyone in the house. In the same way, let your light shine before others, so that they may see your good deeds and glorify your Father in heaven."

In Matthew 5:13-16, Jesus urges us to be both salt and light in the world. Salt preserves and enhances flavour, while light dispels darkness. As followers of Christ, we are called to influence our surroundings positively. To be "salt" means to bring out the best in others, preserving the values of love, compassion, and grace. To be "light" means to shine God's truth and love, dispelling the darkness of ignorance and despair. Living as salt and light involves actively living out our faith, serving as beacons of hope, and reflecting God's glory in our actions.

**Action Plan:**

1. Live Out Your Faith: Demonstrate your Christian values in your daily life. Show kindness, love, and forgiveness in your interactions with others.

2. Share Your Testimony: Don't hide your faith; share it with humility and grace. Your personal story can inspire others to seek God.

3. Pray for Guidance: Pray for God's guidance in how to be salt and light in specific situations. Ask Him to show you where your influence is needed most.

**Prayer:**

Heavenly Father,
We thank you for calling us to be salt and light in the world. Empower us to live out our faith boldly, being a source of love, kindness, and truth. May our actions and words glorify you and draw others closer to your light. Guide us in all we do, that we may truly make a difference in the lives of those around us.
In Jesus name, we pray. Amen.

## DAY 18
## God's Comfort In Times Of Loss

Psalm 34:18 (NIV)
"The Lord is close to the brokenhearted and saves those who are crushed in spirit."

In moments of loss and grief, it's easy to feel alone and overwhelmed. Psalm 34:18 reminds us that in those very moments, God draws near to us. His presence offers solace and strength. When our hearts are broken, He is the mender of wounds. When our spirits are crushed, He is the lifter of our souls. God's comfort in times of loss is a promise of His unwavering love and compassion. He walks with us through the darkest valleys, offering His shoulder to lean on and His light to guide us.

Action Plan:

1. Prayer and Reflection: Dedicate time each day to pray and reflect on your feelings of loss. Pour out your heart to God and invite His comfort into your life.

2. Seek Support: Reach out to friends, family, or support groups. Don't bear your grief alone; sharing your feelings can provide emotional healing.

3. Help Others: Use your experience to help others facing similar losses. Offering support and compassion can be a way to find purpose in your pain.

**Prayer:**

*Heavenly Father,*
*In times of loss and grief, we turn to you for comfort and strength. Thank you for being close to the brokenhearted and for saving those who are crushed in spirit. Help us navigate our pain, find healing, and trust in your love as we journey through the difficult seasons of life. May your presence be a source of solace and peace.*
*In Jesus name, we pray. Amen.*

## DAY 19
## The Power Of God's Word In Transformation

Romans 12:2 (NIV)
"Do not conform to the pattern of this world, but be transformed by the renewing of your mind. Then you will be able to test and approve what God's will is—his good, pleasing and perfect will."

Romans 12:2 calls us to a life of transformation through the renewing of our minds. The Word of God is a potent force in this renewal process. It has the power to reshape our thoughts, beliefs, and actions, aligning them with God's will. As we immerse ourselves in His Word, we are continually transformed into His likeness, shedding old habits and worldly patterns. The Word offers guidance, wisdom, and encouragement, enabling us to navigate life's challenges with faith and purpose.

**Action Plan:**

1. Daily Scripture Study: Commit to daily Bible reading and meditation. Allow God's Word to permeate your thoughts and influence your decisions.

2. Scripture Memorization: Memorise verses that speak to your heart. Carry them with you as a source of strength and guidance throughout the day.

3. God's Word: Share passages and insights with others, encouraging them in their faith journey. Teaching and discussing Scripture can deepen your own understanding.

**Prayer:**

*Heavenly Father,*
*We thank you for the transformative power of your Word. Help us to diligently study and apply it to our lives, so that our minds may be renewed in alignment with your perfect will. Guide us as we seek to live out your Word in our daily actions, and may it be a source of strength and wisdom for us in all circumstances. In Jesus name, we pray. Amen.*

## DAY 20
## Finding Strength In Unity

Psalm 133:1 (NIV)
"How good and pleasant it is when God's people live together in unity!"

Psalm 133:1 beautifully illustrates the value of unity among God's people. In a world often marked by division and discord, unity stands as a powerful testament to God's love and purpose. When we come together in harmony and oneness, we discover strength that transcends our individual abilities. Unity fosters a sense of belonging, support, and purpose, making our journey of faith more rewarding and effective. It reflects the love of Christ and allows us to be His hands and feet in the world.

**Action Plan:**

1. Pray for Unity: Begin by praying for unity among believers, both in your local community and globally. Ask God to guide His people in coming together.

2. Build Relationships: Foster strong relationships within your church or faith community. Get to know one another, support each other, and celebrate one another's successes and milestones.

3. Resolve Conflicts: Address conflicts and disagreements with humility and a commitment to reconciliation. Unity doesn't mean absence of disagreement but rather resolving differences in a Christ-like manner.

**Prayer:**

*Heavenly Father,*
*We thank you for the gift of unity among your people. Help us to value and protect this unity, for it is a reflection of your love and purpose. Guide us in our efforts to strengthen relationships, serve together, and resolve conflicts in a manner that glorifies your name. May our unity be a beacon of hope and a testament to your transformative power.*
*In Jesus name, we pray. Amen.*

## DAY 21
## Surrendering Fear To Faith

2 Timothy 1:7 (NIV)
"For the Spirit God gave us does not make us timid, but gives us power, love, and self-discipline."

2 Timothy 1:7 reminds us that God has not given us a spirit of fear but of power, love, and self-discipline. Fear can be crippling, holding us back from pursuing our dreams, serving others, and fully experiencing life. However, faith empowers us to overcome fear. It's a trust in God's strength, a belief in

His love, and a discipline to focus on His promises rather than our anxieties. Surrendering fear to faith is a journey of letting go of our worries, embracing God's peace, and living boldly, knowing that His Spirit equips us to face any challenge with courage and love.

**Action Plan:**

1. Prayer and Meditation: Begin each day with prayer and meditation on Scripture. Ask God to replace your fears with faith and to remind you of His promises.

2. Challenge Comfort Zones: Regularly step out of your comfort zone, trusting in God's guidance and provision. These experiences will strengthen your faith.

3. Practice Gratitude: Cultivate a habit of gratitude. Focus on the blessings in your life, which will help shift your perspective away from fear.

**Prayer:**

*Heavenly Father,*
*We come before you with our fears and anxieties, asking for the strength to surrender them to faith. Help us trust in your power, love, and self-discipline to overcome all that holds us back. May we live boldly, fully embracing the life you have planned for us, knowing that your Spirit equips us to face every challenge with courage and love.*
*In Jesus name, we pray. Amen.*

## DAY 22
### Trusting God's Timing In Relationships

Ecclesiastes 3:1 (NIV)
"There is a time for everything, and a season for every activity under the heavens."

Ecclesiastes 3:1 reminds us that God has a perfect timing for every aspect of our lives, including relationships. Often, we impatiently rush into relationships or feel disheartened when they don't unfold as we expect. But God's timing is purposeful. It allows us to grow, learn, and prepare for the right person. Trusting God's timing in relationships means surrendering our desire for control and embracing His plan, even when it doesn't align with our own. It's about recognizing that each season of life, whether single or in a relationship, serves a unique purpose in our journey toward love and personal growth.

**Action Plan:**

1. Prayer and Patience: Pray for patience and trust in God's timing. Surrender your desires to Him, asking for guidance in your relationships.

2. Focus on Personal Growth: Use single seasons to focus on personal growth, self-discovery, and strengthening your relationship with God.

3. Stay Open and Hopeful: Stay open to new connections while being discerning. Trust that God's timing will bring the right person into your life when the time is right.

**Prayer:**

*Heavenly Father,*
*We surrender our desires for relationships to your perfect timing. Give us patience and wisdom to trust in your plan, even when it doesn't align with our own. Help us grow in faith and love, whether we are single or in a relationship. May we find peace and hope in your timing, knowing that you have the best in store for us.*
*In Jesus name, we pray. Amen.*

## DAY 23
## Embracing God's Promises For Healing

Jeremiah 30:17 (NIV)
"But I will restore you to health and heal your wounds, declares the Lord."

Jeremiah 30:17 is a beautiful reminder of God's promise to heal and restore us. It speaks to both physical and emotional healing. In times of illness, pain, or emotional distress, we may feel broken and helpless. However, God assures us that He is the ultimate healer. Embracing His promises of healing means placing our trust in His divine plan and timing. It means seeking His comfort and peace, knowing that He can mend not only our physical ailments but also the wounds within our hearts and souls. God's healing is a testimony to His unwavering love and grace.

**Action Plan:**

1. Prayer for Healing: Dedicate time each day to pray for healing, both physical and emotional. Pour out your heart to God, surrendering your pain and seeking His restoration.

2. Seek Medical Help: While praying for healing, also seek medical assistance when needed. God often works through medical professionals to bring healing.

3. Embrace Gratitude: Cultivate gratitude for the healing you have received or witnessed. Recognize the power of God's hand in your life.

**Prayer:**

*Heavenly Father,*
*We come before you seeking the healing and restoration you promise. Whether our wounds are physical or emotional, we trust in your loving care. Be our ultimate healer, granting us strength and faith during times of illness and distress. May your healing touch bring not only physical relief but also the peace that surpasses all understanding.*
*In Jesus name, we pray. Amen.*

## DAY 24

## Navigating Life's Storm With Faith

Matthew 8:26 (NIV)
"He replied, 'You of little faith, why are you so afraid?' Then he got up and rebuked the winds and the waves, and it was completely calm."

Matthew 8:26 recounts a moment when the disciples were caught in a violent storm, and Jesus calmed the tempest with a word. This verse reminds us that, like the disciples, we will face storms in life. These storms can be physical, emotional, or spiritual, and they often stir up fear and doubt. Yet, just as Jesus had control over the wind and waves, He has the power to calm the storms in our lives. Navigating life's storms with faith means trusting in His presence and sovereignty, even when circumstances seem dire. It means recognizing that faith can calm our fears and bring peace in the midst of chaos.

**Action Plan:**

1. Prayer and Surrender: Turn to prayer when facing life's storms. Surrender your fears and worries to God, trusting in His plan and timing.

2. Scripture Study: Find comfort and strength in the Bible. Study verses that speak to God's faithfulness and His ability to calm storms.

3. Seek Support: Reach out to your faith community or a trusted friend for support and encouragement during challenging times.

**Prayer:**

*Heavenly Father,*
*We thank you for being our anchor in life's storms. When fear and doubt threaten to overwhelm us, help us to turn to you in faith. Calm our hearts, just as Jesus calmed the winds and waves, and grant us the peace that surpasses all understanding. May our trust in you grow stronger with each storm we face.*
*In Jesus name, we pray. Amen.*

## DAY 25
## Cultivate A Heart Of Worship

John 4:23-24 (NIV)
"Yet a time is coming and has now come when the true worshipers will worship the Father in the Spirit and in truth, for they are the kind of worshipers the Father seeks. God is spirit, and his worshipers must worship in the Spirit and in truth."

In John 4:23-24, Jesus teaches us that worship isn't confined to a physical place or ritual but is an intimate connection between our hearts and God. Cultivating a heart of worship is about living a life where our thoughts, actions, and attitudes align with a deep reverence for God. It's recognizing His presence in all aspects of life and responding with gratitude, praise, and adoration. True worship is not bound by tradition but flows from a heart transformed by the Spirit and grounded in God's truth.

**Action Plan:**

1. Daily Devotion: Set aside time each day for prayer and reflection. This allows you to connect with God personally and grow in your worship.

2. Gratitude Journal: Keep a gratitude journal to regularly reflect on God's blessings in your life. Cultivating thankfulness is a powerful form of worship.

3. Live in Integrity: Worship involves living in alignment with God's truth. Strive for integrity and authenticity in your thoughts, words, and actions.

**Prayer:**

*Heavenly Father,*
*We desire to be the kind of worshipers you seek, worshiping you in Spirit and in truth. Help us cultivate a heart of worship that permeates every aspect of our lives. May our worship be genuine and our connection with you deep and profound. Guide us in daily devotion, gratitude, integrity, and service, so that our lives may be a continual offering of worship to you.*
*In Jesus name, we pray. Amen.*

## DAY 26
## Living With Joyful Expectation

Romans 15:13 (NIV)
"May the God of hope fill you with all joy and peace as you trust in him, so that you may overflow with hope by the power of the Holy Spirit."

Romans 15:13 reminds us of the profound connection between joy, peace, and hope that comes from our trust in God. Living with joyful expectation means embracing life with a positive outlook, firmly anchored in the hope that God provides. It's about facing each day with confidence, knowing that the God of hope is with us, guiding our steps, and working all things for our good. This joyful expectation isn't based on wishful thinking but on a deep trust in God's faithfulness. It allows us to navigate life's challenges with resilience and optimism, always looking forward to the promise of a better tomorrow.

**Action Plan:**

1. Daily Gratitude: Begin each day by counting your blessings. Cultivate gratitude for the simple joys in life, acknowledging God's goodness.

2. Prayer and Meditation: Spend time in prayer and meditation, seeking God's presence and guidance. Let His Word fill you with hope and joy.

3. Positive Mindset: Train your mind to focus on the positive aspects of situations. Replace negative thoughts with hopeful and optimistic ones.

**Prayer:**

*Heavenly Father,*
*We thank you for being the God of hope who fills us with joy and peace. Help us to live each day with joyful expectation, anchored in the trust that you are with us, guiding our steps. May our lives overflow with hope by the power of your Holy Spirit. Grant us the wisdom to encourage others and cultivate a positive mindset, even in challenging times.*
*In Jesus' name, we pray. Amen.*

## DAY 27
## Embracing God's Forgiveness And Freedom

Galatians 5:1 (NIV)
"It is for freedom that Christ has set us free. Stand firm, then, and do not let yourselves be burdened again by a yoke of slavery."

Galatians 5:1 is a powerful reminder of the freedom we have in Christ. It's a call to release the burdens of guilt, shame, and past mistakes and to embrace the forgiveness and freedom He offers. Often, we carry the weight of our sins, allowing them to define us and limit our potential. But Christ's sacrifice on the cross has set us free from this bondage. Embracing God's forgiveness means acknowledging our imperfections and accepting His grace with gratitude. It's a transformative process that allows us to let go of the past, move forward with hope, and live in the fullness of God's love.

**Action Plan:**

1. Confession and Repentance: Regularly confess your sins to God, acknowledging your need for His forgiveness. Repentance is a path to freedom.

2. Study God's Word: Dive into Scripture to understand the depth of God's forgiveness and the freedom it brings. Seek passages that speak to His love and grace.

3. Forgive Yourself: Forgive yourself for past mistakes. Remember that God has forgiven you, and you can release the burden of guilt.

4. Live in Freedom: Embrace the freedom Christ has given you. Make choices that align with His love and grace, and let go of anything that holds you back.

**Prayer:**

*Heavenly Father,*
*We thank you for the freedom we have in Christ, made possible through your forgiveness. Help us to release the burdens of guilt and shame and fully embrace your grace. May we live in the freedom you've provided, making choices that reflect your love and mercy. Thank you for setting us free and allowing us to walk in the light of your love.*
*In Jesus name, we pray. Amen.*

## DAY 28
## Trusting God's Protection In Adversity

Psalm 91:1-2 (NIV)
"Whoever dwells in the shelter of the Most High will rest in the shadow of the Almighty. I will say of the Lord, 'He is my refuge and my fortress, my God, in whom I trust.'"

Psalm 91:1-2 offers solace and assurance to those facing adversity. It reminds us that when we dwell in God's presence and make Him our refuge, we find safety and protection. Trusting God's protection in adversity means acknowledging that He is our ultimate fortress, our shield against life's storms. It's about letting go of fear and anxiety, knowing that in Him, we have a source of unwavering strength and security. Even when circumstances seem daunting, God's promise of protection empowers us to face adversity with courage, faith, and a sense of peace.

**Action Plan:**

1. Daily Prayer: Begin and end your day with prayer, entrusting your concerns and fears to God. Ask for His protection and guidance.

2. Meditate on Scripture: Spend time meditating on verses that speak of God's protection. Let His promises become a source of strength in times of trouble.

3. Gratitude Journal: Keep a journal of gratitude, recording moments when you have experienced God's protection in the past. This practice will strengthen your trust in His care.

**Prayer:**

*Heavenly Father,*
*We thank you for being our refuge and fortress in times of adversity. Help us to trust in your protection, even when life's challenges seem overwhelming. May we dwell in your presence, finding comfort and strength in your unwavering love. Grant us the courage and faith to face adversity with confidence, knowing that you are our ultimate shield.*
*In Jesus name, we pray. Amen.*

## DAY 29
## Surrendering Anxiety To Prayer

Philippians 4:6 (NIV)
"Do not be anxious about anything, but in every situation, by prayer and petition, with thanksgiving, present your requests to God."

Philippians 4:6 is a powerful verse that encourages us to surrender our anxieties to God through prayer. Anxiety is a common struggle in today's fast-paced world, often stemming from worries about the future, personal challenges, or the unknown. However, this verse provides a beautiful remedy: prayer. Surrendering anxiety to prayer means entrusting our concerns to a loving and all-powerful God. It's about releasing the burdens that weigh us down and finding peace in the assurance that He hears and cares for us. Through prayer, we not only seek God's help but also express gratitude, shifting our focus from fear to faith.

**Action Plan:**

1. Daily Prayer Routine: Establish a daily prayer routine that includes both scheduled and spontaneous moments of conversation with God. Dedicate time to lay your anxieties before Him.

2. Scripture Meditation: Meditate on verses that offer comfort and peace. Memorise passages that resonate with you, allowing them to guide your thoughts.

3. Seek Support: Don't hesitate to seek support from your faith community or a trusted friend. Share your anxieties and ask for prayer, knowing that you're not alone in your struggles.

**Prayer:**

*Heavenly Father,*
*We come before you, surrendering our anxieties through prayer. We thank you for the comfort and peace that come from entrusting our concerns to you. Help us establish a deeper connection with you through daily prayer, journaling, and meditation on your Word. May we find support and strength within our faith community. Teach us to always turn to you in moments of anxiety, knowing that you are our loving and caring Father. In Jesus name, we pray. Amen.*

# DAY 30
## The Power Of God's Love And Grace

Ephesians 2:4-5 (NIV)
"But because of his great love for us, God, who is rich in mercy, made us alive with Christ even when we were dead in transgressions—it is by grace you have been saved."

Ephesians 2:4-5 beautifully captures the essence of God's love and grace. His love for us is immeasurable, and His grace is boundless. It is through His love and grace that we find salvation and new life in Christ. Despite our imperfections and sins, God's love reaches down to rescue us. His grace lifts us from the depths of despair and breathes new life into our souls.
Understanding the power of God's love and grace transforms our relationship

with Him. It compels us to live with gratitude, humility, and a deep desire to extend the same love and grace to others.

**Action Plan:**

1. Daily Reflection: Take time each day to reflect on God's love and grace in your life. Remember moments when His love and grace were evident.

2. Practice Forgiveness: Extend forgiveness to others just as you have received God's forgiveness. This reflects the grace you've experienced.

3. Share His Love: Be intentional about sharing God's love and grace with those around you through acts of kindness, compassion, and understanding.

**Prayer:**

Heavenly Father,
We are in awe of your great love and boundless grace. Thank you for making us alive in Christ despite our flaws and sins. Help us to truly grasp the depth of your love and grace so that it transforms our lives. May we reflect your love and grace in our interactions with others, and may your love shine brightly through us.
In Jesus name, we pray. Amen.

*Proverbs 14:1 A wise woman builds her house, while a foolish woman tears hers down with her own hands. 9. Matthew 15:28 Then Jesus said to her, "O woman, your faith is great; it shall be done for you as you wish." And her daughter was healed at once.*

## DAY 01
### Finding Peace In God's Word

Psalm 119:165 (NIV)
"Great peace, have those who love your law, and nothing can make them stumble."

Psalm 119:165 beautifully illustrates the profound peace that comes from immersing ourselves in God's Word. In a world filled with turmoil, uncertainty, and noise, the Bible serves as a source of solace and stability. Finding peace in God's Word means seeking refuge in His timeless truths, wisdom, and promises. It's about allowing His Word to dwell richly in our hearts, shaping our thoughts and actions. The peace it brings is not just the absence of conflict but a deep, abiding serenity that transcends circumstances. As women of faith, we can rest assured that God's Word is a steadfast anchor in the storms of life, providing the peace that surpasses all understanding.

**Action Plan:**

1. Daily Scripture Reading: Dedicate time each day to read and meditate on Scripture. Choose verses or passages that resonate with your heart.

2. Bible Study Groups: Join or form a Bible study group with other women to explore God's Word together, sharing insights and supporting one another.

3. Application in Daily Life: Purposefully apply the principles and teachings of the Bible to your daily life, seeking to live out the peace it offers.

**Prayer:**

## DAY 02
## Resting In God's Sovereignty

Isaiah 46:10 (NIV)
"I make known the end from the beginning, from ancient times, what is still to come.
I say, 'My purpose will stand, and I will do all that I please.'"

Isaiah 46:10 reminds us of the absolute sovereignty of God. In a world marked by uncertainty, it's a profound comfort to know that God is in control of all things. Resting in God's sovereignty means releasing the need to manipulate or worry about outcomes and trusting that His purposes will prevail. It's acknowledging that God's wisdom transcends our understanding, and His plan for our lives is perfect. This surrender brings peace and a sense of security, allowing us to face life's twists and turns with confidence that God is working all things together for our good, even when we can't see the bigger picture.

**Action Plan:**

1. Meditate on Scripture: Study passages that emphasise God's sovereignty to deepen your understanding and trust in His plan.

2. Pray for Wisdom: Seek wisdom in discerning God's will and trusting His guidance in decision-making.

3. Practice Patience: When facing challenges or uncertainties, exercise patience, knowing that God's timing is perfect.

**Prayer:**

*Heavenly Father,*
*We rest in your sovereignty, trusting that your purposes will prevail in our lives. Help us to surrender daily to your will, finding peace in the knowledge that you are in control. May we*

## DAY 03
## Cultivating A Heart Compassion

Colossians 3:12 (NIV)
"Therefore, as God's chosen people, holy and dearly loved, clothe yourselves with compassion, kindness, humility, gentleness and patience."

Colossians 3:12 calls us to clothe ourselves with compassion as a reflection of our identity as God's chosen and beloved children. Compassion is a heart quality that enables us to empathise with the pain and struggles of others. It goes beyond mere sympathy; it's about actively extending love, care, and understanding. Cultivating a heart of compassion means intentionally developing the capacity to see the world through the eyes of others, offering help and kindness, and walking alongside those in need. It's a beautiful way to mirror God's love and mercy in a broken world.

**Action Plan:**

1. Daily Prayer: Begin and end each day with a prayer for a heart of compassion. Ask God to open your eyes to the needs of others.

2. Practice Empathy: Seek to understand the experiences and emotions of those around you. Listen actively and without judgement.

3. Forgive Freely: Extend forgiveness to those who have wronged you, demonstrating compassion even in difficult situations.

**Prayer:**

*Heavenly Father,*
*We thank you for your compassion toward us, and we desire to reflect that same compassion to those around us. Open our hearts to the needs of others and guide us to practice empathy, kindness, and forgiveness. May our lives be a testament to your boundless love and compassion.*
*In Jesus name, we pray. Amen.*

## Persevering In Faithfulness

1 Corinthians 15:58 (NIV)
"Therefore, my dear sisters, stand firm. Let nothing move you. Always give yourselves fully to the work of the Lord, because you know that your labour in the Lord is not in vain."

1 Corinthians 15:58 encourages us to stand firm and persevere in our faithfulness to the Lord. Life is filled with challenges and uncertainties, and it's easy to become discouraged or swayed by circumstances. However, this verse reminds us that our efforts and service for God are never in vain. Persevering in faithfulness means remaining unwavering in our commitment to God's work, even when we face obstacles or setbacks. It's about giving our whole hearts to serving Him and trusting that He will use our efforts for His glory. Our faithfulness in both good times and bad is a testament to our love for the Lord and our unwavering belief in His promises.

**Action Plan:**

1. Daily Devotion: Establish a daily devotion routine, including prayer, Scripture reading, and reflection to stay spiritually grounded.

2. Encourage Fellow Believers: Lift up and support your fellow sisters in Christ, providing encouragement and strength in their faith journeys.

3. Pray for Perseverance: Ask God for the strength and perseverance to remain faithful in all circumstances, trusting in His plan.

**Prayer:**

Heavenly Father,
We thank you for your faithfulness to us, and we desire to be faithful in return. Grant us the strength to stand firm, unwavering in our commitment to you. Help us to persevere in faithfulness, always giving ourselves fully to your work, knowing that our labour in you is never in vain. May our lives be a testimony to your grace and love.
In Jesus name, we pray. Amen.

## Nurturing Strong Marriage

Ephesians 5:22-33 (NIV)
"Wives, submit yourselves to your own husbands as you do to the Lord... Husbands,
love your wives, just as Christ loved the church and gave himself up for her..."

Ephesians 5:22-33 provides a profound blueprint for nurturing strong and
loving marriages. It underscores the importance of mutual respect, love, and
sacrifice within the marital relationship. For wives, it speaks of respect and
submission, not as inferiority, but as a willing partnership in harmony with
God's design. For husbands, it calls for selfless love, mirroring Christ's love for
the church. Nurturing strong marriages means building a foundation of trust,
open communication, and unwavering support for one another. It's a
partnership that acknowledges each other's strengths and weaknesses,
fostering an environment of love, respect, and mutual growth.

**Action Plans:**

1. Communication: Commit to open and honest communication,
   discussing both joys and challenges in your marriage.

2. Quality Time: Set aside dedicated time for each other, nurturing the
   emotional connection in your marriage.

3. Prayer Together: Pray as a couple, seeking God's guidance and blessings
   for your marriage.

**Prayer:**

Heavenly Father,
We thank you for the gift of marriage and for the wisdom provided in your Word. Help us to
nurture strong and loving marriages, following the example set in Ephesians 5. May our
relationships be marked by mutual respect, love, and selflessness. Grant us the strength to
communicate openly, spend quality time together, and serve one another with joyful hearts.
May our marriages be a reflection of your love for the church.
In Jesus name, we pray. Amen.

# Living As Light In A Dark World

Philippians 2:15 (NIV)
"so that you may become blameless and pure, children of God without fault in a
warped and crooked generation. Then you will shine among them like stars in the
sky."

Philippians 2:15 encourages us to be a light in the midst of a dark and
challenging world. As women of faith, we are called to shine brightly,
embodying the love, grace, and truth of Christ. Living as light means being a
beacon of hope, kindness, and righteousness in a world that often seems lost
in darkness. It's about reflecting God's character in our words and actions,
showing compassion to the hurting, and standing firm in our faith even when
faced with adversity. By doing so, we not only bring glory to God but also draw
others to the transformative power of His light.

**Action Plan:**

1. Prayer and Reflection: Begin each day with prayer, asking God to help
   you shine His light in your daily interactions.

2. Acts of Kindness: Look for opportunities to show kindness and love to
   those around you, even in small ways.

3. Live with Integrity: Strive for a life of integrity, aligning your actions
   with your beliefs, and setting an example for others to follow.

**Prayer:**

Heavenly Father,
We thank you for calling us to be light in a dark world. Help us to shine brightly, reflecting
your love and truth to those around us. May our lives be beacons of hope and kindness,
drawing others closer to you. Grant us the courage to share our faith and live with integrity,
always bringing glory to your name.
In Jesus name, we pray. Amen.

DAY 07

## Embracing God's Promises Of Provision

Philippians 4:19 (NIV)
"And my God will meet all your needs according to the riches of his glory in Christ Jesus."

Philippians 4:19 reassures us of God's unfailing promise to provide for our every need. As women of faith, we often face various challenges and uncertainties, including financial ones. In these moments, it's essential to remember that God's provision extends far beyond our understanding. Embracing His promises means trusting that He knows our needs intimately and is committed to meeting them. It's an invitation to rely on God's abundant riches in Christ Jesus rather than our own efforts or resources. When we fully embrace God's promises of provision, we can release our anxieties and walk in faith, knowing that He will supply all our needs, whether material, emotional, or spiritual.

**Action Plan:**

1. Budget Wisely: Be a good steward of the resources God has entrusted to you. Create a budget that aligns with your values and priorities.

2. Generosity: Give generously to those in need, recognizing that God uses us to be part of His provision for others.

3. Trust and Prayer: In times of financial stress, trust in God's promise and pray for His guidance and provision. Surrender your anxieties to Him.

**Prayer:**

*Heavenly Father,*
*We thank you for your promise of provision in our lives. Help us to fully embrace this promise, trusting that you will meet all our needs according to your glorious riches. May we walk in faith, knowing that you are our ultimate provider. Grant us the wisdom to be good stewards and the generosity to share with those in need.*
*In Jesus name, we pray. Amen.*

DAY 08
Trusting God's Guidance In Parenting

Proverbs 22:6 (NIV)
"Start children off on the way they should go, and even when they are old, they will not turn from it."


Proverbs 22:6 reminds us of the profound responsibility and privilege of parenting. As women entrusted with the care and guidance of our children, we are called to start them on the path of wisdom and faith. Trusting God's guidance in parenting means recognizing that He is the ultimate source of wisdom and love. It's about seeking His counsel through prayer, relying on His Word, and setting an example of faith through our own lives. Parenting can be both rewarding and challenging, but with God's guidance, we can instil values, love, and a strong foundation of faith in our children, believing that His influence will remain with them throughout their lives.

**Action Plan:**

1. Pray for Wisdom: Dedicate time to pray for wisdom in your parenting journey. Ask God for guidance in making decisions that align with His will.

2. Teach God's Word: Regularly engage your children with Scripture, sharing its stories and teachings to instil a love for God's Word.

3. Communication: Foster open and loving communication with your children, allowing them to ask questions and express their thoughts and concerns.

**Prayer:**

*Heavenly Father,*
*We come before you as parents, seeking your guidance in raising our children. Grant us the wisdom to lead them on the path of faith and love. May your Word be our guide, and may our lives reflect your love and grace. Help us to communicate with our children in a way that strengthens their relationship with you. We trust that, with your guidance, our children will grow in wisdom and faith, following you all the days of their lives.*
*In Jesus name, we pray. Amen.*


DAY 09

## Rejoicing In God's Mercy

Psalm 136:26 (NIV)
"Give thanks to the God of heaven. His love endures forever."

Psalm 136:26 invites us to rejoice in God's enduring love and boundless mercy. As women of faith, we find great comfort in knowing that His mercy is constant, never wavering, and always available to us. Rejoicing in God's mercy means celebrating the compassion and forgiveness He extends to us, despite our shortcomings. It's recognizing that His love is not based on our performance but on His unchanging character. When we truly grasp the depth of His mercy, it fills our hearts with gratitude, joy, and a desire to extend the same compassion to others. It's an invitation to live in a state of continuous thankfulness for His everlasting love.

**Action Plan:**

1. Daily Gratitude: Begin and end each day with gratitude for God's mercy in your life.

2. about God's mercy and love for His children.

3. Serve Others: Seek opportunities to show mercy and kindness to those in need, sharing God's love.

**Prayer:**

Heavenly Father,
We rejoice in your enduring love and boundless mercy. Thank you for your compassion and forgiveness, which are freely given to us. Help us to extend this same mercy to others, reflecting your love in our daily lives. May we live in a state of continuous gratitude for your everlasting mercy.
In Jesus name, we pray. Amen.

## DAY 10
## The Blessing Of Giving And Receiving

Acts 20:35 (NIV)

"In everything I did, I showed you that by this kind of hard work we must help the weak, remembering the words the Lord Jesus himself said: 'It is more blessed to give than to receive.'"

Acts 20:35 highlights a profound truth taught by Jesus: that there is a remarkable blessing in both giving and receiving. Often, we focus on the joy of giving, which indeed brings a sense of fulfilment and purpose. However, receiving is equally important. It allows us to experience the love, generosity, and care of others. In receiving, we acknowledge our interdependence within the body of Christ, fostering unity and deepening relationships. It's a reminder that we all have seasons of need, and it's okay to accept help with humility and gratitude. The cycle of giving and receiving reflects God's love and provision in our lives, reminding us that He works through the generosity of His people.

**Action Plan:**

1. Cultivate Generosity: Seek opportunities to give to others in need, whether through acts of kindness, service, or financial support.

2. Practice Gracious Receiving: When others offer help or support, receive it with gratitude and humility, recognizing it as a blessing.

3. Teach the Blessing: Share the message of Acts 20:35 with others, encouraging them to experience the joy of both giving and receiving.

**Prayer:**

Heavenly Father,
Thank you for the blessing of both giving and receiving. Help us to cultivate a spirit of generosity and to receive with gratitude and humility. May our lives reflect the love and provision you offer through the cycle of giving and receiving. In all things, let us remember the words of Jesus, "It is more blessed to give than to receive."
In Jesus name, we pray. Amen.

## DAY 11
## Finding Strength In God's Grace

2 Timothy 2:1 (NIV)
"You then, my son, be strong in the grace that is in Christ Jesus."

2 Timothy 2:1 reminds us of the boundless strength that comes from God's grace. As women of faith, we often face challenges, uncertainties, and moments when our own strength wanes. It's in these times that we can turn to the wellspring of God's grace. Finding strength in His grace means recognizing that His unmerited favour is available to us, empowering us to endure, persevere, and overcome. It's an invitation to lean on His grace as a source of courage, resilience, and unwavering faith. In our weakness, His grace is more than sufficient to carry us through. It's a reminder that we are not alone in our struggles; we have a loving Father who equips us with His grace.

**Action Plans:**

1. Daily Prayer: Begin each day with a prayer for God's grace to strengthen you in all circumstances.

2. Scripture Meditation: Reflect on verses that highlight God's grace and strength. Let His Word renew your spirit.

3. Community Support: Seek encouragement and support from fellow believers, sharing your journey and leaning on one another.

**Prayer:**

*Heavenly Father,*
*We are grateful for the strength that comes from your abounding grace. Help us to be strong in your grace, finding courage and resilience in our daily walk with you. May your grace empower us to persevere through challenges and to extend love and kindness to others. In our weakness, may your grace be our strength.*
*In Jesus name, we pray. Amen.*

## DAY 12
## Surrendering Control To God

Psalm 37:5 (NIV)
"Commit your way to the Lord; trust in him, and he will act."

Psalm 37:5 urges us to commit our ways to the Lord and trust in Him. As women, we often carry the weight of responsibilities, expectations, and desires, and it can be tempting to try to control every aspect of our lives. However, true peace and freedom are found in surrendering control to God. It means acknowledging that He is the ultimate orchestrator of our lives and trusting His perfect plan. Surrender isn't a sign of weakness; it's an act of faith, recognizing that God's ways are higher than ours. When we release our grip on control, we make room for God to work in miraculous ways, guiding us, providing for us, and shaping us into the women He intends us to be.

**Action Plan:**

1. Prayer of Surrender: Begin and end each day with a prayer, surrendering your plans and desires to God.

2. Trust in God's Timing: Practice patience and trust in God's timing, even when things seem uncertain or delayed.

3. Let Go of Anxiety: Replace anxiety with trust, knowing that God cares for you and is in control.

**Prayer:**

*Heavenly Father,*
*We surrender control to you, recognizing that your plans are higher and better than ours. Help us to trust in your wisdom, even when we can't see the way ahead. Guide us in our decisions, and grant us the patience to wait on your perfect timing. May surrender be an act of faith that brings us peace and draws us closer to you.*
*In Jesus name, we pray. Amen.*

## DAY 13
## The Power Of God's Presence

Psalm 16:11 (NIV)
"You make known to me the path of life; you will fill me with joy in your presence, with eternal pleasures at your right hand."

Psalm 16:11 beautifully portrays the transformative power of God's presence. As women of faith, we yearn for a deeper connection with our Creator. In His presence, we find clarity and direction for our lives, and we experience a profound and lasting joy. God's presence isn't limited to a physical place but is a state of being where we abide in Him and He in us. It's a source of comfort in times of trouble, strength in moments of weakness, and unwavering joy that transcends circumstances. When we dwell in His presence, we are filled with the peace that surpasses understanding, and we gain insight into the path of life He has prepared for us.

**Action Plan:**

1. Daily Devotion: Dedicate time each day to be in God's presence through prayer, worship, and reading His Word.

2. Community Worship: Participate in corporate worship and fellowship to experience God's presence with other believers.

3. Seek His Face: In times of decision-making or trouble, seek God's presence for guidance and comfort.

**Prayer:**

*Heavenly Father,*
*We thank you for the gift of your presence in our lives. Help us to seek you daily and dwell in your presence, finding joy and strength there. May your presence guide us in the path of life and fill us with lasting joy and peace. In all circumstances, let us rest in the comfort of your presence.*
*In Jesus name, we pray. Amen.*

## DAY 14
## Resting In God's Promises Of Peace

John 14:27 (NIV)
"Peace I leave with you; my peace I give you. I do not give to you as the world gives. Do not let your hearts be troubled and do not be afraid."

John 14:27 offers a precious promise of peace directly from the lips of Jesus. As women navigating the complexities of life, we often long for peace in our hearts and minds. But the peace Jesus offers is unlike any peace the world can give. It's a deep, abiding tranquillity that transcends circumstances and calms our anxious souls. Resting in God's promises of peace means surrendering our worries and fears to Him, trusting that He is in control. It's an invitation to cast our burdens upon the Prince of Peace, knowing that He will carry them for us. In His peace, we find strength, courage, and a refuge from the storms of life.

**Action Plans:**

1. Daily Surrender: Start and end each day with a prayer of surrender, entrusting your cares to God.

2. Pray for Peace: In moments of stress or anxiety, turn to prayer, seeking God's peace to guard your heart and mind.

3. Practice Mindfulness: Cultivate mindfulness to stay in the present moment, recognizing God's presence and peace within it.

**Prayer:**

Heavenly Father,
We thank you for the gift of your peace that surpasses understanding. Help us to rest in your promises of peace, surrendering our anxieties and fears to you. May your peace guard our hearts and minds, providing strength and refuge in every season of life. In moments of turmoil, let us not be troubled or afraid, but trust in your unfailing peace.
In Jesus name, we pray. Amen.

## DAY 15
### Trusting God's Plan In Uncertainty

Proverbs 3:5-6 (NIV)
"Trust in the Lord with all your heart and lean not on your own understanding; in all your ways submit to him, and he will make your paths straight."

It's often challenging to maintain our composure and hold fast to our trust in God's divine plan. Yet, in Proverbs 3:5-6, we are reminded of the unfaltering promise that when we trust in the Lord with all our hearts, relinquishing our own limited understanding, and submit to Him wholeheartedly, He will guide our steps and make our paths straight.

The beauty of these verses lies in their simplicity, yet the profundity of their message cannot be overstated. In times when the world seems to spiral into chaos, when our own plans crumble, and when doubt and fear threaten to overwhelm us, God beckons us to place our trust in Him. This trust isn't blind, but a confident assurance that God's wisdom far surpasses our own.

We may question why certain events occur, why prayers seem unanswered, or why we face unexpected challenges. It's natural to seek answers, but God calls us to lean not on our own understanding. Instead, He invites us to rest in His unwavering love and trust that every twist and turn in our journey serves a greater purpose.

*Additional Scriptural Reference:*

*Isaiah 41:10 (NIV) "So do not fear, for I am with you; do not be dismayed, for I am your God. I will strengthen you and help you; I will uphold you with my righteous right hand."*

## Action Plan:

1. Reflect daily on Proverbs 3:5-6, reminding yourself to trust in the Lord with all your heart.

2. Keep a gratitude journal to record moments when God's plan became evident in your life.

3. Seek support from fellow believers and engage in prayer and Bible study to strengthen your faith.

## Prayer:

*Heavenly Father, we come before you with humble hearts, acknowledging that your wisdom surpasses our understanding. Help us, O Lord, to trust in your divine plan even when life's uncertainties threaten to shake us. Be our guiding light through the darkest of forests, and grant us the faith to follow where you lead. In Jesus name, we pray. Amen.*

## DAY 16
## Embracing God's For the Broken

Psalm 34:18 (NIV)

"The Lord is close to the brokenhearted and saves those who are crushed in spirit."

In Psalm 34:18, we find solace and hope in the divine promise that the Lord draws near to the brokenhearted and rescues those whose spirits are crushed. In life's most trying moments, when we feel shattered, unloved, and abandoned, God's love shines brilliantly as a beacon of hope.

God's love is not reserved for the perfect or the unbroken. It is precisely in our brokenness that His love is most tenderly bestowed. Our wounds become the canvas upon which He paints His masterpiece of redemption. The cracks in our hearts become channels through which His love flows abundantly.

*Additional Scriptural Reference:*

*Isaiah 42:3 (NIV) "A bruised reed he will not break, and a smouldering wick he will not snuff out."*

## Action Plan:

1. Meditate on Psalm 34:18 daily, reminding yourself that God is close to you in your brokenness.

2. Reach out to those who are hurting and share God's love and compassion with them.

3. Journal your journey of embracing God's love in your brokenness and the moments of healing you experience.

## Prayer:

*Heavenly Father, we thank you for your unfailing love that draws near to us when we are broken and crushed in spirit. Help us to embrace your love and find healing and restoration in your tender care. May our brokenness be a testament to your redeeming power. In Jesus name, we pray. Amen.*
*May you find strength and comfort in God's boundless love as you navigate the brokenness of life.*

## DAY 17
### Rejoicing In God's Faithfulness

Psalm 89:1 (NIV)
"I will sing of the Lord's great love forever; with my mouth I will make your faithfulness known through all generations."

In Psalm 89:1, we are called to rejoice in God's unwavering faithfulness. It's a reminder that His love endures through every season of our lives, a love so deep that it resonates through the ages. Imagine the legacy we can leave by singing of His faithfulness, not only in our own lives but for generations to come.

God's faithfulness isn't just a concept; it's a living reality. In the moments of doubt, when life's storms threaten to overwhelm us, His faithfulness stands as an unshakeable pillar of strength. His promises are our refuge, and His love is our song, a melody of hope that carries us through the trials.

### Action Plan:

1. Reflect daily on Psalm 89:1, finding reasons to rejoice in God's faithfulness.

2. Share your testimony of God's faithfulness with someone, inspiring them to trust Him.

3. Sing a hymn or worship song that celebrates God's faithfulness as a personal act of gratitude.

### Prayer:

*Heavenly Father, we thank you for your unchanging faithfulness that carries us through every season of life. Help us, O Lord, to rejoice in your love and make your faithfulness known to all generations. May our lives be a testament to your enduring grace. In Jesus name, we pray. Amen.*

*May your heart be filled with joy as you rejoice in the steadfast faithfulness of our loving God.*

## DAY 18
## The Blessing Of God's Strength

Isaiah 40:31 (NIV)

"But those who hope in the Lord will renew their strength. They will soar on wings like eagles; they will run and not grow weary, they will walk and not be faint."

Isaiah 40:31 reminds us of the incredible blessing that comes from placing our hope in the Lord. In times of weariness and exhaustion, God's strength is our refuge. It's like the promise of soaring on the wings of eagles, running with unwavering endurance, and walking without growing faint. When we anchor our hope in Him, His strength becomes our own, empowering us to face life's challenges with grace.

*Additional Scriptural Reference:*

*Philippians 4:13 (NIV) "I can do all this through him who gives me strength."*

**Action Plan:**

1. Meditate on Isaiah 40:31 daily, finding hope and strength in God's promises.

2. Identify areas in your life where you need God's strength, and surrender them to Him in prayer.

3. Encourage others by sharing how God's strength has empowered you in difficult times.

**Prayer:**

*Heavenly Father, we thank you for the blessing of your strength that renews us each day. Help us, O Lord, to place our hope in you, knowing that in your strength, we can soar above life's challenges, run with endurance, and walk without growing faint. May your strength be our source of courage and resilience. In Jesus name, we pray. Amen.*
*May you experience the incredible blessing of God's strength as you place your hope and trust in Him each day.*

## DAY 19
## Living With Gratitude In All Circumstances

1 Thessalonians 5:18 (NIV)
"Give thanks in all circumstances; for this is God's will for you in Christ Jesus."

In 1 Thessalonians 5:18, we are called to live with gratitude in all circumstances, recognizing that this aligns with God's divine will for us in Christ Jesus. Gratitude isn't just a fleeting emotion; it's a way of life that transforms our perspective.

Life is a journey filled with highs and lows, joys and challenges. It's easy to give thanks when everything is going smoothly, but God calls us to a deeper level of gratitude. It's in the midst of trials and difficulties that our gratitude truly shines as a beacon of hope. When we thank God in all circumstances, we acknowledge His sovereignty and trust in His plan, even when it's hard to understand.

*Additional Scriptural Reference:*

*Philippians 4:6 (NIV) "Do not be anxious about anything, but in every situation, by prayer and petition, with thanksgiving, present your requests to God."*

**Action Plan:**

1. Start a gratitude journal, recording daily blessings, no matter how small.

2. Practice thankfulness in prayer, presenting your requests to God with a heart of gratitude.

3. Encourage others to join you in cultivating an attitude of gratitude.

**Prayer:**

*Heavenly Father, we thank you for the gift of gratitude that allows us to see your hand at work in all circumstances. Help us, O Lord, to live out 1 Thessalonians 5:18, giving thanks in every situation. May our gratitude be a testament to your faithfulness and love. In Jesus name, we pray. Amen.*

*May your life be a living testament of gratitude, shining brightly even in the midst of life's challenges.*

## DAY 20
## Finding Peace In Surrender

Romans 6:13 (NIV)

"Do not offer any part of yourself to sin as an instrument of wickedness, but rather offer yourselves to God as those who have been brought from death to life; and offer every part of yourself to him as an instrument of righteousness."

In Romans 6:13, we discover the path to finding peace through surrender. It's an invitation to offer ourselves to God, not as instruments of sin but as instruments of righteousness. Surrendering our lives to God can feel daunting, but it's in this act of relinquishing control that we find true peace.

*Additional Scriptural Reference:*

*Philippians 4:7 (NIV) "And the peace of God, which transcends all understanding, will guard your hearts and your minds in Christ Jesus."*

## Action Plan:

1. Reflect on Romans 6:13 daily, seeking opportunities to surrender areas of your life to God.

2. Practice surrender in prayer, entrusting your worries and burdens to Him.

3. Share your journey of surrender with others, encouraging them to find peace in God.

## Prayer:

*Heavenly Father, we thank you for the peace that comes from surrendering our lives to your loving guidance. Help us, O Lord, to offer every part of ourselves to you as instruments of righteousness. May your peace guard our hearts and minds as we trust in your plan. In Jesus name, we pray. Amen.*
*May you find deep and abiding peace as you surrender to God's loving and guiding hand.*

## DAY 21
## Persevering with Hope and Endurance

Hebrews 10:36 (NIV) - "You need to persevere so that when you have done the will of God, you will receive what he has promised."

In the journey of life, we often find ourselves facing trials and tribulations. Hebrews 10:36 reminds us to persevere with hope and endurance. This verse is a beacon of inspiration, calling us to stay steadfast in our faith journey, even when the path is fraught with challenges.

Life's trials can weigh heavy on our hearts, but it's in these moments that our faith is truly tested. We must remember that God's promises are worth the struggle. With hope as our anchor and endurance as our compass, we can navigate through life's storms, knowing that our efforts align with His will.

*Additional Scriptural Reference:*

*Romans 12:12 (NIV) - "Be joyful in hope, patient in affliction, faithful in prayer."*

**Action Plan:**

1. Reflect on the trials you're currently facing and how they align with God's will.

2. Find joy in the hope of God's promises. Practice patience during afflictions, knowing that they refine your faith.

3. Remain faithful in prayer, seeking God's guidance and strength.

**Prayer:**

*Dear Heavenly Father, grant us the strength to persevere with hope and endurance in the face of life's challenges. Help us trust in Your promises and find joy in the hope they bring. May we be patient in affliction and faithful in our prayers, knowing that Your will is the ultimate guide for our lives. In Jesus name, we pray. Amen.*

## DAY 22
## Navigating Life's Challenges with Prayer

Philippians 4:6 (NIV) - "Do not be anxious about anything, but in every situation, by prayer and petition, with thanksgiving, present your requests to God."

Philippians 4:6 is our steadfast anchor. It urges us not to be consumed by anxiety but to find solace in prayer. In the hustle and bustle of daily life, it's easy to become overwhelmed, but this verse is a gentle reminder that prayer is our lifeline.

When we approach God with our anxieties, something remarkable happens. Our burdens grow lighter, and our hearts find peace. Through prayer, we acknowledge our reliance on Him and express our gratitude for His presence in our lives.

*Additional Scriptural Reference:*

*1 Thessalonians 5:17 (NIV) - "Pray continually."*

**Action Plan:**

1. Start your day with a moment of prayer, committing your concerns to God.

2. Throughout the day, maintain an attitude of gratitude through thanksgiving.

3. In challenging moments, pause and offer up a silent prayer for guidance and strength.

**Prayer:**

*Heavenly Father, in the midst of life's challenges, we turn to You with gratitude. Help us to cast away our anxieties through prayer and petition, finding comfort and strength in Your presence. May we pray continually, knowing that You are always near. In Jesus name, we pray. Amen.*

## DAY 23
## Trusting God's Unchanging Character

Hebrews 13:8 (NIV) - "Jesus Christ is the same yesterday and today and forever."

In the ever-changing tapestry of life, we find solace in the unchanging character of God, as beautifully depicted in Hebrews 13:8. This verse is a profound reminder that amidst life's uncertainties, God remains a constant source of strength and unwavering love.

144

The world may shift, circumstances may alter, but the unchanging nature of God provides us with an anchor for our souls. In moments of doubt or fear, we can find reassurance in His consistent presence and enduring love. His promises stand firm, His mercy remains boundless, and His grace never falters.

*Additional Scriptural Reference:*

*Malachi 3:6 (NIV) - "I the Lord do not change. So you, the descendants of Jacob, are not destroyed."*

**Action Plan:**

1. Reflect on the unchanging character of God and the comfort it brings.

2. Seek His guidance and trust in His unchanging promises, even in uncertain times.

3. Share your testimony of God's constancy with others, spreading hope.

**Prayer:**

Dear Heavenly Father, we thank You for Your unchanging character that is our rock in the shifting sands of life. Help us to trust in Your unwavering love and promises. In times of uncertainty, may we find peace in Your unchanging nature. Grant us the strength to share this hope with others. In Jesus name, we pray. Amen.

# DAY 24
## Embracing God's Purpose in Trials

James 1:2-4 (NIV) - "Consider it pure joy, my brothers and sisters, whenever you face trials of many kinds, because you know that the testing of your faith produces perseverance. Let perseverance finish its work so that you may be mature and complete, not lacking anything."

James 1:2-4 reveals a deeper purpose. It invites us to embrace God's divine plan in our trials, to find joy amidst adversity. These verses remind us that through life's challenges, our faith is refined, our endurance strengthened, and our character matured.

God's purpose in trials is to mould us into vessels of greater resilience and spiritual depth. Rather than fearing hardships, we are called to rejoice in them, knowing that they are opportunities for growth.

*Additional Scriptural Reference:*

*Romans 8:28 (NIV) - "And we know that in all things God works for the good of those who love him, who have been called according to his purpose."*

## Action Plan:

1. When trials come, pray for the strength to see God's purpose within them.

2. Keep a journal to record how trials have shaped your faith and character.

3. Encourage others facing trials, sharing the hope of God's purpose.

## Prayer:

*Dear Heavenly Father, grant us the wisdom to see Your purpose in our trials. May we find joy in the refining process and trust that You work all things for our good. Strengthen our faith, and use us to encourage others on their journey. In Jesus name, we pray. Amen.*

## DAY 25
### The Blessing of God's Guidance in Decision-Making

Psalm 32:8 (NIV) - "I will instruct you and teach you in the way you should go; I will counsel you with my loving eye on you."

In the labyrinth of life's decisions, Psalm 32:8 shines as a beacon of hope and assurance. It's a reminder that God's guidance is a precious blessing. He promises to personally instruct, teach, and counsel us with His watchful and loving eye always upon us.

The weight of decision-making can be daunting, but knowing that God is our guide brings comfort. His guidance is not arbitrary; it's tailor-made for our unique journey. His wisdom surpasses human understanding, and His love ensures that every step we take is under His care.

*Additional Scriptural Reference:*

*Proverbs 3:5-6 (NIV) - "Trust in the Lord with all your heart and lean not on your own understanding; in all your ways submit to him, and he will make your paths straight."*

## Action Plan:

1. Seek God's guidance in prayer before making important decisions.

2. Trust His wisdom, even when it doesn't align with your own understanding.

3. Submit every area of your life to Him, inviting His guidance in all things.

## Prayer:

*Heavenly Father, we thank You for Your promise to guide us. In moments of decision-making, we trust in Your wisdom and lean not on our own understanding. May Your loving eye be upon us always, making our paths straight. In Jesus name, we pray. Amen.*

## DAY 26
## Rejoicing in God's Love and Salvation

Psalm 13:5-6 (NIV) - "But I trust in your unfailing love; my heart rejoices in your salvation. I will sing the Lord's praise, for he has been good to me."

In the midst of life's trials, Psalm 13:5-6 is a resounding anthem of hope and rejoicing. It's a heartfelt declaration of unwavering trust in God's unfailing love and an outpouring of gratitude for His salvation.

In our darkest hours, when it seems like all hope is lost, we can find solace in God's steadfast love and the salvation He offers. This verse reminds us that even in our struggles, we can choose to rejoice in His goodness.

*Additional Scriptural Reference:*

*Zephaniah 3:17 (NIV) - "The Lord your God is with you, the Mighty Warrior who saves. He will take great delight in you; in his love, he will no longer rebuke you, but will rejoice over you with singing.*

## Action Plan:

1. Reflect on the times when God's love and salvation have been evident in your life.

2. Choose to rejoice and sing praises to the Lord daily, regardless of your circumstances.

3. Share your testimony of God's goodness with others to inspire hope.

**Prayer:**

*Heavenly Father, we trust in Your unfailing love and rejoice in Your salvation. Even in the midst of challenges, we find solace in Your goodness. Help us to sing Your praises daily and share the joy of Your love with those around us. In Jesus name, we pray. Amen.*

## DAY 27
## Cultivating a Heart of Trust

Psalm 37:3-5 (NIV) - "Trust in the Lord and do good; dwell in the land and enjoy safe pasture. Take delight in the Lord, and he will give you the desires of your heart. Commit your way to the Lord; trust in him and he will do this."

Psalm 37:3-5 offers a profound prescription for cultivating a heart of trust. It urges us to trust in the Lord wholeheartedly, to find joy in His presence, and to commit our ways to Him.

Trusting in God can be a journey of surrender, where we release control and place our faith in His plans. As we do good and seek His delight, we discover that His desires become our own, and our hearts align with His purpose.

*Additional Scriptural Reference:*

*Proverbs 3:5-6 (NIV) - "Trust in the Lord with all your heart and lean not on your own understanding; in all your ways submit to him, and he will make your paths straight."*

**Action Plan:**

1. Reflect on areas in your life where trust in God needs to deepen.

2. Seek joy in His presence through prayer, worship, and thanksgiving.

3. Commit your plans and desires to Him, allowing His guidance to shape your path.

**Prayer:**

## DAY 28
## Resting in God's Provision in Times of Need

Philippians 4:11-12 (NIV) - "I am not saying this because I am in need, for I have learned to be content whatever the circumstances. I know what it is to be in need, and I know what it is to have plenty. I have learned the secret of being content in any and every situation, whether well fed or hungry, whether living in plenty or in want."

In the midst of life's uncertainties, Philippians 4:11-12 is a profound testament to the art of resting in God's provision. The apostle Paul's words resonate deeply, reminding us that contentment is not reliant on our circumstances but on our trust in God.

When we face times of need, whether materially or spiritually, God's provision is unwavering. It may not always align with our expectations, but it aligns perfectly with His plan for our lives. As we learn to trust Him completely, we discover the profound peace of contentment.

*Additional Scriptural Reference:*

*Matthew 6:31-33 (NIV) - "So do not worry, saying, 'What shall we eat?' or 'What shall we drink?' or 'What shall we wear?' For the pagans run after all these things, and your heavenly Father knows that you need them. But seek first his kingdom and his righteousness, and all these things will be given to you as well."*

**Action Plan:**

1. In times of need, turn to God in prayer, seeking His guidance and provision.

2. Practice gratitude daily, acknowledging His blessings, whether big or small.

3. Seek His kingdom and righteousness above all else, trusting that He will provide for your needs.

**Prayer:**

*Heavenly Father, in times of need, we rest in Your unwavering provision. Teach us the secret of contentment, whether in abundance or scarcity. Help us seek Your kingdom above all else, trusting that You will meet our needs. In Jesus name, we pray. Amen.*

## DAY 29
## Trusting God's Timing in Waiting

Psalm 27:14 (NIV) - "Wait for the Lord; be strong and take heart and wait for the Lord."

In the tapestry of life, waiting can be one of the most challenging threads to weave. Psalm 27:14 encourages us to trust God's timing while we wait. It's a gentle reminder that, in the waiting, our faith is tested, and our hearts are refined.

Waiting is not passive; it's an act of strength and courage. It's an opportunity to deepen our reliance on God's perfect timing. In the waiting, we find solace in knowing that God is working behind the scenes, orchestrating His divine plan for our lives.

*Additional Scriptural Reference:*

*Isaiah 40:31 (NIV) - "But those who hope in the Lord will renew their strength. They will soar on wings like eagles; they will run and not grow weary, they will walk and not be faint."*

**Action Plan:**

1. Surrender your timeline to God in prayer, trusting His wisdom.

2. Seek opportunities to grow spiritually and emotionally during the waiting period.

3. Encourage others who are also waiting, sharing the hope found in trusting God's timing.

**Prayer:**

*Dear Heavenly Father, as we wait, help us find strength and courage in You. Teach us to trust Your perfect timing, even when it doesn't align with our own. May we soar on wings like eagles, knowing that our hope is in You. In Jesus name, we pray. Amen.*

## DAY 30
## Embracing God's Promises of Comfort

2 Corinthians 1:3-4 (NIV) - "Praise be to the God and Father of our Lord Jesus Christ, the Father of compassion and the God of all comfort, who comforts us in all our troubles, so that we can comfort those in any trouble with the comfort we ourselves receive from God."

In the midst of life's storms, 2 Corinthians 1:3-4 reveals God as the ultimate source of comfort. He is the Father of compassion, the wellspring of solace in our times of trouble. These verses remind us that His comfort is not just for us to receive but to share with others.

When we embrace God's promises of comfort, we find strength in our weaknesses, hope in our despair, and healing in our pain. It's a comforting thought that our trials are not in vain; they become a testimony of God's faithfulness, equipping us to comfort others.

*Additional Scriptural Reference:*

*Psalm 34:18 (NIV) - "The Lord is close to the brokenhearted and saves those who are crushed in spirit."*

**Action Plan:**

1. Seek God's comfort through prayer and meditation on His promises.

2. Share your experiences of God's comfort with someone in need.

3. Extend compassion and support to those facing troubles, becoming a vessel of God's comfort.

**Prayer:**

*Heavenly Father, we praise You for being our source of comfort in times of trouble. Teach us to embrace Your promises of solace and to share the comfort we receive with others. May Your presence be felt by the brokenhearted, and may we be instruments of Your compassion. In Jesus name, we pray. Amen.*

## DAY 31
## The Blessing of God's Presence in Loneliness

Psalm 139:7-10 (NIV) - "Where can I go from your Spirit? Where can I flee from your presence? If I go up to the heavens, you are there; if I make my bed in the depths, you are there. If I rise on the wings of the dawn, if I settle on the far side of the sea, even there your hand will guide me, your right hand will hold me fast."

In the depths of loneliness, Psalm 139:7-10 offers a profound revelation - God's unwavering presence. It reminds us that there is no place too high or too low, no corner too distant where God's comforting presence cannot be found.

Loneliness often makes us feel isolated, but in those moments, we can take solace in the truth that we are never truly alone. God's presence is our constant companion, our guide, and our refuge. His love fills the void of loneliness, bringing comfort and peace.

*Additional Scriptural Reference:*

*Isaiah 41:10 (NIV) - "So do not fear, for I am with you; do not be dismayed, for I am your God. I will strengthen you and help you; I will uphold you with my righteous right hand."*

**Action Plan:**

1. In moments of loneliness, turn to God in prayer, seeking His comforting presence.

2. Reach out to a friend or loved one for companionship and support.

3. Reflect on God's promise to strengthen and uphold you in times of need.

**Prayer:**

*Heavenly Father, in moments of loneliness, we find comfort in Your abiding presence. Help us to remember that we are never truly alone. May Your love and companionship fill the void of loneliness, bringing peace to our hearts. In Jesus name, we pray. Amen.*

# JUNE

*Jesus is the fountain of "Living Water". He is our source of life, our sustenance of life and, essentially, our "life." When we approach Jesus daily in prayer and obedience, we are blessed to drink from His presence. His presence is the gift of life. It is eternal life, and the very life for which they were created.*

## DAY 01
## Cultivating a Heart of Kindness and Compassion

Ephesians 4:32 (NIV)
"Be kind and compassionate to one another, forgiving each other, just as in Christ God forgave you."

Kindness is the gentle touch that can heal wounded hearts. Compassion is the empathy that bridges divides and brings people together. Forgiveness is the balm that soothes our own souls as much as it mends fractured relationships. When we embody these qualities, we become beacons of hope and agents of change. We create ripples of goodwill that touch the lives of those around us, inspiring them to pay forward the love they've received.

*Additional Scriptural Reference:*

*Colossians 3:12 (NIV) "Therefore, as God's chosen people, holy and dearly loved, clothe yourselves with compassion, kindness, humility, gentleness, and patience."*

**Action Plan:**

1. Forgive Freely: Release the burden of grudges and resentments. Forgive as you have been forgiven.

2. Random Acts of Kindness: Perform small acts of kindness for others, even strangers, without expecting anything in return.

3. Study God's Word: Continuously seek guidance and inspiration from the Scriptures to nurture these virtues.

**Prayer:**

*Dear Heavenly Father, we come before you with hearts open to your guidance. We thank you for the boundless kindness and compassion you've shown us through your Son, Jesus Christ. Help us, Lord, to cultivate these virtues within ourselves, to be beacons of your love in this world. Grant us the strength to forgive as you have forgiven us, and the wisdom to be kind and compassionate to all. In Jesus name, we pray. Amen.*

## DAY 02
## Living with Purpose in Your Calling

Colossians 3:17 (NIV)
"And whatever you do, whether in word or deed, do it all in the name of the Lord Jesus, giving thanks to God the Father through him."

Colossians 3:17 illuminates the profound concept of living with purpose in your calling. It invites us to infuse every aspect of our lives with a sense of divine purpose, reminding us that our actions and words have the power to glorify God and impact the world.

Living with purpose means recognizing that your daily interactions, whether at work, home, or in the community, are significant. It's about conducting yourself in a way that reflects the love, grace, and truth of Christ. It's infusing your calling with a sense of worship, knowing that through your life, God's glory shines.

*Additional Scriptural References:*

*Romans 12:6-8 (NIV)*

*"We have different gifts, according to the grace given to each of us. If your gift is prophesying, then prophesy in accordance with your faith; if it is serving, then serve; if it is teaching, then teach; if it is to encourage, then give encouragement; if it is giving, then give generously; if it is to lead, do it diligently; if it is to show mercy, do it cheerfully."*

**Action Plan:**

1.  Discover Your Calling: Take time to reflect on your unique gifts, talents, and passions. Seek guidance through prayer and self-reflection to understand your purpose.

2.  Daily Dedication: Begin each day with a prayer, dedicating your actions and words to God's glory.

3.  Intentional Living: In your daily activities, strive to exhibit qualities of love, grace, and truth. Be an ambassador of Christ's light.

**Prayer:**

*Heavenly Father, we come before you with hearts filled with gratitude for the unique calling you've placed on each of our lives. Help us, Lord, to live with purpose, to glorify you in all that we do, and to recognize that our words and actions can be a testimony of your love and grace. Guide us as we seek to discover and fulfil our calling, and may our lives be a testament to your glory. In the name of Jesus, we pray. Amen.*

## DAY 03
## The Power of God's Love in Relationships

1 Corinthians 13:4–7 (NIV)
"Love is patient, love is kind. It does not envy, it does not boast, it is not proud. It does not dishonour others, it is not self-seeking, it is not easily angered, it keeps no record of wrongs. Love does not delight in evil but rejoices with the truth. It always protects, always trusts, always hopes, always perseveres."

In the tapestry of life, love is the golden thread that binds our relationships. 1 Corinthians 13:4–7 reveals the transformative power of God's love. It inspires us to love with patience, kindness, and humility. It challenges us to let go of envy and pride, to forgive freely, and to cherish truth. It urges us to protect, trust, hope, and persevere, for true love is an unwavering force.

*Additional Scriptural References:*

*1 John 4:7 (NIV) "Dear friends, let us love one another, for love comes from God."*

**Action Plan:**

1.  Forgive and Let Go: Release grudges and cultivate a heart that forgives as God forgives.

2.  Cherish Truth: Build trust by being honest and authentic in your relationships.

3.  Pray for Love: Seek God's guidance in loving others as He loves you.

**Prayer:**

## DAY 04
## Surrendering Fear to God's Peace

John 14:27 (NIV)
"Peace I leave with you; my peace I give you. I do not give to you as the world gives. Do not let your hearts be troubled and do not be afraid."

In the tumultuous sea of life, fear can be an anchor that drags us down. John 14:27 reminds us of God's extraordinary gift—His peace. It's a peace beyond the world's understanding, a tranquil harbour amid life's storms. This scripture is an invitation to surrender our fears to the comforting embrace of God's peace.

Imagine the burdens you carry—fears of the future, anxieties about the unknown. Now, imagine releasing them, one by one, into God's capable hands. His peace replaces fear, providing a soothing balm for your troubled heart.

*Additional Scriptural References:*

*Isaiah 41:10 (NIV) "So do not fear, for I am with you; do not be dismayed, for I am your God. I will strengthen you and help you; I will uphold you with my righteous right hand."*

**Action Plan:**

1. Prayerful Surrender: Daily, offer your fears to God in prayer, asking for His peace to replace them.

2. Scriptural Meditation: Reflect on passages like John 14:27 and Philippians 4:6–7 for reassurance.

3. Breath of Peace: In moments of anxiety, take deep breaths, envisioning God's peace filling you.

**Prayer:**

## DAY 05
## Finding Strength in Perseverance

Hebrews 12:1 (NIV)
"Therefore, since we are surrounded by such a great cloud of witnesses, let us throw off everything that hinders and the sin that so easily entangles. And let us run with perseverance the race marked out for us."

Life can often feel like a long and challenging race. Hebrews 12:1 reminds us that we are not alone in this journey. We are surrounded by a "great cloud of witnesses," those who have faced trials with faith and perseverance. Their stories inspire us to press on.

Think of the hurdles you've encountered—the obstacles that threaten to slow your pace. This verse encourages us to shed the burdens of doubt and sin that entangle us, allowing us to run with perseverance. It's a call to endure with determination, knowing that our race is marked out by a loving God who equips us for the journey.

*Additional Scriptural References:*

*Romans 5:3–4 (NIV)*

*"Not only so, but we also glory in our sufferings, because we know that suffering produces perseverance; perseverance, character; and character, hope."*

**Action Plan:**

1. Identify Obstacles: Recognize what hinders your journey and seek solutions.

2. Set Goals: Break your journey into achievable milestones, focusing on one step at a time.

3. Pray for Perseverance: Ask God for the strength and endurance to stay the course.

**Prayer:**

*Heavenly Father, in moments of weariness and doubt, we turn to you for strength and perseverance. Thank you for the examples of faith found in Hebrews 12:1. Help us throw off the hindrances that weigh us down, enabling us to run with perseverance the race you've marked out for us. Grant us unwavering determination and hope. In Jesus name, we pray. Amen.*

## DAY 06
## Rejoicing in God's Faithfulness in the Storms

Isaiah 43:2 (NIV)
"When you pass through the waters, I will be with you; and when you pass through the rivers, they will not sweep over you. When you walk through the fire, you will not be burned; the flames will not set you ablaze."

Life's storms can be relentless, threatening to drown us in despair and scorch us with adversity. Yet, Isaiah 43:2 offers solace and unwavering hope. It paints a vivid picture of God's faithfulness, assuring us that even in the fiercest tempests and the hottest fires, He remains our anchor and shield.

Imagine being surrounded by tumultuous waters, but never being swept away. Visualise walking through the scorching flames, yet remaining unburned. God's promise is not just survival but triumph in the face of adversity.

*Additional Scriptural References:*

*Psalm 46:1 (NIV)*

*"God is our refuge and strength, an ever-present help in trouble."*

**Action Plan:**

1. Journal Your Journey: Document instances where God has been faithful in your life.

2. Lean on Scripture: Seek strength in the Bible during difficult times.

3. Encourage Others: Share your stories of God's faithfulness to inspire and uplift.

**Prayer:**

## DAY 07
## Embracing God's Forgiveness and Redemption

Psalm 103:12 (NIV)
"As far as the east is from the west, so far has he removed our transgressions from us."

In the depths of our souls, we often carry the weight of our mistakes and regrets. Yet, Psalm 103:12 paints a breathtaking picture of God's forgiveness. It illustrates His boundless love and grace by comparing the removal of our sins to the infinite expanse between east and west. In this verse, we find a profound reminder of God's ability to wipe our slates clean and offer us redemption.

Imagine a burden lifted, chains broken, and a heart set free. God's forgiveness isn't just a pardon; it's a complete separation from our sins. It's an invitation to embrace His redemption and live in the fullness of His love.

*Additional Scriptural References:*

*1 John 1:9 (NIV)*

*"If we confess our sins, he is faithful and just and will forgive us our sins and purify us from all unrighteousness."*

**Action Plan:**

1. Confession and Repentance: Humbly confess your sins and seek God's forgiveness.

2. Reflect on Psalm 103:12: Meditate on this verse, allowing its truth to penetrate your heart.

3. Forgive Yourself: Release self-condemnation and accept God's forgiveness fully.

**Prayer:**

*Heavenly Father, we stand in awe of your forgiveness and redemption as described in Psalm 103:12. Thank you for removing our sins as far as the east is from the west. Help us accept your grace, forgive ourselves, and live in the freedom of your love. May we share your redemptive power with others. In Jesus name, we pray. Amen.*
*May you embrace God's forgiveness and redemption, finding joy in the knowledge that your sins are forever separated from you, and may His grace and love fill your heart to overflowing.*

## DAY 08
## Trusting God's Plan for Your Future

Jeremiah 29:11 (NIV)
"For I know the plans I have for you," declares the LORD, "plans to prosper you and not to harm you, plans to give you hope and a future."

Life's uncertainties often lead us to question our future, but Jeremiah 29:11 is a beacon of hope. It's a reminder that God's plans for us are filled with promise, purpose, and prosperity. When we trust His plan, we find solace in the knowledge that our future is in the hands of a loving and all-knowing God.

*Additional Scriptural References:*

*Proverbs 3:5–6 (NIV)*

*"Trust in the LORD with all your heart and lean not on your own understanding; in all your ways submit to him, and he will make your paths straight."*

**Action Plan:**

1. Prayerful Surrender: Begin and end your day in prayer, surrendering your future to God.

2. Seek God's Guidance: In decision-making, consult God through prayer and study of His Word.

3. Trust and Patience: When facing uncertainty, trust that God's timing is perfect, even if it doesn't align with your plans.

**Prayer:**

*Heavenly Father, we thank you for your reassuring promise in Jeremiah 29:11. Help us to trust your plan for our future, even when we cannot see the way. Grant us patience and unwavering faith as we walk the path you've designed for us. May our lives be a testimony to your goodness and wisdom. In Jesus name, we pray. Amen.*

## DAY 09
## The Blessing of God's Guidance in Education

Proverbs 1:5 (NIV)
"Let the wise listen and add to their learning, and let the discerning get guidance."

Education is a journey of growth and discovery, and Proverbs 1:5 reminds us of the divine blessing of guidance. It's an invitation to embrace wisdom and discernment as companions on our educational path. God's guidance in education is a beacon of light, illuminating our minds, and enriching our spirits.

*Additional Scriptural References:*

*Proverbs 2:6 (NIV)*

*"For the LORD gives wisdom; from his mouth comes knowledge and understanding."*

**Action Plan:**

1. Daily Prayer for Guidance: Begin your study or educational journey with prayer, asking God for wisdom and understanding.

2. Seek God in Learning: As you learn, look for opportunities to apply His wisdom to your studies.

3. Mentorship: Seek mentors who can guide you in both your educational and spiritual growth.

**Prayer:**

*Heavenly Father, we thank you for the blessing of education and the guidance you provide along this journey. As we seek knowledge, grant us discernment and wisdom. May our learning always lead us closer to you, and may we use the knowledge we gain to bring glory to your name. In Jesus name, we pray. Amen.*

## DAY 10
## Finding Peace in God's Creation

Psalm 19:1 (NIV)
"The heavens declare the glory of God; the skies proclaim the work of his hands."

In the midst of life's chaos, we find solace in Psalm 19:1, a poetic ode to the beauty of God's creation. It invites us to look up at the vast expanse of the heavens and find peace in the intricate tapestry of stars and galaxies. The skies themselves become a proclamation of God's handiwork, a testament to His creative genius.

*Additional Scriptural References:*

*Psalm 104:24-25 (NIV)*

*"How many are your works, Lord! In wisdom, you made them all; the earth is full of your creatures."*

**Action Plan:**

1. Nature Walks: Spend time in nature regularly, whether it's a hike, a walk in the park, or simply sitting in your backyard.

2. Reflect and Meditate: Use these moments to reflect on God's creation, offering gratitude for its beauty.

3. Share the Experience: Invite friends or family to join you in appreciating God's handiwork.

**Prayer:**

*Heavenly Father, we thank you for the beauty and wonder of your creation as described in Psalm 19:1. In moments of stillness and awe, may we find peace in the knowledge of your presence. Help us to connect with you through the beauty of the natural world and to share the joy of your creation with others. In Jesus name, we pray. Amen.*

## DAY 11
## Surrendering Control to God in Finances

Matthew 6:33 (NIV)
"But seek first his kingdom and his righteousness, and all these things will be given to you as well."

The topic of finances often stirs feelings of control and uncertainty. Yet, in Matthew 6:33, Jesus offers a profound lesson in surrendering control to God. He encourages us to prioritise seeking God's kingdom and righteousness over obsessing about financial matters. It's an invitation to trust God as the ultimate provider.

*Additional Scriptural References:*

*Proverbs 3:5-6 (NIV)*

*"Trust in the Lord with all your heart and lean not on your own understanding; in all your ways submit to him, and he will make your paths straight."*

**Action Plan:**

1. Budget with Faith: Create a financial plan that aligns with your values and God's principles.

2. Generosity: Practice giving to God's work and helping those in need.

3. Prayer: Make prayer a regular part of your financial decision-making process.

**Prayer:**

## DAY 12
## The Power of God's Word in Spiritual Growth

1 Peter 2:2 (NIV)
"Like newborn babies, crave pure spiritual milk, so that by it you may grow up in your salvation."

Imagine the hunger of a newborn baby, eagerly seeking nourishment and growth. 1 Peter 2:2 likens our spiritual journey to this craving for pure spiritual milk—God's Word. Just as milk is vital for a baby's physical growth, God's Word is essential for our spiritual growth.

The Bible is more than just words on paper; it's a divine source of wisdom, guidance, and strength. It's a wellspring of truth that nourishes our souls and transforms our lives. When we approach it with a hunger for spiritual growth, we invite God's presence into our hearts, enabling us to mature in our faith.

*Additional Scriptural References:*

*2 Timothy 3:16-17 (NIV)*

*"All Scripture is God-breathed and is useful for teaching, rebuking, correcting, and training in righteousness, so that the servant of God may be thoroughly equipped for every good work."*

**Action Plan:**

1. Daily Reading: Commit to daily reading and meditation on God's Word.

2. Study and Reflect: Dive deeper into Scripture, studying its context and reflecting on its application to your life.

3. Pray for Understanding: Ask God for wisdom and understanding as you engage with His Word.

**Prayer:**

*Heavenly Father, we thank you for the power of your Word as described in 1 Peter 2:2. May we approach it with the hunger of newborns, seeking spiritual nourishment and growth. Grant us insight and understanding as we study your Scriptures, and may your Word be a guiding light in our lives. In Jesus name, we pray. Amen.*

## DAY 13
## Living with Gratitude for God's Blessings

Psalm 118:29 (NIV)
"Give thanks to the LORD, for he is good; his love endures forever."

Gratitude is the golden thread that weaves through every blessing. Psalm 118:29 is a heartfelt call to live with a spirit of thankfulness, recognizing that the goodness of the Lord and His enduring love deserve our eternal gratitude. Imagine a life where gratitude is your default response to God's blessings, both big and small.

Gratitude transforms our perspective, turning moments into memories and trials into testimonies. It's an emotional journey that leads to contentment and joy, even in life's challenges. Living with gratitude is an inspiring way to honour God's goodness.

*Additional Scriptural References:*

*1 Thessalonians 5:18 (NIV)*

*"Give thanks in all circumstances; for this is God's will for you in Christ Jesus."*

**Action Plan:**

1. Daily Gratitude Journal: Start and end each day by listing things you're grateful for.

2. Acts of Kindness: Show gratitude by performing acts of kindness for others.

3. Reflect on Blessings: During challenging times, focus on the blessings you've received.

**Prayer:**

*Heavenly Father, we give thanks to you with hearts full of gratitude, as expressed in Psalm 118:29. Your goodness and enduring love surround us. Help us live with a spirit of thankfulness in all circumstances, knowing that your blessings are abundant. May our lives be a testament to your love and grace. In Jesus name, we pray. Amen.*

## DAY 14
## Cultivating a Heart of Joy

Psalm 30:5 (NIV)
"Weeping may stay for the night, but rejoicing comes in the morning."

Life often carries moments of darkness and sorrow, but Psalm 30:5 paints a vivid picture of hope. It reminds us that joy, like the sunrise after a long night, follows even the deepest of sorrows. This verse inspires us to cultivate a heart of joy, knowing that God's promise of rejoicing awaits us.

Imagine a heart that finds joy not despite life's challenges but because of them. It's a heart anchored in faith, resilient in trials, and overflowing with gratitude. Cultivating joy is an emotional journey of trust in God's unfailing love.

*Additional Scriptural References:*

*Nehemiah 8:10 (NIV)*

*"The joy of the LORD is your strength."*

**Action Plan:**

1. Morning Gratitude: Begin each day with thanksgiving for the gift of a new morning.

2. Count Your Blessings: Keep a gratitude journal to remind yourself of the reasons for joy.

3. Pray for Joy: Ask God to fill your heart with His joy and help you find it in all circumstances.

**Prayer:**

*Heavenly Father, we thank you for the promise of joy as found in Psalm 30:5. May our hearts be filled with the joy that comes from knowing you and trusting in your love. Help us to find joy in the morning, even after the darkest night. In Jesus name, we pray. Amen.*

## DAY 15
## Rejoicing in God's Salvation

Isaiah 12:3 (NIV)
"With joy, you will draw water from the wells of salvation."

Isaiah 12:3 paints a beautiful image of rejoicing in God's salvation, where joy becomes the vessel through which we receive the living water of His grace.

Rejoicing is an emotional response to the realisation of God's salvation. It's the song of your heart when you grasp the depth of His love and the profoundness of His rescue. In moments of despair, you can draw from the wells of salvation, finding sustenance for your spirit.

*Additional Scriptural References:*

*Psalm 51:12 (NIV)*

*"Restore to me the joy of your salvation and grant me a willing spirit, to sustain me."*

**Action Plan:**

1. Daily Reflection: Take moments to reflect on the depth of God's salvation in your life.

2. Gratitude Journal: Keep a journal of God's acts of salvation and thank Him daily.

3. Rejoice in Worship: Participate in worship services with a heart full of gratitude and joy.

**Prayer:**

*Heavenly Father, we rejoice in your salvation as described in Isaiah 12:3. Thank you for the living water that sustains our spirits. May we draw from the wells of salvation with hearts full of joy. Help us to share this joy with others, spreading the good news of your grace. In Jesus name, we pray. Amen.*

*May you continually draw from the wells of God's salvation, finding unending joy in His grace and sharing it with those around you, like a refreshing stream of living water.*

## DAY 16
## Embracing God's Mercy and Grace

Ephesians 1:7 (NIV)
"In him, we have redemption through his blood, the forgiveness of sins, in accordance with the riches of God's grace."

God's mercy is the tender touch that wipes away your tears, and His grace is the unearned gift that frees you from the chains of sin. Embracing His mercy and grace is an emotional journey of transformation, where brokenness is replaced with wholeness and shame with honour.

*Additional Scriptural References:*

*Romans 3:23-24 (NIV)*

*"For all have sinned and fall short of the glory of God, and all are justified freely by his grace through the redemption that came by Christ Jesus."*

**Action Plan:**

1. Daily Reflection: Begin each day reflecting on Ephesians 1:7 and God's grace.

2. Confession and Repentance: Regularly confess your sins and seek God's forgiveness.

3. Forgive Others: Extend the same grace and mercy to others that God has given you.

**Prayer:**

*Heavenly Father, we are humbled and grateful for the mercy and grace described in Ephesians 1:7. Thank you for redeeming us through the sacrifice of your Son. Help us embrace your forgiveness, extending it to others with love. May your grace transform our lives, and may we live in the freedom it offers. In Jesus name, we pray. Amen.*

## DAY 17
## Trusting God's Protection in Times of Danger

Psalm 91:11 (NIV)
"For he will command his angels concerning you to guard you in all your ways."

In the face of danger, Psalm 91:11 offers a profound promise of God's protection. It's a reminder that even in our most vulnerable moments, God sends His angels to watch over us, guiding us through life's perils. Imagine the comfort of knowing that you are never alone, surrounded by divine protection.

This verse evokes powerful emotions - the relief of being sheltered, the assurance of safety, and the warmth of God's love. Trusting God's protection in times of danger is an emotional journey of surrender, where fear gives way to faith.

*Additional Scriptural References:*

*Psalm 34:7 (NIV)*

*"The angel of the LORD encamps around those who fear him, and he delivers them."*

**Action Plan:**

1. Daily Prayer for Protection: Begin and end each day with a prayer, asking for God's protection.

2. Scripture Meditation: Memorise and meditate on Psalm 91:11 during moments of anxiety.

3. Safety Precautions: Be wise in safety decisions, trusting God's guidance.

**Prayer:**

*Heavenly Father, we thank you for the promise of protection found in Psalm 91:11. May we trust in your loving care, knowing that you command your angels concerning us. In times of danger, may our faith in your protection be unwavering. Keep us safe, Lord, and guide us through life's challenges. In Jesus name, we pray. Amen.*

## DAY 18
## Surrendering Anxiety to God's Peace

Philippians 4:7 (NIV)
"And the peace of God, which transcends all understanding, will guard your hearts and your minds in Christ Jesus."

Imagine a storm of anxiety raging within, threatening to overwhelm your heart and mind. Philippians 4:7 is a tranquil oasis in this tempest, offering the promise of God's peace that surpasses all comprehension. It's an emotional refuge, where anxiety gives way to an inexplicable, soothing calm.

This verse evokes feelings of awe and serenity as you realise that God's peace is not dependent on circumstances. It's a divine embrace that envelops your heart and mind, guarding them in the loving shelter of Christ Jesus. Surrendering anxiety to God's peace is an emotional journey of trust and release.

*Additional Scriptural References:*

*Isaiah 26:3 (NIV)*

*"You will keep in perfect peace those whose minds are steadfast because they trust in you."*

**Action Plan:**

1. Daily Surrender: Begin and end each day with a prayer, surrendering your anxieties to God.

2. Deep Breathing and Prayer: In moments of anxiety, practice deep breathing while praying for God's peace to fill you.

3. Philippians 4:8: Focus your thoughts on whatever is true, noble, right, pure, lovely, and of good repute.

**Prayer:**

*Heavenly Father, we surrender our anxieties to you, knowing that your peace, as described in Philippians 4:7, transcends understanding. Guard our hearts and minds in Christ Jesus, enveloping us in your soothing calm. In moments of anxiety, may your peace prevail. We trust in your unfailing love. In Jesus name, we pray. Amen.*

## DAY 19
## The Power of Prayer in Intercession

1 Timothy 2:1 (NIV)
"I urge, then, first of all, that petitions, prayers, intercession and thanksgiving be made for all people."

In 1 Timothy 2:1, we are urged to engage in intercession, the powerful act of lifting up others in prayer. It's a spiritual and emotional journey where we become instruments of God's grace, standing in the gap for those in need.

Intercession stirs deep emotions of compassion, empathy, and love. It's the privilege of partnering with God in His divine plan for people's lives. Through prayer, we can change destinies, heal wounds, and offer hope.

*Additional Scriptural References:*

*James 5:16 (NIV)*

*"The prayer of a righteous person is powerful and effective."*

**Action Plan:**

1. Prayer List: Create a prayer list for individuals and causes close to your heart.

2. Regular Intercession: Dedicate time each day to intercede for those on your list.

3. Ask for Prayer: Don't hesitate to ask others to pray for you or your concerns.

4. Keep a Prayer Journal: Record answered prayers and testimonies of God's faithfulness.

**Prayer:**

*Heavenly Father, we thank you for the privilege of intercession as encouraged in 1 Timothy 2:1. May our hearts be stirred with compassion, and may our prayers bring healing, hope, and transformation to those we intercede for. Teach us to stand in the gap for others, as you have done for us. In Jesus name, we pray. Amen.*

## DAY 20
## Finding Strength in Unity and Fellowship

1 Corinthians 1:10 (NIV)
"I appeal to you, brothers and sisters, in the name of our Lord Jesus Christ, that all of you agree with one another in what you say and that there be no divisions among you, but that you be perfectly united in mind and thought."

1 Corinthians 1:10 calls us to find strength in unity and fellowship, to stand as a united force in the name of Christ. It's an emotional call to bridge divides, heal wounds, and forge bonds of love that withstand all challenges.

In unity, there's a sense of belonging, purpose, and empowerment. It's the profound feeling of being part of a greater whole, where the collective strength far exceeds individual efforts. Finding strength in unity is an emotional journey of forgiveness, reconciliation, and love.

*Additional Scriptural References:*

*Psalm 133:1 (NIV)*

*"How good and pleasant it is when God's people live together in unity!"*

**Action Plan:**

1. Seek Reconciliation: If divisions exist, seek reconciliation with those you may have differences with.

2. Regular Fellowship: Attend and participate in church or community gatherings to build fellowship.

3. Pray for Unity: Regularly pray for unity and love within your church or fellowship.

**Prayer:**

*Heavenly Father, we humbly come before you, seeking the unity and fellowship described in 1 Corinthians 1:10. May our hearts be inclined toward love and reconciliation. Help us find strength in our unity, knowing that we are called to be one body in Christ. Let our actions and words reflect your love and grace. In Jesus name, we pray. Amen.*

*May you find strength, purpose, and joy in the unity and fellowship of the body of Christ, and may your love and unity be a powerful testimony of God's grace to the world.*

## DAY 21
## Cultivating a Heart of Forgiveness and Reconciliation

Matthew 6:14 (NIV)
"For if you forgive other people when they sin against you, your heavenly Father will also forgive you."

Matthew 6:14 illuminates the transformative power of forgiving others. It's an emotional journey that leads to healing, reconciliation, and a heart aligned with God's grace.

Forgiveness is an act of courage and compassion. It evokes profound emotions as you release the burden of hurt, allowing God's love to mend what was broken. Cultivating a heart of forgiveness and reconciliation is a testament to God's boundless mercy.

*Additional Scriptural References:*

*Colossians 3:13 (NIV)*

*"Bear with each other and forgive one another if any of you has a grievance against someone. Forgive as the Lord forgave you."*

**Action Plan:**

1. Self-Reflection: Reflect on any unforgiveness in your heart and the need for reconciliation.

2. Initiate Forgiveness: Reach out to those you need to forgive or seek forgiveness from.

3. Pray for Healing: Pray for emotional healing and reconciliation in broken relationships.

4. Forgive Continuously: Make forgiveness a daily practice, even for small grievances.

**Prayer:**

*Heavenly Father, we seek the grace to cultivate hearts of forgiveness and reconciliation, as guided by Matthew 6:14. Help us release the weight of unforgiveness and embrace the freedom of forgiveness. May our actions and words reflect your boundless mercy. Heal our hearts, Lord, and mend broken relationships. In Jesus name, we pray. Amen.*

## DAY 22
## Trusting God's Love and Faithfulness in All Things

Psalm 36:5 (NIV)
"Your love, LORD, reaches to the heavens, your faithfulness to the skies."

Psalm 36:5 unveils the boundless nature of God's love and faithfulness. It's a truth that should inspire deep emotions within us—awe, gratitude, and trust.

God's love is like an endless ocean, and His faithfulness is like the unchanging constellations above. Trusting in God's love and faithfulness in all things is an emotional journey of surrender, where our worries and doubts are replaced with the unshakable assurance of His unwavering care.

*Additional Scriptural References:*

*Psalm 136:26 (NIV)*

*"Give thanks to the God of heaven. His love endures forever."*

### Action Plan:

1. Gratitude Journal: Keep a journal of moments where you've seen His faithfulness in your life.

2. Scripture Meditation: Memorise and meditate on verses that remind you of God's love and faithfulness.

3. Pray for Trust: Pray for an increased trust in God's love and faithfulness in all situations.

### Prayer:

*Heavenly Father, we stand in awe of your love and faithfulness, as described in Psalm 36:5. Your love reaches to the heavens, and your faithfulness is unchanging. Help us trust in your unwavering care, even in the midst of uncertainty. May your love be our anchor, and your faithfulness our guiding star. In Jesus name, we pray. Amen.*

## DAY 23
## Rejoicing in God's Faithfulness in Past Seasons

Lamentations 3:22-23 (NIV)
"Because of the LORD's great love we are not consumed, for his compassions never fail. They are new every morning; great is your faithfulness."

Recalling past seasons filled with God's faithfulness evokes deep emotions—gratitude for His unmerited grace, comfort in times of hardship, and awe for His constant presence. It's a journey of rejoicing, knowing that His mercies are renewed daily.

Imagine standing at the crossroads of life, gazing back at the footprints of God's faithfulness in past seasons. Lamentations 3:22-23 paints a portrait of His unending love and unfailing compassion. It's an emotional reminder that no matter how tough life gets, His faithfulness remains an unwavering anchor.

*Additional Scriptural References:*

*Psalm 103:2-5 (NIV)*

*"Praise the LORD, my soul, and forget not all his benefits—who forgives all your sins and heals all your diseases, who redeems your life from the pit and crowns you with love and compassion."*

## Action Plan:

1. Count Your Blessings: Daily, recount seasons of God's faithfulness in a gratitude journal.

2. Serve with Gratitude: Volunteer or serve others as an expression of gratitude for God's faithfulness.

3. Morning Thanksgiving: Start each day by thanking God for His faithfulness in past seasons.

## Prayer:

*Heavenly Father, we rejoice in your faithfulness, as depicted in Lamentations 3:22-23. Your compassions never fail, and your love is unwavering. Help us to remember and celebrate your faithfulness in past seasons, knowing that your mercies are renewed daily. May we live each day with hearts full of gratitude and awe. In Jesus name, we pray. Amen.*

## DAY 24
## The Blessing of God's Guidance in Future Plans

Proverbs 16:9 (NIV)
"In their hearts humans plan their course, but the LORD establishes their steps."

Proverbs 16:9 paints a vivid picture of our human desire to plan, yet it humbly acknowledges that God ultimately guides our steps. This truth should evoke emotions of trust, assurance, and hope.

God's guidance in future plans is like a beacon in the night, illuminating our path with His wisdom and love. It's an emotional journey of surrender, where our plans align with His purpose, and our hearts find peace in His leading.

*Additional Scriptural References:*

*Psalm 32:8 (NIV)*

*"I will instruct you and teach you in the way you should go; I will counsel you with my loving eye on you."*

**Action Plan:**

1. Prayerful Planning: Seek God's guidance in every decision, large or small.

2. Reflect on His Word: Meditate on Scripture to discern His will.

3. Trust His Timing: Be patient and trust that His timing is perfect.

**Prayer:**

*Heavenly Father, we acknowledge your sovereign guidance in our future plans, as spoken of in Proverbs 16:9. Help us align our hearts with your purpose, knowing that your wisdom surpasses our understanding. May your guiding hand lead us, and may we find peace and hope in your direction. In Jesus name, we pray. Amen.*

## DAY 25
## Finding Peace in God's Promises of Rest

Matthew 11:28-30 (NIV)
"Come to me, all you who are weary and burdened, and I will give you rest. Take my yoke upon you and learn from me, for I am gentle and humble in heart, and you will find rest for your souls. For my yoke is easy and my burden is light."

Matthew 11:28-30 offers this imagery of rest for the soul. It's an emotional invitation to release the heavy burdens of life and find profound peace in God's promises.

In these verses, Jesus calls us to Him, promising rest and gentleness. The emotional impact of this promise is relief, comfort, and a sense of belonging. It's a deep breath after holding it for too long, a moment of stillness in life's chaos.

*Additional Scriptural References:*

*Psalm 23:1 (NIV)*

*"The LORD is my shepherd, I lack nothing."*

Action Plan:

1. Daily Surrender: Start and end your day in prayer, surrendering your burdens to God.

2. Scripture Meditation: Memorise and reflect on verses that promise rest and peace.

3. Sabbath Rest: Dedicate a day of the week to rest and reflection on God's goodness.

4. Help Others Find Rest: Extend Jesus' invitation to others who are weary.

Prayer:

*Heavenly Father, we come to you, weary and burdened, as mentioned in Matthew 11:28-30. Thank you for your promise of rest for our souls. May we find peace in your gentle embrace and learn from your humility. Help us release our burdens to you and trust in your loving care. In Jesus name, we pray. Amen.*

## DAY 26
## Resting in God's Strength in Daily Battles

Ephesians 6:10 (NIV)
"Finally, be strong in the Lord and in his mighty power."

Ephesians 6:10 take us into this emotional realm of divine empowerment. It's an assurance that in the midst of daily struggles, we can find strength and courage in God's presence.

This verse evokes feelings of confidence, resilience, and security. It's the knowledge that no battle is too great when we rely on God's strength. The emotional journey is one of surrender, where our weaknesses become opportunities for God to display His mighty power.

*Additional Scriptural References:*

*Isaiah 41:10 (NIV)*

*"So do not fear, for I am with you; do not be dismayed, for I am your God. I will strengthen you and help you; I will uphold you with my righteous right hand."*

**Action Plan:**

1. Daily Prayer for Strength: Begin each day by asking God for His strength.

2. Physical and Emotional Self-Care: Prioritise rest, nutrition, and emotional well-being.

3. Acts of Service: Find opportunities to serve others, allowing God's strength to flow through you.

**Prayer:**

*Heavenly Father, as we face daily battles, we turn to Ephesians 6:10 for strength. Clothe us in your mighty power, for we know that in you, we find our courage. Help us rely on your strength, not our own, and face each challenge with unwavering faith. In Jesus name, we pray. Amen.*

## DAY 27
## The Power of God's Word in Renewing the Mind

Romans 12:2 (NIV)
"Do not conform to the pattern of this world, but be transformed by the renewing of your mind. Then you will be able to test and approve what God's will is—his good, pleasing and perfect will."

Romans 12:2 paints a picture of the transformative power of God's Word. It's an emotional journey from conformity to renewal, from uncertainty to clarity.

This verse evokes feelings of hope, transformation, and spiritual growth. It's the assurance that God's Word is a living, breathing force capable of renewing our minds. It's an invitation to explore His will and purpose, to trade anxiety for peace, and confusion for clarity.

*Additional Scriptural References:*

*Psalm 119:105 (NIV)*

*"Your word is a lamp for my feet, a light on my path."*

### Action Plan:

1. Daily Scripture Reading: Commit to regular reading and meditation on God's Word.

2. Renew Your Thoughts: Identify areas of your mind and life that need transformation.

3. Prayer for Renewal: Ask God to renew your mind according to His will.

### Prayer:

*Heavenly Father, we embrace Romans 12:2 as a promise of renewal through your Word. Transform our minds, Lord, and align our thoughts with your will. May your Word be a guiding light, leading us to a deeper understanding of your purpose. In Jesus name, we pray. Amen.*

*May you experience the profound transformation that comes from immersing yourself in God's Word, allowing it to renew your mind and guide you into His perfect will, bringing peace, clarity, and spiritual growth.*

## DAY 28
### Trusting God's Plan in Family Matters

Joshua 24:15 (NIV)
"But as for me and my household, we will serve the LORD."

Imagine your family as a vessel sailing through life's storms, anchored in the unwavering trust of God's plan. Joshua 24:15 is a powerful declaration of trust in family matters. It's an emotional commitment to align your family's journey with the Lord's purpose.

This verse stirs feelings of unity, devotion, and unwavering trust. It's a call to make God the captain of your family's ship, ensuring that His wisdom guides every decision, His love fills every home, and His grace binds every heart Trusting God's Plan in Family Matters

*Additional Scriptural References:*

*Proverbs 22:6 (NIV)*

*"Start children off on the way they should go, and even when they are old they will not turn from it."*

## Action Plan:

1. Family Prayer: Dedicate time for family prayer and Bible study.

2. Lead by Example: Demonstrate trust in God's plan through your own life.

3. Family Values: Establish and uphold values that align with God's principles.

4. Open Communication: Foster open, honest, and loving communication within your family.

## Prayer:

*Heavenly Father, as we reflect on Joshua 24:15, we declare our trust in your plan for our families. May we serve you wholeheartedly and be a shining example of your love and grace. Guide our family in unity and devotion, so that our homes may be a reflection of your presence. In Jesus name, we pray. Amen.*

*May your family be a testimony of trust in God's plan, filled with unity, love, and devotion, and may His wisdom guide every aspect of your family's journey.*

# DAY 29
## Living with Gratitude for God's Daily Provision

Psalm 34:10 (NIV)
"The lions may grow weak and hungry, but those who seek the LORD lack no good thing."

Psalm 34:10 is an emotional testament to His daily care. It's a reminder that in seeking the Lord, we find ourselves lacking nothing.

This verse elicits feelings of gratitude, trust, and contentment. It's the assurance that God's provision is not just about sustenance but also about abundance. Living with gratitude for His daily provision is an emotional journey of recognizing His faithfulness in the smallest details of life.

*Additional Scriptural References:*

*Matthew 6:26 (NIV)*

*"Look at the birds of the air; they do not sow or reap or store away in barns, and yet your heavenly Father feeds them. Are you not much more valuable than them?"*

**Action Plan:**

1. Help Others: Look for opportunities to share God's blessings with those in need.

2. Reflect on His Provision: Keep a journal of how God has provided for you each day.

3. Contentment in Simplicity: Find joy in life's simple pleasures, knowing they are gifts from God.

**Prayer:**

*Heavenly Father, we come before you with hearts full of gratitude for your daily provision, as described in Psalm 34:10. Teach us to trust in your care, knowing that in seeking you, we lack no good thing. May our lives be a testament to your faithfulness. In Jesus name, we pray. Amen.*

## DAY 30
## Cultivating a Heart of Joy in Worship

Psalm 100:2 (NIV)
"Worship the LORD with gladness; come before him with joyful songs."

Psalm 100:2 is an emotional call to cultivate a heart of joy in worship. It's an invitation to approach God with exuberant praise, knowing that He delights in our joyful adoration.

This verse evokes feelings of gratitude, happiness, and spiritual connection. It's a reminder that worship is not a solemn duty but a joyful privilege. Cultivating a heart of joy in worship is an emotional journey where our songs become expressions of love and our praises resound with gladness.

*Additional Scriptural References:*

*Psalm 98:4 (NIV)*

*"Shout for joy to the LORD, all the earth, burst into jubilant song with music."*

**Action Plan:**

1. Daily Worship: Dedicate time each day for personal worship and praise.

2. Express Gratitude: Incorporate thanksgiving into your worship to foster joy.

3. Dance and Sing: Express your joy physically through dance and vocally through song.

**Prayer:**

*Heavenly Father, we come before you with hearts ready to worship you with gladness, as Psalm 100:2 encourages us. Fill us with the joy of your presence as we sing and praise your name. May our worship be a source of joy, both to you and to our own souls. In Jesus name, we pray. Amen.*

*May you cultivate a heart of joy in your worship, knowing that your praises bring delight to God and fill your own spirit with gladness, fostering a deeper connection with Him and a life marked by joyful worship.*

# JULY

## DAY 01
## Embracing God's Mercy and Compassion

Psalm 145:8 (NIV)
"The LORD is gracious and compassionate, slow to anger and rich in love."

Visualise a loving embrace, where the weight of your shortcomings is met with the boundless mercy of God. Psalm 145:8 paints a vivid picture of God's character—gracious, compassionate, patient, and overflowing with love. It's an emotional reminder that His mercy is the balm for our wounded souls.

This verse evokes feelings of awe, relief, and profound gratitude. It's an invitation to embrace God's mercy and compassion as the cornerstone of our faith. It's a journey of emotional release, where guilt and shame give way to the warm embrace of His love.

*Additional Scriptural References:*

*Lamentations 3:22-23 (NIV)*

*"Because of the LORD's great love we are not consumed, for his compassions never fail. They are new every morning; great is your faithfulness."*

**Action Plan:**

1. Forgiveness Practice: Extend mercy and forgiveness to others as a reflection of God's love.

2. Study God's Mercy: Explore Scriptures that reveal God's mercy and compassion.

186

3. Prayer for Grace: Pray for an increased understanding and acceptance of God's mercy.

**Prayer:**

*Heavenly Father, we bow before your gracious and compassionate nature, as expressed in Psalm 145:8. Thank you for your boundless love and unending mercy. Help us to embrace your compassion and extend it to others as a testament to your grace. In Jesus name, we pray. Amen.*

## DAY 02
## Trusting God's Protection in Times of Danger

Psalm 18:2 (NIV)
"The LORD is my rock, my fortress and my deliverer; my God is my rock, in whom I take refuge, my shield and the horn of my salvation, my stronghold."

Imagine standing in the face of danger, yet feeling an unshakable sense of security. Psalm 18:2 is an emotional declaration of trust in God's protection. It's an assurance that even in perilous moments, He is our unyielding fortress, our shield, and our source of salvation.

This verse elicits feelings of courage, peace, and profound reliance on God. It's an invitation to entrust our safety to Him, to find refuge in His unchanging strength, and to know that danger may come, but God's protection is unwavering.

*Additional Scriptural References:*

*Psalm 46:1 (NIV)*

*"God is our refuge and strength, an ever-present help in trouble."*

**Action Plan:**

1. Daily Prayer for Protection: Begin and end your day with a prayer for God's protection.

2. Scripture Meditation: Memorise and reflect on verses about God's protection.

3. Safety Measures: Act wisely and responsibly in times of danger while trusting God.

**Prayer:**

*Heavenly Father, we take refuge in your protective embrace, as expressed in Psalm 18:2. In times of danger, be our fortress and deliverer, our shield and salvation. Help us trust in your unwavering protection, knowing that in you, we find ultimate safety. In Jesus' name, we pray. Amen.*

## DAY 03
## The Power of Prayer in Seeking God's Will

James 1:5 (NIV)
"If any of you lacks wisdom, you should ask God, who gives generously to all without finding fault, and it will be given to you."

James 1:5 is a beacon of hope, an emotional reminder that when we seek God's will through prayer, He grants us wisdom without hesitation. It's an invitation to approach Him with the trust that He is the giver of discernment.

This verse evokes feelings of humility, trust, and hope. It's an acknowledgment that our understanding is limited, but God's wisdom is boundless. The power of prayer in seeking God's will is an emotional journey where our uncertainties are transformed into confident steps guided by divine wisdom.

*Additional Scriptural References:*

*Proverbs 3:5-6 (NIV)*

*"Trust in the LORD with all your heart and lean not on your own understanding; in all your ways submit to him, and he will make your paths straight."*

**Action Plan:**

1. Daily Prayer for Wisdom: Dedicate time for prayer, seeking God's wisdom in decisions.

2. Seek Counsel: Consult with wise and spiritually mature individuals for guidance.

3. Act on Wisdom: Once you receive wisdom, take action in alignment with God's will.

**Prayer:**

*Heavenly Father, we approach you in awe of your wisdom, as James 1:5 encourages us. Grant us discernment as we seek your will through prayer. May your wisdom guide our steps, and may we trust in your generous and faultless provision. In Jesus name, we pray. Amen.*

## DAY 04
## Finding Strength in Community and Fellowship

Hebrews 10:24-25 (NIV)
"And let us consider how we may spur one another on toward love and good deeds, not giving up meeting together, as some are in the habit of doing, but encouraging one another—and all the more as you see the Day approaching."

Visualise a circle of friends, bound by love and a shared faith, lifting each other up in times of joy and trial. Hebrews 10:24-25 embodies the emotional essence of Christian fellowship. It's an invitation to draw strength from a supportive community, where love and encouragement abound.

This verse evokes feelings of warmth, belonging, and spiritual growth. It's a call to cherish the gift of Christian fellowship, recognizing that together, we can inspire love and good deeds, and we can persevere through life's challenges.

*Additional Scriptural References:*

*1 Thessalonians 5:11 (NIV)*

*"Therefore encourage one another and build each other up, just as in fact, you are doing."*

**Action Plan:**

1. Regular Gatherings: Commit to regular meetings with your Christian community.

2. Prayer Partners: Form prayer partnerships within your community.

3. Share Testimonies: Share your faith journey and encourage others with your experiences.

**Prayer:**

*Heavenly Father, we thank you for the precious gift of Christian community, as highlighted in Hebrews 10:24-25. Help us to cherish and cultivate these bonds, spurring one another on toward love and good deeds. May our fellowship be a source of strength, love, and encouragement. In Jesus name, we pray. Amen.*

## DAY 05
## Living as Instruments of God's Grace

Ephesians 2:10 (NIV)
"For we are God's handiwork, created in Christ Jesus to do good works, which God prepared in advance for us to do."

Ephesians 2:10 is an emotional revelation that we are God's masterpieces, uniquely fashioned to extend His grace. It's an invitation to live as instruments of His love and kindness.

This verse evokes feelings of purpose, awe, and the profound significance of your existence. It's a reminder that your life has a grand design, preordained by God for acts of grace and love.

*Additional Scriptural References:*

*1 Peter 4:10 (NIV)*

*"Each of you should use whatever gift you have received to serve others, as faithful stewards of God's grace in its various forms."*

**Action Plan:**

1. Discover Your Gifts: Seek to understand your unique gifts and talents.

2. Act with Love: Commit to daily acts of kindness and grace toward others.

3. Mentorship: Offer guidance and mentorship to those who can benefit from your experience.

**Prayer:**

*Heavenly Father, we are awed by the truth of Ephesians 2:10, that we are your handiwork, created for good works. May we live as instruments of your grace, bringing love and kindness to a world in need. Guide us in discovering our unique purpose and grant us the strength to fulfil it. In Jesus name, we pray. Amen.*

## DAY 06
## Embracing God's Comfort in Times of Loss

2 Corinthians 1:3-4 (NIV)
"Praise be to the God and Father of our Lord Jesus Christ, the Father of compassion and the God of all comfort, who comforts us in all our troubles, so that we can comfort those in any trouble with the comfort we ourselves receive from God."

Envision a comforting embrace in your darkest hour. 2 Corinthians 1:3-4 embodies the emotional essence of God's love and solace in times of loss. It's an invitation to find refuge in His compassionate arms and, in turn, become channels of comfort to others.

This verse evokes feelings of reassurance, empathy, and healing. It's a testimony that our suffering is not in vain, but a wellspring of comfort to offer others. Embracing God's comfort in times of loss is an emotional journey where grief is transformed into compassion.

*Additional Scriptural References:*

*Psalm 34:18 (NIV)*

*"The LORD is close to the brokenhearted and saves those who are crushed in spirit."*

**Action Plan:**

1. Seek God's Comfort: Turn to God in prayer and scripture for solace.

2. Share Your Story: Use your experiences of loss to encourage and uplift others.

3. Pray for Healing: Pray for God's healing and comfort over those who are grieving.

**Prayer:**

Heavenly Father, we praise you as the Father of compassion and the God of all comfort, as described in 2 Corinthians 1:3-4. In times of loss, may we find solace in your arms and extend that comfort to others. Use our experiences of grief to bring healing and hope to those around us. In Jesus name, we pray. Amen.

## DAY 07
## Dedication: The Secret To Fruitful Christianity

John 12:26 (NIV)
"Whoever serves me must follow me; and where I am, my servant also will be. My Father will honour the one who serves me."

John 12:26 is an emotional revelation of the profound truth that our commitment to follow Christ yields the honour of the Father. It's an invitation to dedicate our lives wholeheartedly to His service.

This verse evokes feelings of devotion, purpose, and the deep desire to walk in the footsteps of Jesus. It's a call to pursue a life of meaningful service, knowing that through dedication, we find the secrets to bearing fruit in our Christian journey.

Additional Scriptural References:

Matthew 16:24 (NIV)

"Then Jesus said to his disciples, 'Whoever wants to be my disciple must deny themselves and take up their cross and follow me.'"

**Action Plan:**

1. Fellowship: Join a Christian community for support and encouragement in your dedication.

2. Pray for Guidance: Seek God's guidance in your journey of dedication.

**Prayer:**

Heavenly Father, we acknowledge the importance of dedication as revealed in John 12:26. Help us follow Christ wholeheartedly, serving where He leads us. May our dedication bring honour to you and bear abundant fruit in our Christian walk. In Jesus name, we pray. Amen.

DAY 08
## Stop Procrastinating As A Believer

John 4:35 (NIV)
"Do you not say, 'Four months more and then the harvest'? I tell you, open your eyes and look
at the fields! They are ripe for harvest."

John 4:35 is an emotional call to believers, urging us to seize the present moment. It's a reminder that procrastination can delay the spiritual harvest. This verse evokes feelings of urgency, purpose, and the profound realisation that opportunities for sharing God's love are abundant. It's a call to overcome procrastination in our faith journey, recognizing that every moment is an opportunity to make a difference.

*Additional Scriptural References:*

*James 4:17 (NIV)*

*"If anyone, then, knows the good they ought to do and doesn't do it, it is sin for them."*

**Action Plan:**

1. Immediate Obedience: When prompted by the Holy Spirit, act promptly.

2. Prioritise Spiritual Growth: Allocate time daily for prayer, Bible study, and reflection.

3. Prayer for Diligence: Pray for the strength to overcome procrastination in your spiritual walk.

**Prayer:**

*Heavenly Father, we pray for the wisdom and strength to overcome procrastination in our faith journey, as John 4:35 reminds us that the fields are ripe for harvest. Help us seize the opportunities before us to share your love and grace with others. In Jesus name, we pray. Amen.*

## DAY 09
## Praying For The Salvation Of Souls

Genesis 18:22 (NIV)
"The men turned away and went toward Sodom, but Abraham remained standing before the LORD."

Genesis 18:22 is an emotional testament to the power of prayer for the lost. It's a reminder that our prayers can impact the eternal destiny of others.
This verse evokes feelings of urgency, compassion, and the deep desire to see souls saved. It's an invitation to be like Abraham, fervently praying for the salvation of those who are lost in sin.

Additional Scriptural References:

1 Timothy 2:1-4 (NIV)

"I urge, then, first of all, that petitions, prayers, intercession, and thanksgiving be made for all people... This is good, and pleases God our Saviour, who wants all people to be saved."

**Action Plan:**

1. Prayer List: Create a list of individuals who need salvation and pray for them regularly.

2. Share the Gospel: Look for opportunities to share the message of salvation with those around you.

3. Intercessory Prayer: Dedicate specific times for focused intercession for the salvation of souls.

**Prayer:**

*Heavenly Father, like Abraham in Genesis 18:22, we stand before you, praying for the salvation of souls. May our intercession be fervent, and our hearts burdened for those who need your saving grace. Lord, open the hearts of the lost to receive your love and forgiveness. In Jesus name, we pray. Amen.*

## DAY 10
## Giving for the promotion of God's kingdom

Genesis 22:18 (NIV)
"...and through your offspring all nations on earth will be blessed because you have obeyed me."

Visualise Abraham's willingness to give, knowing that through his obedience, all nations would be blessed. Genesis 22:18 is an emotional reminder of the transformative power of giving for the promotion of God's kingdom. It's an invitation to be like Abraham, joyfully contributing to God's work on earth. This verse evokes feelings of joy, purpose, and the profound impact of our giving. It's a testament that when we give to advance God's kingdom, lives are touched, and blessings flow not only to us but to the nations.

*Additional Scriptural References:*

*Malachi 3:10 (NIV)*

*"Bring the whole tithe into the storehouse, that there may be food in my house. Test me in this,' says the LORD Almighty, 'and see if I will not throw open the floodgates of heaven and pour out so much blessing that there will not be room enough to store it.'"*

**Action Plan:**

1. Pray for Guidance: Seek God's guidance on how and where to contribute to His kingdom.

2. Regular Giving: Commit to regular giving, whether through tithes or offerings.

3. Give Cheerfully: Cultivate a heart of cheerful giving, rejoicing in the opportunity to bless others.

**Prayer:**

*Heavenly Father, we are inspired by the example of Abraham in Genesis 22:18, who gave obediently and saw nations blessed. Guide us in our giving for the promotion of your kingdom, and may our hearts overflow with joy as we contribute to your work on earth. In Jesus name, we pray. Amen.*

## DAY 11
## Enjoying God's kingdom prosperity

Proverbs 12:14 (NIV)
"From the fruit of their lips people are filled with good things, and the work of their hands brings them reward."

Proverbs 12:14 is an emotional revelation that our words and deeds can usher in God's abundance. It's an invitation to experience the richness of His blessings by aligning our lives with His principles.
This verse evokes feelings of hope, gratitude, and the profound impact of our choices. It's a testament that as we speak life, love, and truth, and as we work diligently in His name, we partake in His kingdom prosperity.

*Additional Scriptural References:*

*Psalm 1:3 (NIV)*

*"That person is like a tree planted by streams of water, which yields its fruit in season and whose leaf does not wither—whatever they do prospers."*

**Action Plan:**

1. Guard Your Words: Speak words of life, encouragement, and love.

2. Serve with Purpose: Work diligently in your vocation or ministry, recognizing that it's an opportunity to bring glory to God.

3. Seek God's Kingdom: Prioritise seeking God's kingdom in all aspects of your life.

**Prayer:**

*Heavenly Father, we are inspired by Proverbs 12:14, which reminds us of the power of our words and actions to manifest your kingdom prosperity. Help us to speak life, love, and truth, and to work diligently for your glory. May our lives be filled with the abundance of your blessings. In Jesus name, we pray. Amen.*

## DAY 12
## The Blessing of God's Guidance in Life's Journeys

Psalm 32:8 (NIV)
"I will instruct you and teach you in the way you should go; I will counsel you with my loving eye on you."

The threads of guidance from our Heavenly Father are woven with divine care. Psalm 32:8 assures us of God's intimate involvement in our paths. His promise is our beacon of hope, reminding us that even in uncertainty, His loving eye is upon us.

Imagine a loving Father, gently holding your hand, leading you step by step through the labyrinth of life. It's a comforting thought, isn't it? When challenges loom large, and decisions weigh heavy, His guidance becomes our refuge.

*Additional Scriptures: Proverbs 3:5-6*

**Action Plan:**

1. Seek God's guidance through prayer and meditation on His Word.

2. Listen attentively to that still, small voice in your heart.

3. Trust His wisdom, even when His path seems unconventional.

**Prayer:**

*Heavenly Father, we thank you for your unwavering guidance in our lives. May we always heed your loving counsel and trust your perfect plan. In moments of uncertainty, be our guiding light. In Jesus name, we pray. Amen.*

## DAY 13
## The Power of God's Word in Transforming Lives

Hebrews 4:12 (NIV)
"For the word of God is alive and active. Sharper than any double-edged sword, it penetrates even to divide soul and spirit, joints and marrow; it judges the thoughts and attitudes of the heart."

In the pages of the Bible, we find a treasure trove of transformative power. Hebrews 4:12 reminds us that God's Word is not just ink on paper; it's a living force, a double-edged sword that pierces to our innermost depths. It heals wounds, transforms hearts, and renews minds.

Consider the stories of women throughout history who were touched by God's Word. From Esther's courage to Ruth's loyalty, these heroines drew strength from Scripture. In your life, too, God's Word can be a source of inspiration, comfort, and guidance.

*Additional Scriptures: Psalm 119:105*

**Action Plan:**

1. Daily, spend time in the Word, allowing it to penetrate your heart.

2. Reflect on how specific verses apply to your life.

3. Share the Word with others, spreading its transformative power.

**Prayer:**

*Heavenly Father, your Word is a source of strength and transformation. Help us to embrace it daily, allowing it to shape our lives. May it be a guiding light in our journey of faith. In Jesus name, we pray. Amen.*

## DAY 14
## Trusting God's Plan in Career and Vocation

Proverbs 3:6 (NIV)
"In all your ways submit to him, and he will make your paths straight."

In the maze of our careers and vocations, Proverbs 3:6 offers a guiding light: to trust God's plan completely. It's a journey of surrender, where we relinquish control and align our ambitions with His divine purpose.

Picture a path carved through the wilderness, stones removed, obstacles cleared - this is what happens when we submit to God. His wisdom ensures our steps are steady, our choices sound. In times of uncertainty, remember that He's the architect of your career.

*Additional Scriptures: Jeremiah 29:11*

**Action Plan:**

1. Seek God's guidance in your career decisions through prayer and reflection.

2. Trust His timing, even when it differs from your own.

3. Continually seek opportunities to align your work with His purpose.

**Prayer:**

*Heavenly Father, we surrender our careers and vocations to You. Guide our steps and align our paths with Your perfect plan. May our work be a reflection of Your glory. In Jesus name, we pray. Amen.*

## DAY 15
## Cultivating a Heart of Joy in Everyday Life

Psalm 118:24 (NIV)
"This is the day the Lord has made; let us rejoice and be glad in it."

In the ordinary moments of life, Psalm 118:24 reminds us to cultivate a heart of joy. Each day is a precious gift from God, an opportunity to embrace the beauty of existence, and to find joy in His creation.

Imagine waking up every morning with a heart full of gratitude, seeing the world through the lens of joy. Even in the midst of challenges, joy becomes an anchor, a testament to our trust in God's sovereignty.

*Additional Scriptures: Philippians 4:4*

**Action Plan:**

1. Start each day with a prayer of gratitude for the day ahead.

2. Practice finding joy in small moments, like a sunrise or a kind word.

3. Share your joy with others, spreading God's love.

**Prayer:**

Heavenly Father, thank you for the gift of today. Help us cultivate hearts of joy that glorify You in every circumstance. May our lives be a testimony to Your goodness. In Jesus name, we pray. Amen.

## DAY 16
## Living as Vessels of God's Grace and Love

Ephesians 2:8–9 (NIV)
"For it is by grace you have been saved, through faith—and this is not from yourselves, it is the gift of God—not by works, so that no one can boast."

In Ephesians 2:8–9, we're reminded that our salvation is a gift of God's grace, unearned and undeserved. As women of faith, we are called to be vessels of this grace and love, reflecting God's incredible gift to us.

Imagine your life as a beautiful vessel, filled to the brim with God's grace and love, overflowing onto others. This divine love knows no bounds, and it's our privilege to share it with the world.

*Additional Scriptures: 1 John 4:7*

**Action Plan:**

1. Daily, meditate on God's grace and love in your life.

2. Seek opportunities to extend grace and love to others.

3. Share your testimony of God's grace with someone in need.

**Prayer:**

*Heavenly Father, thank you for your amazing grace and love. Fill us with your spirit so we may be vessels of your goodness in the world. Use us to touch the lives of those around us. In Jesus name, we pray. Amen.*

## DAY 17
## The Power of Prayer in Seeking God's Guidance

Proverbs 3:5–6 (NIV)
"Trust in the Lord with all your heart and lean not on your own understanding; in all your ways submit to him, and he will make your paths straight."

In the complexity of life's decisions, Proverbs 3:5–6 is a beacon of hope. It reminds us that prayer is our conduit to seek God's guidance, acknowledging our reliance on Him. When we trust God wholeheartedly and submit our ways to Him in prayer, He lovingly guides us, making our paths straight.
Picture yourself in prayer, pouring out your concerns, dreams, and doubts before the Creator of the universe. In those moments, you're not alone; you're in the presence of the Almighty.

*Additional Scriptures: Matthew 7:7-8*

**Action Plan:**

1. Dedicate time daily to prayer and meditation.

2. Pour out your heart to God, seeking His guidance.

3. Listen attentively to His still, small voice in your heart.

**Prayer:**

*Heavenly Father, we humbly seek Your guidance in our lives. Help us trust You completely and submit our ways to Your wisdom. May our prayers be a bridge to Your perfect plan. In Jesus name, we pray. Amen.*

## DAY 18
## Rejoicing in God's Faithfulness in Every Season

Psalm 89:8 (NIV)
"O Lord God Almighty, who is like you? You are mighty, O Lord, and your faithfulness surrounds you."

In Psalm 89:8, we are reminded of God's unwavering faithfulness. Like a radiant thread, His faithfulness weaves through every season of our lives, bringing light to our darkest hours.

Imagine the seasons of your life as chapters in a grand story, with God as the author. In each chapter, His faithfulness shines through, whether in times of joy or sorrow. Reflect on the countless moments when His promises were kept, and His presence was felt.

*Additional Scriptures: Lamentations 3:22-23*

**Action Plan:**

1. Daily, reflect on God's faithfulness in your life.

2. Journal moments when you experienced His unwavering love.

3. Share your testimony of God's faithfulness with someone in need.

**Prayer:**

*Heavenly Father, we rejoice in Your faithfulness that transcends every season. May we continually trust in Your promises and find solace in Your presence. In Jesus name, we pray. Amen.*

## DAY 19
## Trusting God's Plan in Parenting and Family

Psalm 127:3-5 (NIV)

"Children are a heritage from the Lord, offspring a reward from him. Like arrows in the hands of a warrior are children born in one's youth. Blessed is the man whose quiver is full of them."

In Psalm 127:3-5, we find the profound truth that our children are a precious gift from God, entrusted to us for a purpose. Parenting and family life can be challenging, but it's in trusting God's plan that we find strength and wisdom. Imagine your family as a quiver full of arrows, each child a unique arrow in the hands of a warrior. God equips us to nurture and guide them toward their destiny. The journey may be unpredictable, but God's plan is always perfect.

*Additional Scriptures: Proverbs 22:6*

## Action Plan:

1. Pray daily for wisdom and patience in parenting.

2. Nurture a loving and God-centred atmosphere in your family.

3. Trust God's plan for each child's life, even when it differs from your own.

## Prayer:

*Heavenly Father, we entrust our families to Your care. Grant us the wisdom and grace to fulfil Your plan in parenting. May our homes be a haven of love and faith. In Jesus name, we pray. Amen.*

## DAY 20
## Cultivating a Heart of Joy in Worship and Praise

Psalm 95:1-2 (NIV)
"Come, let us sing for joy to the Lord; let us shout aloud to the Rock of our salvation. Let us come before him with thanksgiving and extol him with music and song."

In Psalm 95:1-2, we're invited to cultivate hearts filled with joy through worship and praise. Imagine yourself in a sacred moment, surrounded by

fellow believers, lifting your voices in unison, and letting the music of praise fill the air. It's in these moments that our hearts overflow with joy.
Worship isn't just a routine; it's a joyful celebration of the One who saved us. It's a heart-to-heart connection with the Rock of our salvation.

*Additional Scriptures: Psalm 100:1-2*

**Action Plan:**

1. Make worship and praise a daily practice, whether through music, prayer, or reflection.

2. Create a gratitude journal to record moments of joy and thanksgiving.

3. Encourage others in your community to join in joyful worship.

**Prayer:**

*Heavenly Father, we thank You for the gift of worship and the joy it brings. May our hearts be filled with gratitude and praise, lifting up your name in unison. In Jesus name, we pray. Amen.*

## DAY 21
## Trusting God's Love and Faithfulness in All Circumstances

Psalm 136:26 (NIV)
"Give thanks to the God of heaven. His love endures forever."

In Psalm 136:26, we're reminded of the unchanging love and faithfulness of our Heavenly Father. His love endures through every circumstance, a constant anchor in the stormiest seas of life.
Imagine a love so steadfast that it never wavers, even when circumstances seem uncertain or overwhelming. This is the love of God, one that remains a rock of stability in an ever-changing world.

*Additional Scriptures: Lamentations 3:22-23*

**Action Plan:**

1. Start and end each day with gratitude for God's enduring love.

2. Remind yourself of His faithfulness by memorising key verses.

3. Share your testimony of God's love with others who may be struggling.

**Prayer:**

*Heavenly Father, we thank You for your unwavering love and faithfulness. In all circumstances, help us to trust in Your unchanging nature. May our lives reflect the beauty of Your enduring love. In Jesus name, we pray. Amen.*

# DAY 22
## Self-Control

Proverbs 4:23 (NIV)
"Above all else, guard your heart, for everything you do flows from it."

In Proverbs 4:23, we are urged to cultivate self-control as we guard our hearts. Our hearts are the wellsprings of our emotions, thoughts, and actions. When we exercise self-control, we safeguard these precious aspects of our lives. Imagine a heart kept pure and unburdened by the shackles of impulsive reactions. Self-control empowers us to respond thoughtfully rather than react impulsively. It allows us to choose love over anger, patience over frustration, and wisdom over folly.

*Additional Scriptures: Galatians 5:22-23, James 1:19-20*

**Action Plan:**

1. Daily self-examination: Reflect on areas where self-control is needed.

2. Prayer and meditation: Seek God's help in developing self-control.

3. Accountability: Share your struggles and victories with a trusted friend or mentor.

**Prayer:**

*Heavenly Father, grant us the strength to guard our hearts and cultivate self-control. Help us be wise stewards of our emotions and actions. May our lives reflect Your grace and wisdom. In Jesus name, we pray. Amen.*

## DAY 23
## The Spiritual Gift

### Romans 12:6–8 (NIV)
"We have different gifts, according to the grace given to each of us. If your gift is prophesying, then prophesy in accordance with your faith; if it is serving, then serve; if it is teaching, then teach; if it is to encourage, then give encouragement; if it is giving, then give generously; if it is to lead, do it diligently; if it is to show mercy, do it cheerfully."

In Romans 12:6–8, we're reminded that every woman has been uniquely gifted by God to serve His kingdom. These spiritual gifts are a reflection of His grace, equipping us to fulfil our divine purpose.

Imagine a world where every woman embraced her spiritual gift, passionately serving others with love and joy. It's a beautiful tapestry of God's grace woven through our lives, impacting the world in profound ways.

*Additional Scriptures: 1 Corinthians 12:4-11*

**Action Plan:**

1. Pray for discernment to discover your spiritual gift.

2. Seek opportunities to use your gift to bless others.

3. Encourage and support other women in their spiritual gifts.

**Prayer:**

*Heavenly Father, thank You for giving us uniquely to serve Your kingdom. May we use our gifts faithfully, with love and joy, to bring glory to Your name. In Jesus name, we pray. Amen.*

## DAY 24
## Social Responsibilities

Proverbs 19:17 (NIV)
"Whoever is kind to the poor lends to the Lord, and he will reward them for what they have done."

In Proverbs 19:17, we discover the profound concept of social responsibility. It reminds us that when we extend kindness and compassion to those in need, we are, in essence, lending to the Lord Himself. Our actions of love ripple through society, reflecting God's heart for the vulnerable.
Imagine the impact when women embrace this call to social responsibility. Lives are transformed, communities strengthened, and God's love shines brightly. It's a divine partnership that brings hope to a hurting world.

*Additional Scriptures: Matthew 25:35-36*

**Action Plan:**

1. Identify a specific way to help those in need within your community.

2. Regularly allocate time or resources to this cause.

3. Encourage other women to join you in acts of kindness and social responsibility.

**Prayer:**

*Heavenly Father, guide us in our social responsibilities, that we may be vessels of Your love and compassion. Use our actions to bring hope and healing to those in need. In Jesus name, we pray. Amen.*

## DAY 25
## Confident In Times Of Difficulties

Romans 8:28 (NIV)
"And we know that in all things God works for the good of those who love him, who have been called according to his purpose."

In Romans 8:28, we find a profound promise: even in the midst of difficulties, God is at work for our good. It's a reminder that we can face challenges with confidence, knowing that God's plan is unfolding, and He is using every situation to shape us according to His purpose.

Picture the storms of life as refining fires, moulding us into vessels of strength and character. With confidence in God's sovereignty, we can walk through trials, knowing they are not in vain.

*Additional Scriptures: James 1:2-4*

**Action Plan:**

1. Meditate on Romans 8:28 during difficult times to find comfort and strength.

2. Journal about how God has turned past trials into blessings.

3. Encourage others facing difficulties with this promise of God's faithfulness.

**Prayer:**

*Heavenly Father, we place our confidence in Your sovereign plan, even in times of difficulty. Help us trust that You are working for our good and shaping us according to Your purpose. In Jesus name, we pray. Amen.*

## DAY 27
## Anxiety and worry

Proverbs 16:7 (NIV)
"When the Lord takes pleasure in anyone's way, he causes their enemies to make peace with them."

In Proverbs 16:7, we find solace for our anxious hearts. It's a reminder that when we walk in alignment with God's ways, even our enemies can be turned into peacemakers. In times of worry and anxiety, this verse invites us to trust in God's divine intervention.

Picture your worries as adversaries, and imagine God stepping in, orchestrating circumstances for your benefit. With Him at the helm, anxiety can transform into trust, and worry can give way to peace.

*Additional Scriptures: Philippians 4:6-7*

**Action Plan:**

1. Surrender your worries to God through prayer.

2. Replace anxious thoughts with affirmations of trust in His providence.

3. Seek opportunities to practice forgiveness and reconciliation.

**Prayer:**

*Heavenly Father, in moments of anxiety and worry, we turn to You for peace and guidance. Help us trust in Your divine intervention and walk in Your ways. May our lives be a testimony to Your grace. In Jesus name, we pray. Amen.*

## DAY 28
## Power Over Satan

James 4:7 (NIV)
"Submit yourselves, then, to God. Resist the devil, and he will flee from you."

In James 4:7, we discover the powerful truth that as women of faith, we have the authority to resist the schemes of the enemy. When we submit to God and stand firm against Satan, his power diminishes, and he flees from us. Imagine the strength and courage that come from knowing you have power over the enemy. Picture Satan's attempts to ensnare and discourage you from crumbling in the face of your unwavering faith and submission to God.

*Additional Scriptures: Ephesians 6:10-11*

**Action Plan:**

1. Clothe yourself daily with the armour of God (Ephesians 6:13-17).

2. Memorise key scriptures to combat the enemy's lies and temptations.

3. Seek support and accountability within your faith community.

**Prayer**:

*Heavenly Father, we thank You for the power You've given us over the enemy. Help us to submit to You, stand firm in faith, and resist the devil's schemes. May we walk in victory and freedom. In Jesus name, we pray. Amen.*

## DAY 29
## Overcoming Temptation

Isaiah 41:10 (NIV)
"So do not fear, for I am with you; do not be dismayed, for I am your God. I will strengthen you and help you; I will uphold you with my righteous right hand."

In Isaiah 41:10, we find assurance in our battle against temptation. God promises His unwavering presence, strength, and help when we face moments of weakness and allure.
Imagine a lifeline extended from heaven to you, giving you the strength to overcome temptation. In the face of life's enticements, you need not fear, for the Almighty God is with you.

*Additional Scriptures: 1 Corinthians 10:13*

**Action Plan:**

1. Memorise key scriptures that provide strength in moments of temptation.

2. Seek an accountability partner or mentor for support.

3. Replace tempting thoughts with prayer and praise.

**Prayer:**

*Heavenly Father, we thank You for Your promise to strengthen and uphold us in times of temptation. Grant us the wisdom to resist and the humility to seek Your help. May we find victory in Your presence. In Jesus name, we pray. Amen.*

# DAY 30
## parents and children

Ephesians 6:1-4 (NIV)
"Children, obey your parents in the Lord, for this is right. 'Honour your father and mother'—which is the first commandment with a promise—'so that it may go well with you and that you may enjoy long life on the earth.' Fathers, do not exasperate your children; instead, bring them up in the training and instruction of the Lord."

In Ephesians 6:1-4, we glimpse the beautiful dynamic between parents and children, rooted in love, respect, and spiritual nurturing. It's a relationship built on obedience, honour, and guidance.
Imagine a home where children willingly obey, and parents lead with wisdom and gentleness, nurturing their children's faith. This harmonious connection is a glimpse of God's design for families.

*Additional Scriptures: Colossians 3:20-21*

## Action Plan:

1. Parents: Prioritise teaching your children God's ways through Scripture and personal example.

2. Children: Show honour and obedience to your parents, for it pleases the Lord.

3. Pray as a family, seeking God's guidance and unity.

## Prayer:

*Heavenly Father, we seek Your wisdom and grace in our roles as parents and children. May our homes be filled with love, respect, and a deep understanding of Your ways. In Jesus name, we pray. Amen.*

# DAY 31

# Keep yourself Pure

1 Timothy 5:22 (NIV)
"Do not be hasty in the laying on of hands, and do not share in the sins of others. Keep yourself pure."

In 1 Timothy 5:22, we're reminded of the preciousness of purity. It extends beyond physical purity; it encompasses the purity of our hearts, minds, and actions. It's a call to safeguard our integrity and avoid entanglement in the sins of others.

Imagine a heart as a crystal-clear stream, reflecting the beauty of God's holiness. This purity is a testament to our devotion to Him. It's in maintaining this purity that we find strength and resilience against the world's temptations.

*Additional Scriptures: Psalm 51:10*

## Action Plan:

1. Regularly examine your heart and confess any impurities to God.

2. Surround yourself with godly influences and accountability partners.

3. Seek purity not out of legalism but out of love for God.

## Prayer:

*Heavenly Father, help us guard our hearts and minds, keeping them pure and devoted to You. May our lives be a reflection of Your holiness. In Jesus name, we pray. Amen.*

# AUGUST

### 2 Corinthians 1:3-4
*Blessed be the God and Father of our Lord Jesus Christ, the Father of mercies and God of all comfort, who comforts us in all our affliction, so that we may be able to comfort those who are in any affliction, with the comfort with which we ourselves are comforted by God.*

## DAY 01
### Nurturing Self-Compassion

"Love your neighbour as yourself." - Matthew 22:39

In the divine tapestry of life, we often extend love and compassion to others effortlessly, yet we falter when it comes to ourselves. This daily devotion reminds us that, as Matthew 22:39 emphasises, we are called to love our neighbours as ourselves. But what if we haven't truly embraced self-compassion? It begins by recognizing our worth in God's eyes. Just as we extend grace and understanding to others in their imperfections, we should offer the same to ourselves. Embrace your uniqueness, acknowledge your struggles, and forgive your flaws. Be gentle with your heart, for therein lies the strength to love others more profoundly.

*Additional Scripture Reference:*

*"For we are God's handiwork, created in Christ Jesus to do good works, which God prepared in advance for us to do." - Ephesians 2:10*

## Action Plan:

1. Reflect on your self-talk and inner dialogue. Replace self-criticism with self-compassion.

2. Daily, affirm your worth in Christ, remembering you are fearfully and wonderfully made.

3. Extend the same kindness you offer to others to yourself.

## Prayer:

*Dear Heavenly Father, help us to cultivate self-compassion as a reflection of your love. May we see ourselves through your eyes, recognizing our inherent worth and embracing our imperfections with grace. Grant us the strength to extend the same love and compassion to ourselves that we pour out to others, magnifying your boundless love in our lives. In Jesus name, we pray. Amen.*

## DAY 02
## Pursuing Your Dreams Fearlessly

"For I know the plans I have for you, declares the Lord, plans for welfare and not for evil, to give you a future and a hope." - Jeremiah 29:11

In the pages of Jeremiah 29:11, we find a promise from God—a promise of hope, of dreams fulfilled. As women on a journey of faith, we are called to pursue our dreams with unwavering courage. Fear may whisper doubts, but remember, God's plans for you are full of promise. Your dreams are not mere wishes; they are a part of His grand design. Embrace them fearlessly, for it is in pursuing them that we discover our true purpose. Step into the unknown, for it is there that God's providence unfolds.

*Additional Scripture Reference:*

*"For we are his workmanship, created in Christ Jesus for good works, which God prepared beforehand, that we should walk in them." - Ephesians 2:10*

### Action Plan:

1. Identify your dreams, no matter how big or small they may seem.

2. Break your dreams into actionable steps and set goals to achieve them.

3. Seek support and guidance from mentors or fellow believers who can encourage your journey.

### Prayer:

*Heavenly Father, we thank you for the dreams and aspirations you've placed in our hearts. Help us to step out fearlessly, knowing that your plans for us are filled with hope and purpose. Grant us the courage to pursue our dreams with unwavering faith, for we trust that you are guiding our steps. In Jesus name, we pray. Amen.*

## DAY 03
## The Gift of Patience

"But if we hope for what we do not see, we wait for it with patience." - Romans 8:25

In Romans 8:25, we glimpse the virtue of patience, a precious gift we often undervalue. As women navigating life's complexities, we long for immediate answers, swift resolutions. Yet, God calls us to embrace the beauty of patience. It's in the waiting that our faith strengthens, and character deepens. Patience is a testament of trust in His perfect timing. Today, let's cultivate this gift. Embrace the moments of waiting as opportunities for growth. Be patient with your journey, for God's plan unfolds at the perfect pace, filling our lives with His grace.

*Additional Scripture Reference:*

*"The Lord is good to those who wait for him, to the soul who seeks him." - Lamentations 3:25*

**Action Plan:**

1. Identify areas in your life where patience is needed.

2. Practice mindfulness during moments of waiting, using them as opportunities for reflection and prayer.

3. Share your journey with a friend, supporting each other in embracing patience.

**Prayer:**

*Dear Lord, grant us the gift of patience, for we trust in Your perfect timing. Help us find contentment in the waiting and strength in our trust in You. May patience be a reflection of our faith and an opportunity for growth. In Jesus name, we pray. Amen.*

## DAY 04
## Grace in Imperfection

*"But he said to me, 'My grace is sufficient for you, for my power is made perfect in weakness.'" - 2 Corinthians 12:9*

2 Corinthians 12:9 reminds us of the beauty of grace in our imperfections. As women, we often strive for perfection, yet it's in our weaknesses that God's grace shines most brilliantly. Our flaws are not failures but opportunities for His strength to be revealed. Embrace your imperfections as part of your unique story, a canvas for His grace to paint upon. Today, release the weight of perfectionism, and let His grace be your guide. For it's in our brokenness that His power truly shines, and His love completes us.

*Additional Scripture Reference:*

*"But he gives more grace." - James 4:6*

## Action Plan:

1. Reflect on areas of your life where you've struggled with perfectionism.

2. Seek moments of vulnerability where you can share your imperfections with trusted friends.

3. Whenever you feel self-criticism, replace it with gratitude for God's grace.

## Prayer:

*Heavenly Father, we thank you for your all-sufficient grace that covers our imperfections. Help us embrace our weaknesses, knowing they are opportunities for your strength to shine. May your grace be our source of strength and our reminder of your perfect love. In Jesus name, we pray. Amen.*

## DAY 05
## Facing Challenges with Courage

"Have I not commanded you? Be strong and courageous. Do not be frightened, and do not be dismayed, for the Lord your God is with you wherever you go." - Joshua 1:9

In Joshua 1:9, we're reminded that God commands us to be strong and courageous in the face of challenges. As women, life often tests our strength. Challenges can seem insurmountable, yet God's promise is unwavering. Courage isn't the absence of fear but the determination to move forward despite it. Draw strength from His presence, for the Lord is with you always. Embrace challenges as opportunities for growth and testimony to His faithfulness. Today, let courage define your response to adversity, knowing that you are never alone in your journey.

*Additional Scripture Reference:*

*"The Lord is my strength and my shield; in him my heart trusts, and I am helped." - Psalm 28:7*

## Action Plan:

1. Identify a current challenge you face and commit it to prayer.

2. Seek guidance and support from a trusted friend or mentor.

3. When faced with fear, repeat Joshua 1:9 as a mantra for courage.

**Prayer:**

*Gracious God, grant us the courage to face life's challenges, knowing You are our strength and shield. May fear be replaced by faith in Your unwavering presence. Help us grow through adversity, becoming living testimonies to Your grace. In Jesus mighty name, we pray. Amen.*

## DAY 06
## The Beauty of Sisterhood

"Two are better than one because they have a good return for their labour. For if either of them falls, the one will lift up his companion. But woe to the one who falls when there is not another to lift him up." - Ecclesiastes 4:9-10

Ecclesiastes 4:9-10 reminds us of the profound beauty of sisterhood. As women, we are not meant to journey alone. Our sisters, both in faith and friendship, offer companionship in life's valleys and mountaintops. Together, we multiply joy and divide sorrow, creating a tapestry of love and support. Embrace sisterhood as a divine gift, an intricate part of God's plan. Today, reach out to a sister, offer encouragement, or simply be present. In unity, we find strength, and in sisterhood, we experience the profound beauty of God's love.

*Additional Scripture Reference:*

*"A friend loves at all times, and a brother is born for adversity." - Proverbs 17:17*

**Action Plan:**

1. Cultivate deeper connections with your sisters in faith and friendship.

2. Offer your support to a sister in need, whether through prayer or a helping hand.

3. Reflect on the ways sisterhood has enriched your life, and express gratitude for these relationships.

**Prayer:**

*Heavenly Father, we thank you for the gift of sisterhood, both in faith and friendship. May we cherish these bonds and nurture them with love and grace. Strengthen us through unity and remind us of the beauty of Your love reflected in our relationships. In Jesus name, we pray. Amen.*

## DAY 07
## God's Unconditional Love

"But God commendeth his love toward us, in that, while we were yet sinners, Christ died for us." - Romans 5:8

In Romans 5:8, we encounter the profound truth of God's unconditional love. As women, we often seek love and approval, but His love surpasses human comprehension. He loved us not because we were perfect, but while we were still imperfect sinners. Embrace this love that knows no bounds, that extends even in our brokenness. It's a love that offers forgiveness, redemption, and unending grace. Today, bask in the warmth of His unconditional love, knowing you are cherished beyond measure.

*Additional Scripture Reference:*

*"See what kind of love the Father has given to us, that we should be called children of God; and so we are." - 1 John 3:1*

### Action Plan:

1. Meditate on Romans 5:8 daily, letting the truth of God's love sink deep into your heart.

2. Share the concept of God's unconditional love with others, spreading hope and reassurance.

3. Express gratitude for His love through prayer, acknowledging His unmerited favour in your life.

### Prayer:

*Heavenly Father, Your unconditional love is a gift beyond measure. Thank you for loving us despite our imperfections. Help us internalise this truth and share it with others. May your love be a beacon of hope in our lives, guiding our actions and illuminating our path. In Jesus name, we pray. Amen.*

## DAY 08

# Finding Joy in the Little Things

"Rejoice always." - 1 Thessalonians 5:16

In 1 Thessalonians 5:16, we're reminded of a simple yet profound command: to rejoice always. Life's busyness often distracts us from the beauty of the present moment. As women, we can rediscover joy by appreciating the little things: a sunrise's colours, a child's laughter, or a friend's smile. Joy is woven into these everyday moments. Let's savour them. In gratitude, we find joy, for it's in these glimpses of grace that God's love shines brightly. Today, commit to noticing and rejoicing in the little things, and let your heart overflow with gratitude.

*Additional Scripture Reference:*

*"This is the day that the Lord has made; let us rejoice and be glad in it." - Psalm 118:24*

**Action Plan:**

1. Start a gratitude journal to record daily moments of joy.

2. Practice mindfulness to fully immerse yourself in the little things.

3. Share your joy with others, spreading positivity and encouragement.

**Prayer:**

*Heavenly Father, thank you for the gift of joy in life's simplest pleasures. Help us to see your love and grace in the little things and find joy in them. May our hearts overflow with gratitude for each moment you've given us. In Jesus name, we pray. Amen.*

## DAY 09
## Resilience in Adversity

"Count it all joy, my brothers, when you meet trials of various kinds, for you know that the testing of your faith produces steadfastness." - James 1:2-3

In James 1:2-3, we're encouraged to find joy in trials, for they cultivate resilience. As women, we encounter hardships that test our resolve. Yet, it's in adversity that we unearth our inner strength. Resilience isn't the absence of pain but the tenacity to endure and grow. Every challenge becomes a stepping stone, not a stumbling block. Embrace adversity with courage, for it refines faith and fosters unwavering endurance. Know that God walks with you through every storm, and your resilience is a testament to His grace.

*Additional Scripture Reference:*

*"I can do all things through Christ who strengthens me." - Philippians 4:13*

**Action Plan:**

1. Identify a recent or ongoing adversity in your life and reflect on the lessons it offers.

2. Seek inspiration from resilient women in history or your community.

3. Practice gratitude for the strength you gain through adversity.

**Prayer:**

*Heavenly Father, grant us the strength and resilience to face adversity with unwavering faith. May we find joy in trials, knowing that they shape us into women of steadfastness. Walk beside us in our challenges, and may our resilience be a testament to Your grace and love. In Jesus name, we pray. Amen.*

## DAY 10
## Overcoming Self-Doubt

"For God gave us a spirit not of fear but of power and love and self-control." - 2 Timothy 1:7

In 2 Timothy 1:7, we are reminded that God has bestowed upon us a spirit of power, love, and self-control, not one of fear or self-doubt. As women, self-doubt can be a relentless adversary, whispering that we are not enough. Yet, our Creator has equipped us with strength and purpose. It's time to silence self-doubt's voice and embrace the truth of our inherent worth. When you doubt yourself, remember God's promises, and let His love dispel fear. Today, rise above self-doubt, for you are fearfully and wonderfully made.

*Additional Scripture Reference:*

*"I can do all things through him who strengthens me." - Philippians 4:13*

**Action Plan:**

1. Recognize and challenge negative self-talk.

2. Seek daily inspiration in God's Word to reinforce your self-worth.

3. Share your journey of overcoming self-doubt with a trusted friend or mentor.

**Prayer:**

*Heavenly Father, help us overcome self-doubt and fear, knowing that You have equipped us with power and love. Strengthen our faith in Your plan and purpose for our lives. May we walk in confidence, remembering that we can do all things through Christ who strengthens us. In Jesus name, we pray. Amen.*

## DAY 11
## Walking in Faith, Not Fear

"For God gave us a spirit not of fear but of power and love and self-control." - 2 Timothy 1:7

In 2 Timothy 1:7, we're reminded that God's spirit within us is not one of fear but of power, love, and self-control. As women, we often grapple with fear's paralysing grip, especially in the face of uncertainty. However, faith invites us to step boldly into the unknown, trusting that God is our refuge and strength. Fear limits us, but faith empowers us to conquer life's challenges. Today, choose faith over fear, for His perfect love casts out all fear. Embrace each day with courage, knowing you walk in the light of His grace.

*Additional Scripture Reference:*

*"When I am afraid, I put my trust in you." - Psalm 56:3*

**Action Plan:**

1. Identify areas in your life where fear holds you back and commit them to prayer.

2. Seek daily inspiration from the Bible, focusing on verses that strengthen faith.

3. Encourage others to walk in faith by sharing your own experiences and testimonies.

**Prayer:**

## DAY 12
## The Power of Forgiveness

"Forgive us our sins, as we forgive those who sin against us." - Matthew 6:12

Matthew 6:12 imparts the profound message of forgiveness. As women, we often bear the weight of hurt and grudges, unaware of the freedom forgiveness offers. Forgiving others is an act of love, mirroring God's forgiveness of us. It doesn't excuse wrongdoing but releases us from the chains of bitterness. Forgiveness is a healing balm for the soul. Embrace its transformative power, for in letting go, we find peace and restoration. Today, choose to forgive, for it is in forgiving that we experience the depth of God's love.

*Additional Scripture Reference:*

*"Be kind to one another, tenderhearted, forgiving one another, as God in Christ forgave you." - Ephesians 4:32*

**Action Plan:**

1. Reflect on any unresolved conflicts or unforgiveness in your life.

2. Pray for the strength to forgive those who have wronged you, releasing the burden.

3. Extend forgiveness to yourself, knowing that God's grace is sufficient.

**Prayer:**

## DAY 13
## The Power of Surrender

"Then Jesus said to his disciples, 'Whoever wants to be my disciple must deny themselves and take up their cross and follow me.'" - Matthew 16:24

Matthew 16:24 reveals the profound truth of surrender. As women, we often strive for control, only to find ourselves weary. Surrendering to Christ, we yield our burdens, fears, and plans, finding freedom in His embrace. Surrender is not weakness but a testament to trust. It's releasing our grip on life's steering wheel and letting God navigate. Today, choose surrender, for in yielding, we discover His purpose and peace. Let go, take up your cross, and follow Christ. Surrender is the gateway to a life transformed by His love.

*Additional Scripture Reference:*

*"But he said to me, 'My grace is sufficient for you, for my power is made perfect in weakness.'" - 2 Corinthians 12:9*

**Action Plan:**

1. Identify areas of your life where you struggle to surrender concontrol. In prayer, release these concerns into God's hands, trusting His plan.

2. Seek guidance in His Word and through fellowship to deepen your surrender.

**Prayer:**

*Heavenly Father, teach us the power of surrender, for in yielding to You, we find strength. Help us relinquish our burdens, fears, and desires, knowing that Your grace is sufficient. May we follow Your lead with unwavering trust, discovering the transformative beauty of surrender. In Jesus name, we pray. Amen.*

## DAY 14
### Finding Peace in Simplicity

"Better is a little with the fear of the Lord than great treasure and trouble with it." - Proverbs 15:16

Proverbs 15:16 reminds us of the profound peace found in simplicity. In our hectic lives, we often chase after material wealth and status, only to discover emptiness. Simplicity invites us to cherish life's essentials and nurture our souls. It's in the quiet moments of gratitude, in the warmth of relationships, that true richness emerges. Today, embrace simplicity. Let go of unnecessary clutter, both physical and mental. Seek peace in the little things, for in simplicity, we rediscover the profound beauty of God's presence.

*Additional Scripture Reference:*

*"Do not be anxious about anything, but in everything by prayer and supplication with thanksgiving let your requests be made known to God. And the peace of God, which surpasses all understanding, will guard your hearts and your minds in Christ Jesus." - Philippians 4:6-7*

## Action Plan:

1. Reflect on areas of your life where you can simplify and find greater peace.

2. Practice gratitude daily, acknowledging the simple blessings in your life.

3. Share the joy of simplicity with others, encouraging a life of contentment.

## Prayer:

Heavenly Father, guide us to find peace in simplicity, recognizing the value of life's essential blessings. Help us release the burdens of excess and embrace the beauty of Your presence in the ordinary. May Your peace, which surpasses understanding, guard our hearts. In Jesus name, we pray. Amen.

## DAY 15
## The Power of Encouragement

*"Therefore encourage one another and build one another up, just as you are doing." - 1 Thessalonians 5:11*

In 1 Thessalonians 5:11, we discover the transformative power of encouragement. As women, our words and actions can uplift weary souls. Encouragement is a balm that soothes wounds and ignites hope. It's a reminder that we are not alone on life's journey. Today, be an encouragement. Offer a kind word, lend a listening ear, or extend a helping hand. In lifting others, we reflect Christ's love. Embrace the opportunity to make a positive difference in someone's life. Encouragement has the power to heal, mend, and inspire.

*"Let us consider how to stir up one another to love and good works." - Hebrews 10:24*

**Action Plan:**

1. Be mindful of opportunities to encourage those around you.

2. Write notes of encouragement to friends, family, or coworkers.

3. Seek ways to support and uplift others in your community.

**Prayer:**

*Heavenly Father, teach us the profound impact of encouragement. Help us be beacons of hope and support to those around us. May our words and actions reflect your love, inspiring others to persevere in faith. In Jesus name, we pray. Amen.*

## DAY 16
## Nurturing Your Creative Spirit

*"So God created mankind in his own image, in the image of God he created them; male and female he created them." - Genesis 1:27*

Genesis 1:27 reminds us that we are created in the image of a Creator. As women, we carry within us a creative spark, a reflection of God's divine artistry. Nurturing your creative spirit is a sacred journey, a way to draw closer to your Creator. It's in the act of creating that we often find solace, purpose, and joy. Today, embrace your creativity. Whether through art, music, writing, or any form of self-expression, let your creative spirit flourish. In doing so, you connect with the very essence of your Maker.

*Additional Scripture Reference:*

*"He has filled them with skill to do all kinds of work as engravers, designers, embroiderers in blue, purple and scarlet yarn and fine linen, and weavers—all of them skilled workers and designers." - Exodus 35:35*

**Action Plan:**

1. Dedicate time for creative expression regularly.

2. Explore new artistic endeavours to stretch your creative boundaries.

3. Share your creative talents with others, inspiring them to nurture their own creative spirits.

**Prayer:**

*Heavenly Father, thank you for the gift of creativity, a reflection of Your divine nature. Help us to nurture our creative spirits, drawing inspiration from Your limitless creativity. May our creative endeavours bring joy, purpose, and inspiration to our lives and the lives of others. In Jesus name, we pray. Amen.*

## DAY 17
## The Blessing of Rest and Renewal

"Come to me, all who labour and are heavy laden, and I will give you rest." - Matthew 11:28

Matthew 11:28 extends an invitation from Jesus, offering rest to weary souls. As women, we often carry the weight of many roles and responsibilities. In the hustle and bustle, we forget the blessing of rest. Rest is not idleness; it's a sacred pause to recharge our spirits. It's in quiet moments of reflection and connection with God that we find renewal. Today, embrace the gift of rest. Create moments of stillness to listen to God's voice. Find solace in His presence, for it's in rest that our souls are refreshed.

*Additional Scripture Reference:*

*"He makes me lie down in green pastures. He leads me beside still waters. He restores my soul." - Psalm 23:2-3*

**Action Plan:**

1. Schedule regular periods of rest and reflection in your daily life.

2. Seek out peaceful places in nature to unwind and connect with God.

3. Encourage others to prioritise rest and renewal, recognizing its importance for spiritual well-being.

**Prayer:**

*Heavenly Father, we thank you for the blessing of rest and renewal. Help us find solace in Your presence and recognize the importance of resting our souls in You. Restore our spirits and grant us the wisdom to prioritise moments of quiet reflection. In Jesus name, we pray. Amen.*

## DAY 18
## Celebrating Your Accomplishments

"I praise you because I am fearfully and wonderfully made; your works are wonderful, I know that fully well." - Psalm 139:14

Psalm 139:14 reminds us that we are fearfully and wonderfully made by God. Yet, as women, we often downplay our accomplishments, deflecting praise. Today, celebrate your achievements, both big and small. Recognize that your successes are a reflection of God's grace and the unique gifts He has given you. Taking pride in your accomplishments doesn't stem from arrogance but from acknowledging His hand in your life. It's an act of gratitude and a testament to His faithfulness. Embrace the joy of celebrating your journey, for each step is a testament to His marvellous work in you.

*Additional Scripture Reference:*

*"I can do all things through him who strengthens me." - Philippians 4:13*

**Action Plan:**

1. Reflect on your recent accomplishments and give thanks for God's role in them.

2. Share your successes with loved ones, allowing them to celebrate with you.

3. Encourage others to celebrate their achievements, affirming the value of recognizing God's work in our lives.

**Prayer:**

*Heavenly Father, we thank you for fearfully and wonderfully creating us. Help us celebrate our accomplishments as a reflection of your grace. May we humbly acknowledge your hand in our successes and inspire others to do the same. In Jesus name, we pray. Amen.*

## DAY 19
## Letting Go of Regret

"For I will forgive their wickedness and will remember their sins no more." - Jeremiah 31:34

Jeremiah 31:34 offers the promise of God's forgiveness and the release from regret. As women, we often carry the weight of past mistakes, letting them overshadow our present and future. But God's grace calls us to let go of regret. His forgiveness is complete and unconditional, allowing us to start anew. Regret keeps us trapped in yesterday's pain, hindering our growth. Today, release the burden of regret. Accept God's forgiveness and extend it to yourself. Embrace the freedom that comes from surrendering your regrets to Him and trusting in His grace.

*Additional Scripture Reference:*

*"Brothers, I do not consider that I have made it my own. But one thing I do: forgetting what lies behind and straining forward to what lies ahead." - Philippians 3:13*

### Action Plan:

1. Reflect on areas of your life where regret has held you back.

2. Pray for God's forgiveness and guidance in letting go of regret.

3. Focus on the present and future, striving to make positive choices.

### Prayer:

*Heavenly Father, grant us the strength to let go of regret and trust in Your forgiveness. Help us forget what lies behind and press forward toward Your plan for our lives. May we find freedom and hope in Your grace. In Jesus name, we pray. Amen.*

## DAY 20
## Embracing Change with Open Arms

"See, I am doing a new thing! Now it springs up; do you not perceive it? I am making a way in the wilderness and streams in the wasteland." - Isaiah 43:19

Isaiah 43:19 reminds us that God is constantly at work, bringing new opportunities and blessings even in challenging times. As women, change can be unsettling, but it's often the catalyst for growth. Embracing change with open arms requires trust in God's plan. Instead of fearing the unknown, we can see it as an adventure with the Creator. Today, welcome change as a chance for renewal. Embrace it with faith, knowing that God's love and guidance will always light your path.

*"Commit your way to the Lord; trust in him, and he will act." - Psalm 37:5*

**Action Plan:**

1. Reflect on a recent or upcoming change in your life and how you can approach it with faith.

2. Seek guidance and wisdom through prayer, entrusting your plans to God.

3. Embrace change as an opportunity for personal growth and spiritual development.

**Prayer:**

*Heavenly Father, help us embrace change with open arms, trusting in Your divine plan. May we see the new beginnings and blessings You bring in every season of life. Grant us the faith to follow Your lead and the wisdom to see Your purpose in all things. In Jesus name, we pray. Amen.*

## DAY 21
## Cultivating a Heart of Graciousness

"Let your conversation be always full of grace, seasoned with salt, so that you may know how to answer everyone." - Colossians 4:6

Colossians 4:6 guides us to cultivate gracious hearts. As women, our words and actions hold immense power to uplift or wound. Graciousness is a reflection of God's love in our interactions. It's extending kindness, even when it's not deserved. Today, choose graciousness. Let your words be seasoned with grace, offering understanding, forgiveness, and empathy. In doing so, you mirror Christ's love. Cultivating a heart of graciousness transforms relationships, fostering harmony and healing. May your daily interactions radiate God's grace, touching the lives of those you encounter.

*Additional Scripture Reference:*

*"A gentle answer turns away wrath, but a harsh word stirs up anger." - Proverbs 15:1*

**Action Plan:**

1. Reflect on your recent interactions and identify opportunities for more gracious responses.

2. Prioritise active listening and empathy in your conversations.

3. Practice daily gratitude, fostering a heart of graciousness in all aspects of life.

**Prayer:**

*Heavenly Father, help us cultivate hearts of graciousness, reflecting Your love in our words and actions. Grant us the wisdom to respond with kindness and understanding, even in challenging moments. May our graciousness be a testament to Your grace in our lives. In Jesus name, we pray. Amen.*

## DAY 22
## Nurturing Your Faith Daily

"But grow in the grace and knowledge of our Lord and Savior Jesus Christ. To him be the glory both now and to the day of eternity. Amen." - 2 Peter 3:18

2 Peter 3:18 reminds us to continually nurture our faith. For women, the demands of life can be overwhelming, but daily faith nourishment is vital. Like a garden, faith needs consistent care. Spend time in prayer, reading Scripture, and reflecting on God's love. This daily nourishment strengthens your relationship with Him. Faith isn't a one-time event; it's a lifelong journey. Today, commit to nurturing your faith daily. Delve into God's Word, pray fervently, and seek opportunities for growth. As your faith flourishes, so does your connection with the divine.

*Additional Scripture Reference:*

*"Your word is a lamp to my feet and a light to my path." - Psalm 119:105*

**Action Plan:**

1. Set aside dedicated time each day for prayer and Scripture reading.

2. Join a Bible study group or devotional community for accountability and shared growth.

3. Reflect on how your faith journey can inspire and encourage others in your life.

**Prayer:**

*Heavenly Father, we seek to nurture our faith daily, growing in the grace and knowledge of our Lord Jesus Christ. May your Word guide our steps, and may our faith flourish as we seek You with all our hearts. Strengthen our connection with You and use us to inspire faith in others. In Jesus name, we pray. Amen.*

## DAY 23
### The Blessing of Hope

"Now may the God of hope fill you with all joy and peace in believing, so that you will abound in hope by the power of the Holy Spirit." - Romans 15:13

Romans 15:13 reminds us of the profound blessing of hope. As women, life's challenges can weigh heavily, but hope is our anchor. It's the unwavering belief that God's promises will come to pass. Hope fuels our spirits, offering joy and peace amidst adversity. It's a gift from the God of hope, who never abandons us. Today, embrace the blessing of hope. Let it be your source of strength, allowing it to fill your heart with joy and peace. As you abound in hope, you'll radiate His light to a world in need.

*Additional Scripture Reference:*

*"But those who hope in the Lord will renew their strength. They will soar on wings like eagles; they will run and not grow weary, they will walk and not be faint." - Isaiah 40:31*

## Action Plan:

1. Reflect on areas in your life where hope is needed, and pray for renewed strength.

2. Encourage others with words of hope and share testimonies of God's faithfulness.

3. Cultivate a spirit of gratitude, anchoring your hope in God's unwavering love and promises.

**Prayer:**

*Heavenly Father, thank you for the profound blessing of hope. May we be filled with joy and peace as we anchor our trust in You. Renew our strength, O Lord, and help us soar on wings like eagles. May our hope inspire others to believe in Your promises. In Jesus name, we pray. Amen.*

## Embracing Your Spiritual Journey

"Commit your way to the Lord; trust in him, and he will act." - Psalm 37:5

Psalm 37:5 encourages us to commit our way to the Lord, trusting in His guidance. As women, our spiritual journey is a profound and unique adventure. It's a path of growth, discovery, and transformation. Embrace it with an open heart. Just as a caterpillar transforms into a butterfly, your journey leads to spiritual metamorphosis. Trust in God's plan, even in uncertainty. Today, commit your way to the Lord, and let Him lead. Embracing your spiritual journey is an act of faith and surrender, ultimately drawing you closer to His divine purpose.

*Additional Scripture Reference:*

*"Your word is a lamp to my feet and a light to my path." - Psalm 119:105*

**Action Plan:**

1. Reflect on your spiritual journey and identify areas for growth.

2. Seek daily inspiration from God's Word to guide your path.

3. Share your journey with fellow believers, encouraging one another along the way.

**Prayer:**

Heavenly Father, guide us on our spiritual journey, illuminating our path with Your wisdom and love. May we commit our ways to You, trusting in Your divine plan. Strengthen our faith and lead us closer to Your purpose. In Jesus name, we pray. Amen.

## Letting Go of Negative Habits

"Do not conform to the pattern of this world, but be transformed by the renewing of your mind." - Romans 12:2

Romans 12:2 urges us not to conform to the world's patterns but to renew our minds. As women, negative habits can ensnare us, hindering our growth.

Letting go is challenging, but transformation begins with surrender. Today, release these habits that weigh you down. Whether it's self-doubt, gossip, or unhealthy routines, surrender them to God. Embrace His transformative power. Replace negative habits with prayer, Scripture, and positive actions. With each step, you'll experience renewal, moving closer to God's purpose.

*Additional Scripture Reference:*

*"I can do all things through him who strengthens me." - Philippians 4:13*

## Action Plan:

1. Identify negative habits in your life and pray for strength to overcome them.

2. Replace them with positive alternatives and seek accountability from a friend or mentor.

3. Trust in God's power to transform your mind and heart.

## Prayer:

*Heavenly Father, grant us the strength to let go of negative habits and conform to Your will. Renew our minds, making us vessels of Your transformation. May we find strength in You and overcome these hindrances to grow closer to Your purpose. In Jesus name, we pray. Amen.*

## DAY 26
### The Power of Prayer and Meditation

"Do not be anxious about anything, but in everything by prayer and supplication with thanksgiving let your requests be made known to God." - Philippians 4:6

Philippians 4:6 reminds us of the transformative power of prayer and meditation. As women, the demands of life can be overwhelming, but these practices anchor our souls. Prayer is our conversation with God, where burdens are lifted, and hearts find solace. Meditation allows God's Word to dwell richly in our hearts, providing guidance and peace. Today, embrace the power of prayer and meditation. Dedicate time to commune with God, seeking His wisdom and sharing your heart's desires. Through these practices, you'll find strength, serenity, and a deeper connection with the Divine.

*Additional Scripture Reference:*

*"Let the words of my mouth and the meditation of my heart be acceptable in your sight, O Lord, my rock and my redeemer." - Psalm 19:14*

**Action Plan:**

1. Set aside daily quiet time for prayer and meditation, seeking God's presence and guidance.

2. Choose a Scripture verse or passage to meditate on, allowing it to shape your thoughts and actions.

3. Keep a prayer journal to record your reflections, requests, and answered prayers.

**Prayer:**

*Heavenly Father, we thank you for the power of prayer and meditation. May our hearts be attuned to your presence, finding strength and peace in these practices. Help us align our thoughts and words with your will. May our daily communion with you deepen our faith and bring transformation. In Jesus name, we pray. Amen.*

## DAY 28
### Courage to Face the Unknown

*"Be strong and courageous. Do not be afraid; do not be discouraged, for the Lord your God will be with you wherever you go." - Joshua 1:9*

Joshua 1:9 imparts the courage to face the unknown. As women, life often leads us into uncharted territories. Fear may whisper doubt, but God's promise is clear: He walks beside us. Courage isn't the absence of fear but the strength to press onward despite it. Today, muster the courage to embrace uncertainty. Step into the unknown with faith, for the Lord is your steadfast companion. Trust His guidance, and let courage be your compass. As you journey, you'll discover His grace is sufficient, and His love unfailing.

*Additional Scripture Reference:*

*"For I am the Lord your God who takes hold of your right hand and says to you, Do not fear; I will help you." - Isaiah 41:13*

**Action Plan:**

1. Identify an area in your life where fear holds you back and commit it to God in prayer.

2. Seek counsel and encouragement from trusted friends or mentors.

3. Keep a journal of your courageous steps, noting God's faithfulness along the way.

**Prayer:**

*Heavenly Father, grant us the courage to face the unknown, knowing You are with us. Strengthen our hearts and dispel our fears as we journey forward in faith. May we trust in Your unwavering presence and find comfort in Your promises. In Jesus name, we pray. Amen.*

## DAY 29
## Overcoming Life's Challenges

"I can do all things through Christ who strengthens me." - Philippians 4:13

Philippians 4:13 reminds us that with Christ's strength, we can conquer life's challenges. As women, we face a myriad of obstacles, from personal struggles to societal pressures. Yet, we are not defined by our challenges, but by our capacity to rise above them. Through faith, we tap into a wellspring of resilience. Today, remember that you are not alone. With Christ's empowerment, you can endure, learn, and grow from life's trials. Trust His guidance, rely on His strength, and face challenges with unwavering faith. As you overcome, you'll inspire others and find deeper purpose.

*Additional Scripture Reference:*

*"Consider it pure joy, my brothers and sisters, whenever you face trials of many kinds because you know that the testing of your faith produces perseverance." - James 1:2-3*

**Action Plan:**

1. Identify a current challenge you're facing and seek God's guidance through prayer.

2. Reflect on past challenges and the strength and wisdom gained through them.

3. Encourage and support others facing challenges, sharing the hope found in Christ.

**Prayer:**

*Heavenly Father, grant us the strength and faith to overcome life's challenges. May we find joy in trials, knowing they produce perseverance and growth. Equip us to inspire and support others facing difficulties, bearing witness to Your transformative power. In Jesus name, we pray. Amen.*

## DAY 30
## Finding Joy in Simplicity

"Keep your life free from love of money, and be content with what you have, for he has said, 'I will never leave you nor forsake you.'" - Hebrews 13:5

Hebrews 13:5 reminds us to find contentment in simplicity, for God's presence is our true wealth. In a world that often equates happiness with possessions, as women, we yearn for lasting joy. It's not in the accumulation of things but in gratitude for what we already possess that we find true contentment. Today, seek joy in life's simple blessings: the warmth of the sun, a shared laughter, or a moment of solitude. Embrace the beauty of simplicity, knowing that God's abiding presence brings the deepest and most enduring joy.

*Additional Scripture Reference:*

*"Better a little with the fear of the Lord than great wealth with turmoil." - Proverbs 15:16*

**Action Plan:**

1. Reflect on the simple joys in your life and express gratitude for them in your daily prayers.

2. Declutter your physical and mental space, creating room for serenity and contentment.

3. Share the joy of simplicity by volunteering or helping those in need.

**Prayer:**

*Heavenly Father, help us find joy in simplicity, recognizing that true wealth lies in Your abiding presence. May we be content with what we have and cultivate gratitude for life's simple blessings. Let our hearts overflow with joy that radiates Your love to others. In Jesus name, we pray. Amen.*

# DAY 31
## Embracing Your Passions

"Delight yourself in the Lord, and he will give you the desires of your heart." - Psalm 37:4

Psalm 37:4 reminds us that as we delight in the Lord, He places the desires of our hearts within us. Women often juggle numerous roles, sometimes neglecting their passions. Yet, God has uniquely gifted each of us with talents and dreams. Today, embrace your passions, for they are a reflection of God's purpose in your life. Whether it's a creative pursuit, a career, or a cause dear to your heart, follow your passions with faith. God's plan unfolds when we align our desires with His will. As you do, you'll find fulfilment, purpose, and His abundant blessings.

*Additional Scripture Reference:*

*"Commit to the Lord whatever you do, and he will establish your plans." - Proverbs 16:3*

## Action Plan:

1. Reflect on your passions and how they align with your faith and purpose.

2. Set achievable goals to pursue your passions, committing them to the Lord.

3. Seek opportunities to use your passions to serve others and honour God.

## Prayer:

*Heavenly Father, help us embrace our passions and align them with Your divine plan. May our desires be an offering to You, and may You establish our plans. Guide us as we seek fulfilment and purpose in following our passions, using them to glorify Your name. In Jesus name, we pray. Amen.*

# SEPTEMBER

## DAY 01
## The Strength of Endurance

"But they who wait for the Lord shall renew their strength; they shall mount up with wings like eagles; they shall run and not be weary; they shall walk and not faint." - Isaiah 40:31

Isaiah 40:31 reminds us that in endurance, we find renewed strength. As women, life's challenges can be exhausting, but endurance isn't about enduring silently; it's about rising above. It's summoning the strength to persevere through difficulties, trusting that God's grace is sufficient. Today, draw inspiration from those who've faced adversity with unwavering faith. Embrace life's struggles as opportunities for growth and character refinement. Your endurance is a testament to God's sustaining power, allowing you to soar on wings like eagles.

*Additional Scripture Reference:*

*"Let us not become weary in doing good, for at the proper time, we will reap a harvest if we do not give up." - Galatians 6:9*

**Action Plan:**

1. Identify a challenge or hardship in your life and commit to enduring it with faith and perseverance.

2. Seek support from your faith community or friends who can provide encouragement.

3. Keep a journal to document your journey of endurance and reflect on God's faithfulness.

**Prayer:**

## DAY 02
## The Gift of Gratitude

"Give thanks in all circumstances; for this is the will of God in Christ Jesus for you." - 1 Thessalonians 5:18

1 Thessalonians 5:18 teaches us the profound gift of gratitude. As women, life's busyness can eclipse the beauty around us. Gratitude, however, opens our eyes to the abundance of blessings. It's an act of acknowledging God's goodness even in adversity. Today, embrace the gift of gratitude. Count your blessings, both big and small, and offer thanks to God. In gratitude, hearts find joy, and spirits are uplifted. Cultivate a thankful heart, and watch it transform your perspective, relationships, and overall well-being. Gratitude is a path to contentment and a reflection of God's grace.

*Additional Scripture Reference:*

*"Do not be anxious about anything, but in everything by prayer and supplication with thanksgiving, let your requests be made known to God." - Philippians 4:6*

**Action Plan:**

1. Start a gratitude journal, recording at least three things you're thankful for each day.

2. Express gratitude to those around you, nurturing your relationships.

3. In times of hardship, intentionally seek reasons to be thankful, focusing on God's provision and love.

**Prayer:**

*Heavenly Father, we thank you for the gift of gratitude. May we give thanks in all circumstances, recognizing Your goodness in every aspect of our lives. Help us cultivate hearts of thanksgiving, bringing joy and contentment. In Jesus name, we pray. Amen.*

## DAY 03
### Restoring Broken Dreams

"The Lord will restore their fortunes; I will heal their wounds." - Jeremiah 30:17

Jeremiah 30:17 assures us that God can restore what's broken. As women, life's disappointments can shatter our dreams, leaving scars. Yet, God is the ultimate healer and dream-restorer. Today, surrender your shattered dreams to Him. With God's touch, what's broken can be made whole. Trust in His promise to heal your wounds and restore your fortunes. Embrace this as an opportunity for renewed hope. With God, broken dreams can become beautiful testimonies of His grace and redemption.

*Additional Scripture Reference:*

*"And after you have suffered a little while, the God of all grace, who has called you to his eternal glory in Christ, will himself restore, confirm, strengthen, and establish you." - 1 Peter 5:10*

**Action Plan:**

1. Reflect on any broken dreams or disappointments in your life, and bring them to God in prayer.

2. Seek counsel and support from friends or mentors to help navigate the journey of restoration.

3. Embrace a mindset of hope and trust that God can turn setbacks into comebacks.

**Prayer:**

*Heavenly Father, we entrust our broken dreams to You, knowing that You are the ultimate healer and restorer. Heal our wounds and renew our hope. May our stories of restoration bring glory to Your name. In Jesus name, we pray. Amen.*

## Finding Peace in Solitude

"Be still, and know that I am God. I will be exalted among the nations; I will be exalted in the earth!" - Psalm 46:10

Psalm 46:10 reminds us to find peace in solitude, where God's presence is most profound. As women, our lives are often filled with noise and busyness, leaving little room for stillness. Yet, it's in quiet moments that we encounter God's comforting embrace. Today, seek solace in solitude. Step away from the clamour of life and bask in His presence. In stillness, hearts find healing, minds find clarity, and souls find peace. Amidst the chaos, remember that God is exalted in the stillness of your soul.

*Additional Scripture Reference:*

*"The Lord is my shepherd; I shall not want. He makes me lie down in green pastures. He leads me beside still waters." - Psalm 23:1-2*

**Action Plan:**

1. Dedicate time each day for solitude and meditation on Scripture or prayer.

2. Create a peaceful space where you can retreat and find solace.

3. Reflect on the inner peace that comes from knowing God.

**Prayer:**

*Heavenly Father, in the stillness, we find You. May our hearts be quieted by Your presence, and may we discover peace that surpasses understanding. Help us prioritise moments of solitude to draw closer to You. In Jesus name, we pray. Amen.*

## Embracing Your Worthiness

"So God created mankind in his own image, in the image of God he created them; male and female he created them." - Genesis 1:27

Genesis 1:27 reminds us that we are fearfully and wonderfully made in God's image. As women, society's standards may challenge our worthiness, but in God's eyes, we are deeply cherished. Today, embrace your worthiness as a child of God. You are valued, loved, and uniquely created for a divine purpose. Let go of self-doubt, and recognize your inherent worth. With this newfound confidence, step into the world as a beacon of God's love and grace.

*Additional Scripture Reference:*

*"For we are God's handiwork, created in Christ Jesus to do good works, which God prepared in advance for us to do." - Ephesians 2:10*

**Action Plan:**

1. Reflect on your God-given gifts and talents, and use them to serve others.

2. Surround yourself with people who affirm your worth and encourage your spiritual growth.

3. Daily affirm your worthiness in Christ through prayer and meditation on Scripture.

**Prayer:**

*Heavenly Father, we thank you for creating us in your image and declaring our worthiness. Help us embrace our identity as your cherished children, confident in our purpose. May our lives reflect your love and grace to the world. In Jesus name, we pray. Amen.*

## DAY 06
## Letting Go of Worry

"Do not be anxious about anything, but in every situation, by prayer and petition, with thanksgiving, present your requests to God." - Philippians 4:6

Philippians 4:6 urges us to release worry through prayer and gratitude. As women, life's demands can fuel anxiety, robbing us of peace. Worry is a weight that hinders our faith and joy. Today, surrender your worries to God, knowing He cares for you. Replace anxious thoughts with prayers of trust and thanksgiving. In doing so, you'll find solace in His presence. Letting go of worry is an act of faith, a testament to your belief in God's loving care.

*Additional Scripture Reference:*

*"Cast all your anxiety on him because he cares for you." - 1 Peter 5:7*

**Action Plan:**

1. Identify areas causing worry in your life and commit them to God through prayer.

2. Maintain a gratitude journal, listing daily blessings, to shift your focus.

3. Share your worries and concerns with a trusted friend or mentor for support and encouragement.

**Prayer:**

*Heavenly Father, we release our worries to You, knowing that Your care is steadfast. Grant us the faith to trust in Your loving provision and the wisdom to replace anxiety with gratitude and prayer. In Jesus name, we pray. Amen.*

## DAY 07
## The Power of Contentment

"But godliness with contentment is great gain." - 1 Timothy 6:6

1 Timothy 6:6 reminds us of the immense value of contentment. In a world that often encourages us to constantly seek more, contentment is a rare treasure. As women, we may chase after success, beauty, or recognition, but true fulfilment comes in embracing the present with gratitude. Today, find power in contentment. Seek joy in the simple moments, savouring the blessings already bestowed upon you. Contentment is not complacency but a deep understanding that our worth is not determined by possessions or achievements. It's an inner peace that transcends circumstances, a reflection of our trust in God's provision.

*Additional Scripture Reference:*

*"I have learned in whatever situation I am to be content." - Philippians 4:11*

**Action Plan:**

1. Take time daily to reflect on your blessings and express gratitude to God.

2. Practice contentment by focusing on the present rather than dwelling on what you lack.

3. Seek contentment in relationships, knowing that meaningful connections are more valuable than material wealth.

**Prayer:**

Heavenly Father, grant us the strength to embrace the power of contentment. Help us find joy and peace in the present, knowing that our worth is rooted in You. May our hearts overflow with gratitude, and may our lives be a testament to the fulfilment found in godliness and contentment. In Jesus name, we pray. Amen.

## DAY 08
## Finding Purpose in Your Journey

"For I know the plans I have for you, declares the Lord, plans for welfare and not for evil, to give you a future and a hope." - Jeremiah 29:11

Jeremiah 29:11 assures us that God has a purpose for our lives, filled with hope and promise. As women, our life journeys may take unexpected turns, leading us to question our purpose. Yet, every experience, even the difficult ones, plays a part in God's divine plan. Today, find purpose in your journey. Trust that God is orchestrating every step, moulding you into the woman He intended you to be. Embrace each moment, knowing that your life has significance in His grand design. Your journey is a testimony of His faithfulness and love.

*Additional Scripture Reference:*

*"The steps of a man are established by the Lord, when he delights in his way." - Psalm 37:23*

## Action Plan:

1. Seek clarity through prayer and reflection on your passions and talents.

2. Align your actions with your sense of purpose, serving others in meaningful ways.

3. Embrace life's ups and downs as opportunities for growth and trust in God's plan.

## Prayer:

Heavenly Father, we trust in Your divine plan for our lives. Help us find purpose and hope in our journey, knowing that every step is guided by Your wisdom and love. May our lives be a reflection of Your grace and purpose. In Jesus name, we pray. Amen.

## DAY 09
## Embracing Change with Grace

"For I am about to do something new. See, I have already begun! Do you not see it? I will make a pathway through the wilderness. I will create rivers in the dry wasteland." - Isaiah 43:19

Isaiah 43:19 reminds us of God's promise to lead us through change with grace. As women, transitions and uncertainties can feel daunting, yet God assures us that He is orchestrating something new and beautiful. Embrace change with grace, for it's an opportunity for growth. Trust that God is paving a path, even in the wilderness of change. Let your heart be open to His transformative work. Change may challenge you, but it can also usher in blessings beyond imagination.

*Additional Scripture Reference:*

*"May the God of hope fill you with all joy and peace in believing, so that by the power of the Holy Spirit you may abound in hope." - Romans 15:13*

**Action Plan:**

1. Pray for God's guidance and wisdom during times of change.

2. Reflect on past transitions and the growth they brought into your life.

3. Share your experiences with others to encourage and inspire them as they face change.

**Prayer:**

*Heavenly Father, help us embrace change with grace, trusting in Your promise to lead us through. Fill us with hope, joy, and peace as we navigate transitions, knowing that Your plans are filled with purpose and blessing. In Jesus name, we pray. Amen.*

## DAY 10
## Letting Go of Comparison

*"Make a careful exploration of who you are and the work you have been given, and then sink yourself into that. Don't be impressed with yourself. Don't compare yourself with others." - Galatians 6:4*

Galatians 6:4 reminds us to avoid the trap of comparison. As women, it's easy to measure our worth against others' achievements, appearances, or successes, leading to insecurity and discontentment. Yet, God created each of us uniquely, with distinct purposes. Today, let go of comparison. Embrace your individuality and the path God has set before you. Celebrate your own journey and gifts, knowing that true fulfilment comes from living authentically. Rejoice in others' successes and support their endeavours, fostering a community of empowerment rather than competition.

*Additional Scripture Reference:*

*"But each one must test their own actions, and then they will take pride in themselves alone, without comparing themselves to someone else." - Galatians 6:4 (NIV)*

## Action Plan:

1. Reflect on your own strengths, passions, and purpose, embracing them fully.

2. Challenge negative thoughts of comparison with affirmations of self-worth.

3. Encourage others to pursue their unique paths and celebrate their accomplishments.

## Prayer:

*Heavenly Father, free us from the trap of comparison. Help us recognize our worth and purpose as unique creations in Your image. May we celebrate our own journeys and empower others to do the same. In Jesus name, we pray. Amen.*

## DAY 11
## The Blessing of Graciousness

"Be kind and compassionate to one another, forgiving each other, just as in Christ God forgave you." - Ephesians 4:32

Ephesians 4:32 reminds us of the profound blessing of graciousness. As women, life often presents opportunities for acts of kindness and forgiveness. Graciousness is a gift, bestowed upon us by God's grace. Today, embrace the blessing of graciousness. Extend kindness, compassion, and forgiveness to others, mirroring the love and forgiveness we have received from Christ. Graciousness transforms relationships, fostering understanding and healing. It's a reflection of God's boundless love. By offering grace to others, we multiply blessings in our own lives.

*Additional Scripture Reference:*

*"Bear with each other and forgive one another if any of you has a grievance against someone. Forgive as the Lord forgave you." - Colossians 3:13*

**Action Plan:**

1. Practice forgiveness by letting go of grudges and offering second chances.

2. Look for opportunities to show kindness and compassion in your daily interactions.

3. Reflect on the graciousness God has shown you and share that grace with others.

**Prayer:**

*Heavenly Father, we thank you for the blessing of graciousness. May we extend kindness, compassion, and forgiveness to others as you have done for us. Let our lives reflect your boundless love and grace. In Jesus name, we pray. Amen.*

## DAY 12
## Embracing Your Worth in Christ

"So God created mankind in his own image, in the image of God he created them; male and female he created them." - Genesis 1:27

Genesis 1:27 affirms that we are created in the image of God. As women, the world may challenge our worth, but our true identity is found in Christ. Today, embrace your worth in Him. Recognize that you are fearfully and wonderfully made, uniquely gifted and loved by God. Let go of insecurities and comparisons, and find confidence in your identity as His cherished child. In Christ, you are chosen, valued, and empowered to live a purposeful life.

*"You are a chosen people, a royal priesthood, a holy nation, God's special possession." - 1 Peter 2:9*

**Action Plan:**

1. Daily affirm your worth in Christ through prayer and meditation on Scripture.

2. Encourage and uplift other women, helping them recognize their worth.

3. Pursue your passions and talents with confidence, knowing they are gifts from God.

**Prayer:**

*Heavenly Father, help us embrace our worth in Christ. May we find our identity in You and live boldly as Your chosen and beloved children. Equip us to empower others to recognize their worth. In Jesus' name, we pray. Amen.*

## DAY 13
### Letting Go of Regret

"Forget the former things; do not dwell on the past." - Isaiah 43:18

Isaiah 43:18 urges us to release the burdens of regret. As women, we often carry the weight of past mistakes and missed opportunities. Yet, dwelling on regret can hinder our growth and joy. Today, choose to let go. Embrace forgiveness, starting with yourself. God's grace offers a fresh start, unburdened by past regrets. Regret serves as a reminder, not to wallow in guilt, but to learn, grow, and move forward. As you release regrets, you open your heart to the beauty of new beginnings, empowered by God's love and redemption.

*Additional Scripture Reference:*

*"Therefore, there is now no condemnation for those who are in Christ Jesus." - Romans 8:1*

**Action Plan:**

1. Reflect on past regrets, seeking lessons learned and ways to make amends.

2. Practice self-compassion, recognizing that you are a work in progress.

3. Commit to living in the present and embracing each day as a gift from God.

**Prayer:**

*Heavenly Father, help us let go of regret and embrace your forgiveness. May we find strength in your grace, knowing that we are free from condemnation. Guide us to live fully in the present, seeking your purpose for our lives. In Jesus name, we pray. Amen.*

## DAY 14
## Letting Go of Perfectionism

"But he said to me, 'My grace is sufficient for you, for my power is made perfect in weakness.'" - 2 Corinthians 12:9

2 Corinthians 12:9 reminds us of God's sufficiency in our imperfections. As women, the quest for perfection can be exhausting and discouraging. The pursuit of flawless appearances or achievements can lead to stress and anxiety. Today, release the chains of perfectionism. Embrace your humanity and vulnerabilities, knowing that God's power shines through our weaknesses. Allow His grace to fill the gaps where you fall short, for in imperfection, you find beauty and authenticity. Letting go of perfectionism is an invitation to experience God's sufficiency and peace.

*Additional Scripture Reference:*

*"For all have sinned and fall short of the glory of God." - Romans 3:23*

**Action Plan:**

1. Reflect on areas where perfectionism holds you back and acknowledge your imperfections.

2. Seek support and encouragement from friends or mentors who understand your struggles.

3. Embrace grace and self-compassion, recognizing that God loves you as you are.

**Prayer:**

*Heavenly Father, we surrender our perfectionist tendencies to You. Help us find sufficiency in Your grace and strength in our weaknesses. May we live authentically, knowing that Your love transcends our imperfections. In Jesus name, we pray. Amen.*

## DAY 15
## The Strength of Faith

"For we live by faith, not by sight." - 2 Corinthians 5:7

2 Corinthians 5:7 reminds us that faith is our guiding light in life's uncertainties. As women, we face challenges that test our resolve, but faith empowers us to overcome. It's a force that transcends logic and circumstances. In moments of doubt, remember the remarkable stories of faith in Scripture—women like Esther, Ruth, and the persistent widow. Today, strengthen your faith. Trust in God's plan, even when the path ahead seems unclear. Faith is the anchor for our souls, a source of strength that allows us to persevere through trials.

*Additional Scripture Reference:*

*"Now faith is confidence in what we hope for and assurance about what we do not see." - Hebrews 11:1*

**Action Plan:**

1. Nurture your faith through daily prayer, Scripture reading, and meditation.

2. Recall moments when your faith carried you through challenges, and share these stories to inspire others.

3. When facing uncertainties, choose to lean on faith rather than fear.

**Prayer:**

## DAY 16
## Embracing Your God-Given Talents

"Each of you should use whatever gift you have received to serve others, as faithful stewards of God's grace in its various forms." - 1 Peter 4:10

1 Peter 4:10 reminds us that our talents are divine gifts meant to serve others. As women, we often underestimate our abilities or fear comparison. Yet, God has uniquely equipped us with talents to make a positive impact. Today, embrace your God-given talents. Recognize their significance in His grand design. Whether it's a gift for encouragement, leadership, creativity, or compassion, use it to bless others. Your talents are instruments of God's grace, meant to bring light and love to a world in need.

*Additional Scripture Reference:*

*"Whatever you do, work at it with all your heart, as working for the Lord, not for human masters." - Colossians 3:23*

**Action Plan:**

1. Identify your God-given talents and seek ways to use them for the benefit of others.

2. Overcome self-doubt and comparison by focusing on your unique strengths.

3. Continually develop and refine your talents to honour God's calling.

**Prayer:**

*Heavenly Father, thank you for blessing us with unique talents. Help us recognize and embrace them as tools to serve others and glorify Your name. May our talents be a reflection of Your grace and love in the world. In Jesus name, we pray. Amen.*

## DAY 17
## Restoring Hope in Adversity

"Why are you cast down, O my soul, and why are you in turmoil within me? Hope in God; for I shall again praise him, my salvation and my God." - Psalm 42:11

Psalm 42:11 encourages us to anchor our hope in God during times of adversity. As women, we encounter trials that can shake our faith. Yet, adversity also offers an opportunity for hope to flourish. When the world seems bleak, remember that God is our source of unwavering hope. He brings light to our darkest days. Today, restore hope in adversity. Trust in God's promises and His ability to turn trials into testimonies. Let your heart be filled with the assurance that, through Him, you will overcome all challenges, finding renewed strength and hope.

*Additional Scripture Reference:*

*"I can do all things through him who strengthens me." - Philippians 4:13*

**Action Plan:**

1. Seek solace in prayer, pouring out your fears and doubts to God.

2. Surround yourself with a supportive community of faith to lift you up in challenging times.

3. Focus on gratitude for the blessings in your life, even amid adversity.

**Prayer:**

*Heavenly Father, in times of adversity, we turn to You for hope and strength. Restore our faith and fill our hearts with unwavering hope, knowing that through You, we can overcome any challenge. In Jesus name, we pray. Amen.*

## DAY 18
## Nurturing Your Inner Peace

"Peace I leave with you; my peace I give you. I do not give to you as the world gives. Do not let your hearts be troubled and do not be afraid." - John 14:27

John 14:27 reminds us that God's peace transcends worldly worries. As women, the demands of life often tug at our inner serenity. Yet, inner peace is a precious gift, bestowed upon us by Christ. Today, nurture your inner peace. Embrace moments of stillness and reflection in His presence. Let go of anxieties, knowing that His peace is a constant, a refuge amidst life's storms. As you cultivate inner peace, you radiate tranquillity, becoming a source of comfort and inspiration to others.

*Additional Scripture Reference:*

*"You will keep in perfect peace those whose minds are steadfast because they trust in you." - Isaiah 26:3*

**Action Plan:**

1. Dedicate time each day to prayer, meditation, or mindfulness to centre your heart on God.

2. Identify stressors and develop healthy coping mechanisms to maintain inner peace.

3. Share your journey toward inner peace with fellow women, encouraging one another in faith.

**Prayer:**

*Heavenly Father, grant us the gift of inner peace that surpasses understanding. May our hearts remain steadfast in trust and confidence in You. Help us nurture and share this peace with others. In Jesus name, we pray. Amen.*

## DAY 19
## The Beauty of Grace

"But he said to me, 'My grace is sufficient for you, for my power is made perfect in weakness.'" - 2 Corinthians 12:9

2 Corinthians 12:9 reveals the profound beauty of God's grace. As women, we often grapple with feelings of inadequacy and imperfection. Yet, it's in our weakness that God's grace shines brilliantly. It's the unmerited favour that lifts us up when we stumble, fills us with hope when we despair, and forgives us when we fall short. Today, bask in the beauty of grace. Accept that you are cherished and redeemed, not because of your perfection, but because of His love. Grace empowers us to embrace our flaws and extend compassion to others.

*Additional Scripture Reference:*

*"For it is by grace you have been saved, through faith—and this is not from yourselves, it is the gift of God." - Ephesians 2:8*

**Action Plan:**

1. Practice self-compassion, recognizing that you are a recipient of God's grace.

2. Extend grace to others, forgiving and showing kindness, as Christ has done for you.

3. Reflect on the countless ways God's grace has touched your life, fostering gratitude.

**Prayer:**

*Heavenly Father, we marvel at the beauty of Your grace. May it fill our hearts with humility, compassion, and gratitude. Help us extend this precious gift to others, showing the world the beauty of Your love. In Jesus name, we pray. Amen.*

## DAY 20
## Letting Go of Resentment

"Get rid of all bitterness, rage, and anger, brawling, and slander, along with every form of malice. Be kind and compassionate to one another, forgiving each other, just as in Christ God forgave you." - Ephesians 4:31-32

Ephesians 4:31-32 exhorts us to release the burden of resentment. As women, we may carry the weight of past hurts, creating a barrier to joy and peace. Yet, forgiveness is a transformative act of love. Today, choose to let go of resentment. Embrace the freedom that forgiveness brings, both for yourself and others. Just as Christ forgave us, we can extend grace to those who have wronged us. By releasing resentment, we open our hearts to healing, reconciliation, and a brighter future.

*Additional Scripture Reference:*

*"Bear with each other and forgive one another if any of you has a grievance against someone. Forgive as the Lord forgave you." - Colossians 3:13*

## Action Plan:

1. Reflect on any lingering resentments and their impact on your well-being.

2. Seek reconciliation where possible, and if not, choose to forgive in your heart.

3. Cultivate a spirit of kindness and compassion, promoting harmony in your relationships.

## Prayer:

*Heavenly Father, grant us the strength to release resentment and embrace forgiveness. Help us follow Christ's example, extending grace to others as You have done for us. May our hearts be free from bitterness, filled instead with love and compassion. In Jesus name, we pray. Amen.*

## DAY 21
## God's Unconditional Love

"But God demonstrates his own love for us in this: While we were still sinners, Christ died for us." - Romans 5:8

Romans 5:8 reveals the profound depth of God's unconditional love. As women, we often grapple with feelings of unworthiness and the need to earn love. Yet, God's love is different. It's not based on our performance or merits but on His character. His love is unwavering, reaching us at our lowest points. Today, immerse yourself in God's unconditional love. Embrace the truth that you are cherished and accepted as you are. Let His love heal wounds, bring hope, and ignite a profound love for Him in return.

*Additional Scripture Reference:*

*"See what great love the Father has lavished on us, that we should be called children of God!" - 1 John 3:1*

## Action Plan:

1. Meditate on God's love through daily Scripture reading and prayer.

2. Share His love by extending kindness, forgiveness, and compassion to others.

3. Cultivate gratitude for His unconditional love, knowing it transforms lives.

## Prayer:

*Heavenly Father, we stand in awe of Your unconditional love. May it envelop our hearts and overflow into our lives, touching everyone we encounter. Help us grasp the depth of Your love and live as Your beloved children. In Jesus name, we pray. Amen.*

## DAY 22
## Courage to Face Challenges

"Be strong and courageous. Do not be afraid or terrified because of them, for the Lord your God goes with you; he will never leave you nor forsake you." - Deuteronomy 31:6

Deuteronomy 31:6 reassures us that God's presence grants us the courage to face any challenge. As women, we often encounter formidable obstacles that test our resolve. Yet, with God as our steadfast companion, we need not fear. Courage rises from knowing we're not alone. Today, summon the courage to confront challenges head-on. Trust that God's strength empowers you. Embrace difficulties as opportunities for growth and transformation. In moments of doubt, remember the brave women of the Bible, like Esther and Mary, who faced adversity with unwavering courage.

*"Have I not commanded you? Be strong and courageous. Do not be afraid; do not be discouraged, for the Lord your God will be with you wherever you go." - Joshua 1:9*

**Action Plan:**

1. Seek God's guidance and wisdom through prayer when facing challenges.

2. Encourage and support fellow women in their journeys of courage.

3. Keep a journal of your courageous moments, celebrating victories big and small.

**Prayer:**

*Heavenly Father, grant us the courage to face challenges with unwavering faith in Your presence. May we find strength in Your promises and be a source of encouragement to others. In Jesus name, we pray. Amen.*

## DAY 23
## Letting Go of Guilt and Shame

"As far as the east is from the west, so far has he removed our transgressions from us." - Psalm 103:12

Psalm 103:12 reminds us of God's boundless grace, erasing guilt and shame. As women, we often carry the heavy burden of past mistakes and regrets. Yet, God's forgiveness is a beacon of hope. Today, release the chains of guilt and shame. Embrace the freedom found in His forgiveness and acceptance. Know that you are not defined by your past, but by God's love and grace. Allow His healing touch to mend your heart, empowering you to move forward with confidence.

*"Therefore, there is now no condemnation for those who are in Christ Jesus." - Romans 8:1*

## Action Plan:

1. Reflect on areas of guilt and shame, and surrender them to God through prayer.

2. Seek support from trusted friends or a counsellor to process and heal from past wounds.

3. Live in the freedom of God's forgiveness, extending grace to yourself and others.

## Prayer:

*Heavenly Father, we thank You for the forgiveness that removes our guilt and shame. Grant us the strength to let go of our past and walk in the freedom of Your grace. Help us embrace our identity in Christ, knowing there is no condemnation. In Jesus name, we pray. Amen.*

## DAY 24
### The Power of Perseverance

*"Let us not become weary in doing good, for at the proper time we will reap a harvest if we do not give up." - Galatians 6:9*

Galatians 6:9 reminds us that perseverance yields a harvest of blessings. As women, we face trials that may tempt us to quit. But true strength emerges in our determination to press on. Today, tap into the power of perseverance. Your journey may be challenging, but remember the resilient women in the Bible, like Ruth and Mary, who persevered despite adversity. Keep your faith alive, knowing that God's timing is perfect, and your efforts will bear fruit. Hold on, for a brighter tomorrow awaits.

*"But those who hope in the Lord will renew their strength. They will soar on wings like eagles; they will run and not grow weary, they will walk and not be faint." - Isaiah 40:31*

**Action Plan:**

1. Seek inspiration from the stories of persevering women in Scripture.

2. Set specific goals and maintain a consistent effort towards them.

3. Lean on God's strength when you feel weary, trusting in His promises

**Prayer:**

*Heavenly Father, grant us the perseverance to endure through life's challenges. May we find strength and hope in You, knowing that our efforts are not in vain. Renew our spirits, O Lord, and help us press on toward the blessings You have in store. In Jesus name, we pray. Amen.*

## DAY 25
## Finding Peace in Times of Chaos

"Peace I leave with you; my peace I give you. I do not give to you as the world gives. Do not let your hearts be troubled and do not be afraid." - John 14:27

John 14:27 offers the promise of divine peace, unlike the world's fleeting tranquillity. As women, we often confront chaos and uncertainty. Yet, true peace transcends circumstances. It's an inner serenity rooted in our relationship with Christ. Today, seek peace in the midst of chaos. Anchor your heart in God's unchanging love. Let His peace guard your thoughts and actions, enabling you to navigate life's storms with grace and calmness. Embrace the serenity that comes from trusting in His plan.

*Additional Scripture Reference:*

*"The Lord gives strength to his people; the Lord blesses his people with peace." - Psalm 29:11*

**Action Plan:**

1. Dedicate quiet moments to prayer and meditation, inviting God's peace into your life.

2. Practice gratitude, focusing on the blessings that bring peace.

3. Share the peace you've found with others, spreading calmness in turbulent times.

**Prayer:**

*Heavenly Father, grant us Your divine peace that surpasses understanding. In moments of chaos, may our hearts remain steadfast, anchored in Your love. Help us be beacons of peace in a troubled world. In Jesus name, we pray. Amen.*

## DAY 26
## Letting Go of Bitterness

*"Get rid of all bitterness, rage, and anger, brawling, and slander, along with every form of malice. Be kind and compassionate to one another, forgiving each other, just as in Christ God forgave you." - Ephesians 4:31-32*

Ephesians 4:31-32 urges us to release the weight of bitterness and embrace forgiveness. As women, we may harbour hurt from past wounds, poisoning our hearts. But bitterness only holds us captive. Today, choose to let go. Forgiveness is a gift to yourself, releasing the grip of anger and resentment. Remember Christ's forgiveness of your own sins. Let this awareness guide your actions. Embrace kindness and compassion. Through forgiveness, you find freedom, healing, and a heart ready to receive God's abundant blessings.

*Additional Scripture Reference:*

*"Forgive as the Lord forgave you." - Colossians 3:13*

**Action Plan:**

1. Reflect on areas of bitterness and make a conscious choice to forgive.

2. Seek reconciliation when possible, fostering healing in relationships.

3. Practice kindness and compassion daily, extending grace to others.

**Prayer:**

*Heavenly Father, help us release bitterness and embrace forgiveness. Grant us the strength to show the same grace You've shown us. May our hearts be free, ready to receive Your love and blessings. In Jesus name, we pray. Amen.*

## DAY 27
## Finding Joy in Giving Back

"It is more blessed to give than to receive." - Acts 20:35

Acts 20:35 reminds us of the immeasurable joy found in giving. As women, we're often consumed by life's demands. Yet, the act of selflessly giving back enriches our lives. It's in reaching out to help others that we discover a profound sense of purpose and joy. Today, embrace the joy of giving. Whether through acts of kindness, charity, or volunteering, find opportunities to be a blessing to others. In doing so, you'll experience the beauty of selflessness, echoing Christ's love and the promise of blessings returned.

*Additional Scripture Reference:*

*"Give, and it will be given to you. A good measure, pressed down, shaken together and running over, will be poured into your lap." - Luke 6:38*

**Action Plan:**

1. Identify ways to give back to your community or those in need.

2. Keep a giving journal, recording the moments that bring you joy.

3. Encourage others to join you in the joy of giving, amplifying the impact.

**Prayer:**

## DAY 28
## Letting Go of Anger

"In your anger, do not sin: Do not let the sun go down while you are still angry." - Ephesians 4:26

Ephesians 4:26 encourages us to manage anger without sinning. As women, we may grapple with anger's consuming force, causing harm to ourselves and others. But harbouring anger only darkens our hearts. Today, choose to let go. Instead of nurturing anger, seek healing and reconciliation. Recognize that forgiveness is a powerful antidote. Just as God forgives us, we can forgive others. This frees us from the bondage of anger, paving the way for peace and restoration. Let your actions reflect God's grace, turning anger into compassion.

*Additional Scripture Reference:*

*"Get rid of all bitterness, rage, and anger." - Ephesians 4:31*

**Action Plan:**

1. When anger arises, pause and reflect on its root cause.

2. Practice forgiveness, releasing the grip of anger, and seek reconciliation when possible.

3. Replace anger with acts of kindness and compassion, promoting peace.

**Prayer:**

*Heavenly Father, grant us the strength to let go of anger and embrace forgiveness. May our hearts be free from bitterness, filled instead with Your love and grace. Help us walk in the path of peace, following the example of Christ. In Jesus name, we pray. Amen.*

## The Blessing of Rest

"He makes me lie down in green pastures, he leads me beside quiet waters." - Psalm
23:2

Psalm 23:2 illustrates the profound blessing of rest that God provides. As
women, we often lead busy lives, filled with responsibilities and demands. Yet,
God invites us to find rest in Him. Rest is not only physical but also spiritual.
It's a rejuvenation of the soul, a time to pause and dwell in His presence.
Today, embrace the blessing of rest. Make it a priority to find moments of
quietude, allowing God to refresh your spirit. In stillness, you'll discover His
peace and renewed strength.

*Additional Scripture Reference:*

*"Come to me, all you who are weary and burdened, and I will give you rest." -
Matthew 11:28*

**Action Plan:**

1. Dedicate time each day to be still, meditating on God's Word.

2. Prioritise self-care, ensuring adequate rest for your physical well-being.

3. Encourage others to embrace the blessing of rest, nurturing their souls.

**Prayer:**

*Heavenly Father, we thank You for the blessing of rest that You provide. Help us find solace
in Your presence, renewing our spirits. May we rest in the assurance of Your love and care.
In Jesus name, we pray. Amen.*

## Finding Peace in Prayer

"Do not be anxious about anything, but in every situation, by prayer and petition,
with thanksgiving, present your requests to God. And the peace of God, which

transcends all understanding, will guard your hearts and your minds in Christ
Jesus." - Philippians 4:6-7

Philippians 4:6-7 assures us that through prayer, we find peace that surpasses understanding. As women, we often carry the weight of worries and anxieties. Yet, in the quiet moments of prayer, we discover a refuge. It's a place where we pour out our hearts, find solace, and experience God's peace embracing us. Today, immerse yourself in the soothing river of prayer. Surrender your concerns and fears, and in return, receive the peace that guards your heart and mind. In prayer, you'll find strength to face any storm.

*Additional Scripture Reference:*

*"The Lord is near to all who call on him, to all who call on him in truth." - Psalm 145:18*

### Action Plan:

1. Establish a daily prayer routine, setting aside time to commune with God.

2. Keep a prayer journal to document your petitions, witnessing God's faithfulness.

3. Share the gift of prayer with others, offering to pray for their needs.

### Prayer:

*Heavenly Father, thank You for the gift of peace through prayer. Draw us near to You as we seek Your presence in our daily lives. May our hearts find serenity in the midst of life's challenges. In Jesus name, we pray. Amen.*

# OCTOBER

*Zech. 9. [9] Rejoice greatly, O daughter of Zion; shout, O daughter of Jerusalem: behold, thy King cometh unto thee: he is just, and having salvation; lowly, and riding upon an ass, and upon a colt the foal of an ass.*

## DAY 01
### Living a Life of Love

"A new command I give you: Love one another. As I have loved you, so you must love one another." - John 13:34

John 13:34 implores us to love one another as Christ has loved us. As women, we're called to radiate love in our daily lives. It's the essence of our faith, reflecting God's boundless love for us. Love is more than a feeling; it's an intentional, selfless choice. Today, commit to living a life of love. Be a source of compassion, kindness, and forgiveness to those around you. By loving others, you emulate Christ's love and fulfil His greatest commandment.

*Additional Scripture Reference:*

*"Above all, love each other deeply, because love covers over a multitude of sins." - 1 Peter 4:8*

**Action Plan:**

1. Practice love daily through acts of kindness and understanding.

2. Forgive freely, as Christ forgave us.

3. Share the message of God's love with others, spreading His love.

**Prayer:**

*Heavenly Father, help us live a life of love as a reflection of Your love for us. Empower us to love one another deeply, just as You have loved us. May our lives be a testament to Your boundless love. In Jesus name, we pray. Amen.*

266

## Restoring Hope in Hardship

"I pray that God, the source of hope, will fill you completely with joy and peace because you trust in him. Then you will overflow with confident hope through the power of the Holy Spirit." - Romans 15:13

Romans 15:13 reminds us that hope is a gift from God, even in the midst of hardship. As women, we face trials that test our strength and faith. But in these moments, God offers a lifeline of hope. It's a hope rooted in trust, joy, and peace, found in our unwavering faith in Him. Today, let's restore hope in hardship. Lean into God's promises, seek His guidance, and trust that through the Holy Spirit, we can face any challenge with confident hope.

*Additional Scripture Reference:*

*"Why, my soul, are you downcast? Why so disturbed within me? Put your hope in God, for I will yet praise him, my Savior and my God." - Psalm 42:11*

**Action Plan:**

1. Daily prayer and reflection on God's promises to rekindle hope.

2. Encourage others facing adversity, sharing the hope found in Christ.

3. Seek opportunities to serve and bring hope to those in need.

**Prayer:**

*Heavenly Father, in times of hardship, we turn to You for hope and strength. Fill us with Your joy and peace, and let confident hope overflow through the power of the Holy Spirit. Restore hope in our lives, so we may praise You even in difficult times. In Jesus name, we pray. Amen.*

DAY 03
## Embracing Your Worth in Christ

"You are precious in my eyes, and honoured, and I love you." - Isaiah 43:4

Isaiah 43:4 reveals God's profound love for you, highlighting your immeasurable worth in His eyes. As women, we often struggle with self-doubt and insecurities. Yet, God sees us as precious and honoured. Our worth isn't defined by worldly standards but by our identity in Christ. Today, choose to embrace your worth in Him. Recognize that you are fearfully and wonderfully made (Psalm 139:14). Let His love define your value, boosting confidence and self-worth. In Christ, you are cherished, empowered, and dearly loved.

*Additional Scripture Reference:*

*"So God created mankind in his own image, in the image of God he created them." - Genesis 1:27*

**Action Plan:**

1. Daily affirm your worth in Christ through prayer and Scripture.

2. Encourage other women to recognize their value in God's eyes.

3. Practice self-compassion and self-love, reflecting your identity in Christ.

**Prayer:**

*Heavenly Father, help us embrace our worth in Christ and recognize the value You have placed in us. May Your love strengthen our confidence, allowing us to walk boldly in our identity as Your cherished daughters. In Jesus name, we pray. Amen.*

### DAY 04
### Courage to Step Out in Faith

*"Be strong and courageous. Do not be afraid; do not be discouraged, for the Lord your God will be with you wherever you go." - Joshua 1:9*

Joshua 1:9 reminds us that God's presence gives us the courage to step out in faith. As women, we encounter moments of uncertainty and fear when we must take bold steps. These steps may lead to new opportunities, personal growth, or fulfilling God's calling. But they require courage. Today, find the strength to embrace uncertainty with faith. Trust that God goes before you, holding your hand on the journey. In your courageous steps, you'll discover His faithfulness.

*Additional Scripture Reference:*

*"For we live by faith, not by sight." - 2 Corinthians 5:7*

**Action Plan:**

1. Identify an area where you need to step out in faith.

2. Pray for guidance and strength, seeking God's will.

3. Take that courageous step, trusting in God's promises.

**Prayer:**

*Heavenly Father, grant us the courage to step out in faith, knowing that You are with us every step of the way. Remove our fears and doubts, replacing them with unwavering trust in Your guidance. May our lives be a testament to Your faithfulness. In Jesus name, we pray. Amen.*

## DAY 05
### Loving Your Neighbour

"Love your neighbour as yourself." - Mark 12:31

Mark 12:31 encapsulates the essence of Christ's teaching—to love our neighbour as ourselves. As women, we often encounter opportunities to extend love to those around us. It's a call to selflessness, compassion, and empathy. Loving your neighbour transcends boundaries of race, culture, and circumstance. It's a reflection of God's love for us. Today, let's make a conscious effort to love our neighbours in practical ways. Reach out, lend a helping hand, or simply offer a listening ear. In loving our neighbours, we embody the love of Christ and fulfil His commandment.

*"A new command I give you: Love one another. As I have loved you, so you must love one another." - John 13:34*

**Action Plan:**

1. Find a neighbour in need and take action to support them.

2. Practice kindness and empathy in your daily interactions.

3. Pray for God's guidance in loving your neighbours more effectively.

**Prayer:**

*Heavenly Father, teach us to love our neighbours as You have loved us. Help us see opportunities to extend Your love to those around us, regardless of differences. May our lives be a testament to Your love and compassion. In Jesus name, we pray. Amen.*

## DAY 06
## Finding Purpose in Your Pain

"And we know that in all things God works for the good of those who love him, who have been called according to his purpose." - Romans 8:28

Romans 8:28 assures us that God can bring purpose from our pain. As women, we encounter trials that seem unbearable, but in those very moments, God is at work. Your pain doesn't define you; it's a chapter in the story He's writing. It can be a source of strength, empathy, and growth. Today, seek to find purpose in your pain. Look beyond the suffering, recognizing God's redemptive hand. Your trials can be a testimony of His grace.

*Additional Scripture Reference:*

*"For our light and momentary troubles are achieving for us an eternal glory that far outweighs them all." - 2 Corinthians 4:17*

Action Plan:

1. Reflect on past challenges and how they shaped your character.

2. Share your journey with others to encourage them in their struggles.

3. Trust that God can use your pain for His greater purpose.

**Prayer:**

*Heavenly Father, help us find purpose in our pain and trust Your sovereign plan. May our trials draw us closer to You and serve as a testament to Your faithfulness. In Jesus name, we pray. Amen.*

## DAY 07
### Restoring Broken Hearts

"The Lord is close to the brokenhearted and saves those who are crushed in spirit." - Psalm 34:18

Psalm 34:18 assures us that God draws near to those with broken hearts. As women, we may experience the pain of shattered dreams, lost love, or grief. Yet, in our brokenness, God's grace abounds. He's the ultimate healer of wounded hearts. Today, embrace the hope that comes from God's closeness. Seek restoration for your heart through His comforting presence. Allow Him to mend your brokenness and bring forth new beginnings.

*Additional Scripture Reference:*

*"He heals the brokenhearted and binds up their wounds." - Psalm 147:3*

**Action Plan:**

1. Open your heart to God, sharing your pain and seeking His healing.

2. Extend compassion and support to others experiencing heartbreak.

3. Trust in God's promise of restoration.

**Prayer:**

*Heavenly Father, we bring our broken hearts to You, trusting in Your healing and restoration. Draw near to us and mend our wounds. May our renewed hearts bear witness to Your grace and love. In Jesus name, we pray. Amen.*

## DAY 08
## The Power of Words

"Kind words are like honey—sweet to the soul and healthy for the body." - Proverbs 16:24

Proverbs 16:24 reminds us of the profound impact words hold. As women, our words possess the power to uplift, heal, and inspire. They can also wound and discourage. Today, consider the weight of your words. Choose to speak kindness, love, and encouragement. Your words have the potential to bring sweetness to the souls of those around you. In a world often filled with negativity, let your words stand as a beacon of hope, pointing others toward the love of Christ.

*Additional Scripture Reference:*

*"Let your conversation be always full of grace, seasoned with salt, so that you may know how to answer everyone." - Colossians 4:6*

**Action Plan:**

1. Think of your recent conversations and evaluate their impact.

2. Practice intentional kindness and encouragement in your speech.

3. Pray for God's guidance in using your words to bless others.

**Prayer:**

*Heavenly Father, may our words be a source of sweetness, healing, and inspiration to those around us. Guide our speech to reflect Your love and grace. Help us use our words to uplift and encourage, pointing others toward You. In Jesus name, we pray. Amen.*

## DAY 09
## Navigating Life's Transitions

"For I know the plans I have for you, declares the Lord, plans for welfare and not for evil, to give you a future and a hope." - Jeremiah 29:11

Jeremiah 29:11 reminds us that God has a plan for our lives, even amidst transitions. As women, life's changes can be daunting—career shifts, family adjustments, or personal transformations. In these moments of uncertainty, cling to God's promise of hope. Transitions are opportunities for growth and divine guidance. Embrace change with faith, knowing that God's plans for you are filled with hope and blessings. Trust His direction as you navigate the path ahead.

*Additional Scripture Reference:*

*"Your word is a lamp to my feet and a light to my path." - Psalm 119:105*

**Action Plan:**

1. Seek God's guidance through prayer and meditation on His Word.

2. Accept change with a positive outlook, viewing it as a chance for growth.

3. Encourage others facing transitions, offering support and prayer.

**Prayer:**

*Heavenly Father, guide us through life's transitions with unwavering faith in Your plans. May Your hope be our anchor as we navigate the unknown. Help us trust Your divine direction and embrace change as an opportunity for growth. In Jesus name, we pray. Amen.*

## DAY 10
### Celebrating Your Uniqueness

"I praise you because I am fearfully and wonderfully made; your works are wonderful, I know that fully well." - Psalm 139:14

Psalm 139:14 reminds us that we are fearfully and wonderfully made by our Creator. As women, it's easy to compare ourselves to others, but our true worth lies in our uniqueness. Each of us is a masterpiece, crafted with love and purpose. Embrace your individuality with gratitude, recognizing that your strengths, quirks, and experiences make you who you are. Celebrate your uniqueness as a testament to God's creative brilliance.

*Additional Scripture Reference:*

*"God is not unjust; he will not forget your work and the love you have shown him as you have helped his people and continue to help them." - Hebrews 6:10*

**Action Plan:**

1. Reflect on your unique qualities and talents, thanking God for them.

2. Encourage others to celebrate their uniqueness as well.

3. Take steps to use your unique gifts to help and uplift others.

**Prayer:**

*Heavenly Father, we thank You for crafting us fearfully and wonderfully. Help us embrace our uniqueness and use it to serve Your purpose. May we celebrate the individuality of others, recognizing that we are all part of Your divine plan. In Jesus name, we pray. Amen.*

## DAY 11
## Embracing Diversity and Inclusion

"For there is no distinction between Jew and Greek; for the same Lord is Lord of all, bestowing his riches on all who call on him." - Romans 10:12

Romans 10:12 reminds us that in Christ, there is no distinction or bias. As women, we're called to embrace diversity and inclusion, reflecting God's love for all. Our differences, whether of race, background, or experiences, are a testament to God's creativity. Today, let's strive to foster an inclusive spirit. Embrace diversity with open hearts, showing love and respect to all. In doing so, we mirror Christ's love, breaking down barriers and building a more compassionate and united world.

*"So in Christ Jesus, you are all children of God through faith." - Galatians 3:26*

**Action Plan:**

1. Reflect on your own biases and commit to breaking them down.

2. Seek opportunities to learn from and build relationships with people from diverse backgrounds.

3. Pray for unity and understanding among all God's children.

**Prayer:**

*Heavenly Father, help us embrace diversity and inclusion as a reflection of Your love. May we see all people as Your children and treat them with respect and kindness. Guide us to build bridges and foster unity in a world that often divides. In Jesus name, we pray. Amen.*

## DAY 12
## Loving Yourself Unconditionally

*"Love your neighbour as yourself." - Mark 12:31*

Mark 12:31 reminds us to love our neighbours as ourselves, emphasising the importance of self-love. As women, we often prioritise caring for others but neglect self-compassion. Today, embrace the truth that you are fearfully and wonderfully made by God. Love yourself unconditionally, just as God loves you. Your worth isn't determined by external standards; it's intrinsic. Let go of self-doubt, forgive your mistakes, and celebrate your uniqueness. In doing so, you can pour love and kindness into the lives of others more abundantly.

*Additional Scripture Reference:*

*"Beloved, let us love one another, for love is from God, and whoever loves has been born of God and knows God." - 1 John 4:7*

**Action Plan:**

1. Practice self-compassion daily, offering yourself the same grace you extend to others.

2. Surround yourself with positive affirmations and scripture that remind you of your worth.

3. Share the message of self-love with other women to empower them as well.

**Prayer:**

*Heavenly Father, help us love ourselves unconditionally, knowing that we are Your beloved creations. May we treat ourselves with kindness and forgiveness, reflecting Your boundless love. Use our self-love to overflow into the lives of others, drawing them closer to You. In Jesus name, we pray. Amen.*

## DAY 13
## Finding Joy in Simple Pleasures

"Rejoice always, pray continually, give thanks in all circumstances; for this is God's will for you in Christ Jesus." - 1 Thessalonians 5:16-18

1 Thessalonians 5:16-18 encourages us to find joy in all circumstances. As women, we can discover immense joy in life's simple pleasures— a warm embrace, a heartfelt conversation, or the beauty of nature. These moments remind us of God's presence in the everyday. Today, pause and savour the little things. Be present in the moment, give thanks, and let your heart overflow with joy. In appreciating life's simplicity, we align with God's will for us.

*Additional Scripture Reference:*

*"The Lord has done great things for us, and we are filled with joy." - Psalm 126:3*

**Action Plan:**

1. Create a gratitude journal to record daily blessings.

2. Spend quality time with loved ones, cherishing simple moments together.

3. Commit to finding joy in at least one simple pleasure each day.

**Prayer:**

*Heavenly Father, we thank You for the simple pleasures that bring us joy. Open our eyes to Your presence in the everyday moments of life. Help us cultivate gratitude and find joy in the beauty of simplicity. In Jesus name, we pray. Amen.*

## DAY 14
## Strengthening Your Faith Walk

"Trust in the Lord with all your heart and lean not on your own understanding; in all your ways submit to him, and he will make your paths straight." - Proverbs 3:5-6

Proverbs 3:5-6 reminds us to trust God completely. As women, our faith journeys can be filled with twists and turns. Yet, through it all, faith strengthens us. It's an anchor in life's storms, a light in the darkness. Today, nurture your faith by surrendering your worries, seeking God's guidance, and deepening your relationship with Him. As your faith grows, God will illuminate your path, making it straight.

*Additional Scripture Reference:*

*"Now faith is confidence in what we hope for and assurance about what we do not see." - Hebrews 11:1*

**Action Plan:**

1. Spend time daily in prayer and meditation to deepen your faith.

2. Seek opportunities to share your faith journey with others.

3. Trust God's plan even in moments of uncertainty.

**Prayer:**

*Heavenly Father, strengthen our faith as we trust in You with all our hearts. Guide us on this journey and grant us the confidence to walk by faith, not by sight. May our faith be a testimony of Your love and grace. In Jesus name, we pray. Amen.*

## DAY 15
## Overcoming Obstacles with Faith

"I can do all things through him who strengthens me." - Philippians 4:13

Philippians 4:13 reminds us that through Christ, we find the strength to overcome any obstacle. As women, life often presents challenges that seem insurmountable. But faith transforms obstacles into opportunities for growth and resilience. When we face adversity with unwavering faith, we tap into God's limitless power. Today, embrace your obstacles as stepping stones toward God's purpose for your life. With faith as your guide, you can conquer the highest mountains and navigate the deepest valleys.

*Additional Scripture Reference:*

*"The Lord is my strength and my shield; in him my heart trusts, and I am helped." - Psalm 28:7*

**Action Plan:**

1. Identify a current obstacle and pray for the faith to overcome it.

2. Seek wisdom and support from your faith community.

3. Share your testimonies of overcoming obstacles to inspire others.

**Prayer:**

*Heavenly Father, grant us the faith to conquer obstacles and the courage to trust in Your strength. With You as our shield, we face challenges with unwavering confidence. May our faith be a beacon of hope to others. In Jesus name, we pray. Amen.*

## DAY 16
## The Power of Hope

"For I know the plans I have for you, declares the Lord, plans for welfare and not for evil, to give you a future and a hope." - Jeremiah 29:11

Jeremiah 29:11 assures us of God's plans for our future filled with hope. As women, hope is our anchor during life's storms. It's the light that guides us through the darkest nights. Hope reminds us that, no matter the challenges we face, God's purpose for our lives is filled with goodness. Today, hold on to hope with unwavering faith. Let it empower you to overcome obstacles, find joy in adversity, and trust in God's promises.

*Additional Scripture Reference:*

*"But those who hope in the Lord will renew their strength." - Isaiah 40:31*

**Action Plan:**

1. Reflect on areas of your life where hope is needed.

2. Pray for renewed hope and guidance in those areas.

3. Encourage others to find hope in God's promises.

**Prayer:**

*Heavenly Father, we thank You for the hope You provide in our lives. May we always trust in Your plans, knowing they lead to a future filled with Your goodness. Renew our hope, strengthen our faith, and use us to inspire hope in others. In Jesus name, we pray. Amen.*

## DAY 17
## Letting Go of Control

"Trust in the Lord with all your heart and lean not on your own understanding." - Proverbs 3:5

Proverbs 3:5 reminds us to trust God completely and release our grip on control. As women, we often carry the weight of trying to manage every aspect of our lives. But true peace comes when we surrender control to the One who knows our path. Letting go isn't a sign of weakness; it's an act of faith. Today, release your worries, burdens, and plans to God. Embrace the freedom that comes from trusting His wisdom and timing.

*Additional Scripture Reference:*

*"Be still, and know that I am God." - Psalm 46:10*

**Action Plan:**

1. Identify an area where you struggle to let go of control.

2. Practice surrendering it to God through prayer and meditation.

3. Trust that His plans are greater than your own.

**Prayer:**

*Heavenly Father, help us release control and trust in Your perfect plan. Teach us to be still and know that You are God. May our lives be a testament to Your guidance and sovereignty. In Jesus name, we pray. Amen.*

## DAY 18
## The Strength of Patience

"But if we hope for what we do not yet have, we wait for it patiently." - Romans 8:25

Romans 8:25 reminds us of the power of patience in our journey of hope. As women, our lives often rush by in a whirlwind of expectations and desires. Yet, true strength is found in patiently waiting for God's perfect timing. Patience isn't passivity; it's a courageous act of trust. Today, embrace the beauty of waiting, for in it, you build resilience, deepen your faith, and discover God's blessings beyond your imagination.

*Additional Scripture Reference:*

*"But the fruit of the Spirit is love, joy, peace, patience..." - Galatians 5:22*

**Action Plan:**

1. Identify an area where you struggle with impatience.

2. Practice patience through prayer and mindfulness.

3. Trust that God's timing is always perfect.

**Prayer:**

*Heavenly Father, grant us the strength to wait patiently and hope unwaveringly. May we be filled with Your patience, knowing that Your timing is always perfect. In Jesus name, we pray. Amen.*

## DAY 19

## Discovering Your Spiritual Gifts

"Now to each one, the manifestation of the Spirit is given for the common good." - 1 Corinthians 12:7

In 1 Corinthians 12:7, we're reminded that each of us possesses unique spiritual gifts from God. As women, recognizing and embracing these gifts is a transformative journey. These gifts are not just for our benefit but for the greater good of our communities. Today, take time to discover your spiritual gifts through prayer and self-reflection. Your gifts are a source of inspiration and empowerment, allowing you to make a positive impact in the world.

*Additional Scripture Reference:*

*"As each has received a gift, use it to serve one another, as good stewards of God's varied grace." - 1 Peter 4:10*

**Action Plan:**

1. Reflect on your passions and talents.

2. Seek guidance through prayer and community.

3. Take steps to use your gifts to serve others.

**Prayer:**

## DAY 20
## Finding Beauty in Diversity

"For just as each of us has one body with many members, and these members do not all have the same function, so in Christ, we, though many, form one body, and each member belongs to all the others." - Romans 12:4-5

Romans 12:4-5 teaches us that, as women, we are part of a diverse and interconnected body in Christ. Our uniqueness adds to the beauty of this unity. Embrace diversity not only in race and culture but also in thoughts and perspectives. Today, seek the beauty in the differences around you. Celebrate the richness it brings to your life and the world.

*Additional Scripture Reference:*

*"There is neither Jew nor Gentile, neither slave nor free, nor is there male and female, for you are all one in Christ Jesus." - Galatians 3:28*

**Action Plan:**

1. Engage in conversations with people from diverse backgrounds.

2. Educate yourself about different cultures and viewpoints.

3. Pray for unity and understanding among all God's children.

**Prayer:**

*Dear Lord, open our hearts to see the beauty in diversity and to appreciate the unique gifts each person brings. Help us to love and embrace one another as we are, united in Your love. In Jesus name, we pray. Amen.*

## DAY 21
## Living a Life of Abundance

"I came that they may have life and have it abundantly." - John 10:10

In John 10:10, Jesus offers a profound promise of abundant life. As women, this means embracing life with gratitude and generosity, recognizing that true abundance goes beyond material wealth. It's a life filled with love, purpose, and a heart ready to share blessings with others. Today, let go of scarcity mentality and embrace God's abundant love and provision. Overflow with gratitude, sow seeds of kindness, and watch as your life becomes a testament to His boundless blessings.

*Additional Scripture Reference:*

*"And my God will supply every need of yours according to his riches in glory in Christ Jesus." - Philippians 4:19*

**Action Plan:**

1. Reflect on the abundance of blessings in your life.

2. Identify one way you can bless someone today.

3. Practice gratitude through journaling.

**Prayer:**

*Dear Lord, thank You for the promise of abundant life in Christ. Help us live generously, sharing the blessings You've bestowed upon us. May our lives overflow with gratitude and love for others. In Jesus name, we pray. Amen.*

## DAY 22
### The Gift of Encouraging Others

"Therefore encourage one another and build one another up, just as you are doing." - 1 Thessalonians 5:11

1 Thessalonians 5:11 reminds us of the incredible power of encouragement. As women, we hold the gift to uplift others in their journeys. A word of encouragement can mend a wounded heart, reignite hope, and inspire

greatness. Today, purposefully seek opportunities to encourage those around you. Let your words and actions be a source of light and strength to others, nurturing their spirits with love and kindness.

*Additional Scripture Reference:*

*"Let each of us please his neighbour for his good, to build him up." - Romans 15:2*

**Action Plan:**

1. Reach out to someone who may be in need of encouragement.

2. Share a genuine compliment or word of affirmation.

3. Pray for the wisdom to be a beacon of encouragement in others' lives.

**Prayer:**

*Heavenly Father, grant us the grace to be sources of encouragement to those in need. May our words and actions uplift and inspire, reflecting Your love. In Jesus name, we pray. Amen.*

## DAY 23
### Facing Trials with Hope

"Count it all joy, my brothers, when you meet trials of various kinds, for you know that the testing of your faith produces steadfastness." - James 1:2-3

James 1:2-3 reminds us that trials, though challenging, can lead to growth and perseverance. As women, we often encounter various trials in our lives, from personal struggles to external challenges. In these moments, let hope be your anchor. Trust that God is using these trials to strengthen your faith and character. Embrace each difficulty with the knowledge that, in the end, it will produce resilience and a deeper connection with God.

*Additional Scripture Reference:*

*"We rejoice in our sufferings, knowing that suffering produces endurance, and endurance produces character, and character produces hope." - Romans 5:3-4*

**Action Plan:**

1. When facing a trial, pause and pray for strength and hope.

2. Seek support and encouragement from a faith community or friends.

3. Reflect on past trials and how they've shaped your character.

**Prayer:**

*Dear Lord, help us face trials with unwavering hope, knowing that You are with us, refining our faith. Grant us the strength to endure and the wisdom to see Your purpose in every challenge. In Jesus name, we pray. Amen.*

# DAY 24
## Walking in God's Light

"Your word is a lamp to my feet and a light to my path." - Psalm 119:105

Psalm 119:105 beautifully illustrates how God's Word guides our path, illuminating our journey. As women, we often face the complexities of life, and it's in God's light that we find clarity, purpose, and direction. Embrace His word as your guiding light, allowing it to shine on every decision, challenge, and opportunity. By walking in His light, you'll discover the peace and assurance that come from living in alignment with His plan for your life.

*Additional Scripture Reference:*

*"I am the light of the world. Whoever follows me will not walk in darkness but will have the light of life." - John 8:12*

**Action Plan:**

1. Dedicate time each day to read and reflect on Scripture.

2. Seek God's guidance in prayer for your daily decisions.

3. Share a verse that has inspired you with a friend or family member.

**Prayer:**

Heavenly Father, illuminate our paths with Your divine light. May Your Word guide our steps, bringing clarity and wisdom to our lives. Help us walk in Your light daily. In Jesus name, we pray. Amen.

## DAY 25
## Resolving Conflict with Love

"Above all, love each other deeply, because love covers over a multitude of sins." - 1 Peter 4:8

Conflict is inevitable, but how we respond defines our character. 1 Peter 4:8 reminds us that love can mend even the deepest wounds. As women, we hold the power to resolve conflicts with grace and compassion. Approach disagreements with love, seeking understanding and forgiveness. Remember that love's strength lies in its ability to heal and reconcile. Let love be the guiding force in your relationships, paving the way for peace and unity.

*Additional Scripture Reference:*

*"Bear with each other and forgive one another if any of you has a grievance against someone. Forgive as the Lord forgave you." - Colossians 3:13*

**Action Plan:**

1. Pray for guidance in resolving conflicts lovingly.

2. Practice active listening to better understand others.

3. Extend forgiveness as the Lord has forgiven you.

**Prayer:**

*Dear Lord, grant us the wisdom to resolve conflicts with love. Help us bear with one another and forgive as You have forgiven us. May Your love be the cornerstone of our relationships. In Jesus name, we pray. Amen.*

## DAY 26
## Finding Healing and Wholeness

"He heals the brokenhearted and binds up their wounds." - Psalm 147:3

In life's journey, we may carry wounds and brokenness within us. Yet, Psalm 147:3 assures us that God is the ultimate healer of our broken hearts. As women, we can find profound healing and wholeness through our faith. Embrace God's loving touch to mend your spirit and find restoration. Let His grace fill the spaces where pain once resided, turning scars into stories of His redemption.

*Additional Scripture Reference:*

*"The Lord is close to the brokenhearted and saves those who are crushed in spirit." - Psalm 34:18*

**Action Plan:**

1. Surrender your brokenness to God through prayer.

2. Seek counselling or support if needed.

3. Share your journey of healing with others to inspire hope.

**Prayer:**

*Heavenly Father, we come before You with our brokenness, trusting in Your promise to heal our hearts. Be close to us in our pain, and may our wounds be a testament to Your transformative power. In Jesus name, we find healing and wholeness. Amen.*

## DAY 27
## Living with Grace and Gentleness

"Let your gentleness be evident to all. The Lord is near." - Philippians 4:5 (NIV)

Philippians 4:5 reminds us to embrace a life of grace and gentleness, reflecting the nearness of the Lord in our actions. As women, we are called to exemplify these qualities in our daily interactions. In a world often filled with haste and harshness, our gentleness can be a beacon of God's love. Let us approach others with kindness, patience, and empathy, extending the grace we ourselves have received.

*Additional Scripture Reference:*

*"Be completely humble and gentle; be patient, bearing with one another in love." - Ephesians 4:2 (NIV)*

**Action Plan:**

1. Practice gentleness in your words and deeds.

2. Extend forgiveness and understanding to others.

3. Reflect on the impact of gentleness in your relationships.

**Prayer:**

*Heavenly Father, help us embody grace and gentleness in our daily lives, showing the world Your love through our actions. May our interactions be a testament to Your nearness. In Jesus name, we seek the strength to live with grace and gentleness. Amen.*

## DAY 28
## Building Healthy Habits

"Do you not know that your bodies are temples of the Holy Spirit, who is in you, whom you have received from God? You are not your own." - 1 Corinthians 6:19 (NIV)

As women, our bodies are temples of the Holy Spirit. God calls us to care for these vessels with love and intention. By cultivating healthy habits, we honour His divine creation. Whether it's nourishing our bodies with wholesome food or nurturing our minds with positive thoughts, each choice we make impacts our well-being. Let us embark on this journey of self-care, knowing that God walks beside us.

*"So whether you eat or drink or whatever you do, do it all for the glory of God." - 1 Corinthians 10:31 (NIV)*

**Action Plan:**

1. Set achievable health goals.

2. Prioritise self-care, including exercise, rest, and mindfulness.

3. Seek support and accountability in your journey.

**Prayer:**

*Heavenly Father, guide us in building healthy habits that honour the temples You have entrusted to us. May our choices reflect Your glory, and may we find strength in You as we pursue wellness. In Jesus name, we commit to this journey of self-care. Amen.*

## DAY 29
## The Power of Words and Positivity

"Gracious words are a honeycomb, sweet to the soul and healing to the bones." - Proverbs 16:24 (NIV)

Our words have the remarkable ability to shape our world. When we speak words of kindness, encouragement, and positivity, we create an atmosphere of love and hope. In a world often filled with negativity, our words can stand as beacons of light. Let us remember that our tongue has the power to uplift and heal. As women of faith, we are called to be purveyors of grace through our speech.

*Additional Scripture Reference:*

*"Let your conversation be always full of grace, seasoned with salt, so that you may know how to answer everyone." - Colossians 4:6 (NIV)*

**Action Plan:**

1.  Practice speaking words of encouragement daily.

2.  Be mindful of your words, choosing grace over criticism.

3.  Share positive affirmations with others.

**Prayer:**

*Heavenly Father, empower us to use our words as instruments of love and healing. May our speech be a reflection of Your grace and positivity, spreading hope to those around us. In Jesus name, we commit to speaking life and love. Amen.*

## DAY 30
## Courage to Step Out of Your Comfort Zone

"Have I not commanded you? Be strong and courageous. Do not be afraid; do not be discouraged, for the Lord your God will be with you wherever you go." - Joshua 1:9 (NIV)

God often calls us to step out of our comfort zones to fulfil His purpose. It's natural to feel fear and uncertainty when facing the unknown, but remember that God promises to be with you in every step. Embrace these moments as opportunities for growth, knowing that your faith can overcome fear.

*Additional Scripture Reference:*

*"For God has not given us a spirit of fear, but of power and of love and of a sound mind." - 2 Timothy 1:7 (NKJV)*

**Action Plan:**

1.  Identify an area in your life where you need to step out of your comfort zone.

2.  Pray for God's guidance and strength.

3.  Take that courageous step, trusting in God's presence.

**Prayer:**

## DAY 31
## Walking in Humility

"Take my yoke upon you and learn from me, for I am gentle and humble in heart, and you will find rest for your souls." - Matthew 11:29 (NIV)

In a world that often celebrates self-promotion, Christ's call to walk in humility stands as a powerful reminder. Emulating Jesus' gentle and humble nature can transform our relationships and lead to inner peace. Humility doesn't mean self-deprecation but recognizing that our worth comes from God, not worldly success. As we walk humbly, we model Christ's character.

*Additional Scripture Reference:*

*"Do nothing out of selfish ambition or vain conceit. Rather, in humility, value others above yourselves." - Philippians 2:3 (NIV)*

**Action Plan:**

1. Reflect on areas where you can practice humility in your life.

2. Strive to put others' needs before your own.

3. Seek God's strength in cultivating a humble heart.

**Prayer:**

Heavenly Father, teach us to walk in humility, as Jesus did. Help us value others and find our worth in You alone. May our lives reflect Your gentle and humble character. In Jesus name, we pray for hearts of humility. Amen.

# NOVEMBER

*"And blessed is she who believed that there would be a fulfilment of what was spoken to her from the Lord." The Good News: When we ask for anything from the Lord, He listens and provides. "A gracious woman gets honour, and violent men get riches."*

## DAY 01
## Unleashing Creativity

"For we are God's handiwork, created in Christ Jesus to do good works, which God prepared in advance for us to do." - Ephesians 2:10

God, the ultimate Creator, has woven creativity into our very beings. Each of us is a masterpiece crafted by His hands. In embracing our creativity, we honour the divine spark within. Creativity isn't limited to arts; it's about approaching life with fresh perspectives, problem-solving, and expressing love in unique ways.

*Additional Scripture Reference:*

*"Commit your work to the Lord, and your plans will be established." - Proverbs 16:3*

**Action Plan:**

1. Explore a creative endeavour that brings you joy.

2. Pray for guidance and inspiration in your creative pursuits.

3. Share your creativity to bless others.

**Prayer:**

*Heavenly Father, thank you for making us creative beings. Guide us in using our gifts to glorify You and bless others. May we approach life with wonder and imagination. In Jesus name, we pray for a creative heart. Amen.*

## DAY 02
### Honouring Your Emotions

"Trust in the Lord with all your heart and lean not on your own understanding." - Proverbs 3:5

Dear sister, our emotions are a gift from God, a tapestry of joy, sadness, and everything in between. It's crucial to honour and express them honestly. Remember, even Jesus wept (John 11:35). Emotions connect us to our humanity and to God's empathy for our struggles. When you embrace your feelings, you open a path for healing and growth.

*Additional Scripture Reference:*

*"The Lord is close to the brokenhearted and saves those who are crushed in spirit." - Psalm 34:18 (NIV)*

**Action Plan:**

1. Journal your emotions to understand them better.

2. Seek counsel from a trusted friend or therapist.

3. Pray for God's guidance and comfort in your emotional journey.

**Prayer:**

*Heavenly Father, we thank You for the gift of emotions. Help us navigate them with wisdom, drawing closer to You and others. In our vulnerability, may we find strength and healing. Amen.*

## DAY 03
### Fostering Healthy Boundaries

"Guard your heart above all else, for it determines the course of your life." - Proverbs 4:23

Dear sister, setting boundaries is an act of love, both for yourself and others. It's not about building walls but defining spaces where love and respect can flourish. In a world that often blurs lines, remember that God calls you to safeguard your heart. Healthy boundaries ensure you protect your time, energy, and emotional well-being.

*Additional Scripture Reference:*

*"Let your yes be yes and your no be no." - Matthew 5:37 (ESV)*

**Action Plan:**

1. Reflect on areas where you need boundaries.

2. Communicate your boundaries kindly and firmly.

3. Prioritise self-care and seek God's guidance.

**Prayer:**

*Heavenly Father, guide us in setting boundaries that honour You and nurture our relationships. Grant us the wisdom to protect our hearts and live in love and grace. In Jesus name, We pray. Amen.*

## DAY 04
### Loving Your Body

"Do you not know that your bodies are temples of the Holy Spirit, who is in you, whom you have received from God? You are not your own; you were bought at a price. Therefore honour God with your bodies." - 1 Corinthians 6:19-20

Dear sister, your body is a sacred vessel, a divine creation. Embrace it with love and gratitude, for it houses the Spirit of God. In a world that often criticises appearances, remember that your true beauty lies in your soul's radiance. Treat your body with care, nourish it, and celebrate its uniqueness.

*"I praise you because I am fearfully and wonderfully made." - Psalm 139:14 (NIV)*

## Action Plan:

1. Practice self-compassion daily.

2. Focus on nourishing, not punishing, your body.

3. Cultivate a positive body image.

## Prayer:

*Heavenly Father, help us cherish our bodies as temples of Your presence. Grant us the strength to love and care for ourselves, embracing the beauty You've created within us. In Jesus name, we pray. Amen.*

## DAY 06
## Living a Life of Integrity

"Whoever walks in integrity walks securely, but whoever takes crooked paths will be found out." - Proverbs 10:9

Sister, integrity is the foundation of a meaningful life. It's the commitment to moral and ethical principles, even when no one is watching. In a world often tempted by shortcuts, let your integrity shine. It builds trust, strengthens relationships, and reflects the light of Christ in you.

*Additional Scripture Reference:*

*"The integrity of the upright guides them, but the unfaithful are destroyed by their duplicity." - Proverbs 11:3 (NIV)*

## Action Plan:

1. Reflect on your values and align your actions with them.

2. Practice honesty, even in small matters.

3. Seek accountability through prayer and community.

**Prayer:**

*Heavenly Father, grant us the strength to live lives of unwavering integrity. May our actions and words always reflect Your truth and love. In Jesus name, we pray. Amen.*

## DAY 07
## Balancing Work and Life

"Come to me, all you who are weary and burdened, and I will give you rest." - Matthew 11:28 (NIV)

Dear sister, the juggle between work and life can be overwhelming, but remember that God offers rest to the weary. In the chaos, seek His peace. Prioritise your time, knowing that God values both your professional and personal roles. Find harmony by leaning on Him.

*Additional Scripture Reference:*

*"Better a little with the fear of the Lord than great wealth with turmoil." - Proverbs 15:16 (NIV)*

**Action Plan:**

1. Create a balanced schedule with designated time for rest and reflection.

2. Trust God to guide your priorities.

3. Seek support from a faith community.

**Prayer:**

*Gracious Father, help us find balance and rest in the midst of life's demands. May our work glorify You, and our lives be a testament to Your love. In Jesus name, we pray. Amen.*

## DAY 08

## Practicing Mindfulness and Presence

"Be still, and know that I am God." - Psalm 46:10

Dear sister, in the hustle of life, let us heed the call to be still in God's presence. In these moments of mindfulness, we find clarity, peace, and a deeper connection with Him. Be fully present in each moment, for it's in this presence that God's grace unfolds.

*Additional Scripture Reference:*

*"Do not conform to the pattern of this world, but be transformed by the renewing of your mind." - Romans 12:2 (NIV)*

**Action Plan:**

1. Dedicate time daily to mindfulness and prayer.

2. Practice gratitude for the present moment.

3. Let go of distractions to focus on God's presence.

**Prayer:**

*Heavenly Father, help us to be fully present with You and find solace in Your divine presence. Renew our minds and grant us serenity. In Jesus name, we pray. Amen.*

## DAY 09
## Embracing a Life of Eternal Impact

"For we are God's handiwork, created in Christ Jesus to do good works, which God prepared in advance for us to do." - Ephesians 2:10 (NIV)

In the tapestry of life, each thread represents a moment where you can make an eternal impact. God has designed you uniquely, with a purpose that transcends the temporal. Embrace this truth, for in every act of kindness, in every word of encouragement, you are weaving threads of love and hope into the lives of others. Your existence is a divine masterpiece, orchestrated by God Himself.

*Additional Scripture Reference:*

*"Let your light shine before others, that they may see your good deeds and glorify your Father in heaven." - Matthew 5:16 (NIV)*

## Action Plan:

1. Reflect on your unique gifts and talents.

2. Identify one way you can use them to positively impact someone's life today.

## Prayer:

*Dear Heavenly Father, thank you for creating me with a purpose to make an eternal impact. Help me recognize the opportunities you place before me daily. May my actions reflect your love and bring glory to your name. In Jesus name, we pray. Amen.*

## DAY 10
### Living with Abundant Love

*"A new command I give you: Love one another. As I have loved you, so you must love one another." - John 13:34 (NIV)*

Living with abundant love means imitating the boundless love of Christ. His love is a wellspring that never runs dry. It's a love that forgives, uplifts, and serves unconditionally. When we embrace this love, our lives become a beacon of hope, radiating kindness and grace to those around us.

*Additional Scripture Reference:*

*"And over all these virtues put on love, which binds them all together in perfect unity." - Colossians 3:14 (NIV)*

## Action Plan:

1. Practice forgiveness and grace in your interactions today.

2. Find an opportunity to show love to someone in need.

**Prayer:**

*Heavenly Father, help me live each day with the abundant love you have shown me. Teach me to love as you do, unconditionally and selflessly. Use me as an instrument of your love, that others may experience your grace through me. In Jesus name, we pray. Amen.*

## DAY 11
## Surrendering Anxieties to God

"Do not be anxious about anything, but in every situation, by prayer and petition, with thanksgiving, present your requests to God." - Philippians 4:6 (NIV)

Surrendering anxieties to God is a profound act of trust. It's acknowledging that despite life's uncertainties, God's sovereignty reigns supreme. Anxiety can be an oppressive burden, but in surrender, we find liberation. Pour out your worries to the One who knows your heart intimately. He offers peace that transcends understanding. As you release your anxieties, you make room for faith to flourish.

*Additional Scripture Reference:*

*"Cast all your anxiety on him because he cares for you." - 1 Peter 5:7 (NIV)*

**Action Plan:**

1. Take a moment to write down your anxieties and concerns.

2. Spend time in prayer, presenting them to God and trusting in His perfect plan.

**Prayer:**

*Heavenly Father, I surrender my anxieties to You, recognizing Your love and care for me. Grant me the strength to trust Your wisdom and find peace amidst life's uncertainties. May my faith in You grow stronger each day. In Jesus name, we pray. Amen.*

DAY 12
## The Power of Persistent Prayer

"Pray continually." - 1 Thessalonians 5:17 (NIV)

The power of persistent prayer lies in the unwavering connection it forges with God. It's a heartfelt conversation with the Divine, a lifeline of faith. Through persistent prayer, we demonstrate our trust in God's love and His perfect timing. Like a persistent widow seeking justice, let your prayers be relentless, knowing that God hears and responds to the cries of His children. Be inspired to persevere in prayer, for it is in this persistence that miracles are born.

*Additional Scripture Reference:*

*"Ask and it will be given to you; seek and you will find; knock and the door will be opened to you." - Matthew 7:7 (NIV)*

**Action Plan:**

1. Set aside dedicated time each day for prayer.

2. Keep a prayer journal to track your requests and God's responses.

**Prayer:**

*Heavenly Father, I'm grateful for the gift of persistent prayer. Help me to persevere in seeking Your will and trusting Your timing. May my prayers be a testament to my unwavering faith in Your goodness. In Jesus name, we pray. Amen.*

DAY 13
## The Power of a Thankful Heart

"Give thanks in all circumstances; for this is God's will for you in Christ Jesus." - 1 Thessalonians 5:18 (NIV)

The power of a thankful heart is transformative. It transcends circumstances, infusing life with joy and gratitude. When we choose gratitude, we align our hearts with God's will. Even in trials, a thankful heart finds blessings. It is a beacon of hope, radiating positivity and drawing us closer to God. Today, let gratitude be your guiding light, and watch as it illuminates the beauty in every moment.

*Additional Scripture Reference:*

*"Do not be anxious about anything, but in every situation, by prayer and petition, with thanksgiving, present your requests to God." - Philippians 4:6 (NIV)*

**Action Plan:**

1. Start a gratitude journal, listing three things you're thankful for daily.

2. Express your gratitude to someone who has impacted your life.

**Prayer:**

*Heavenly Father, thank You for the power of a thankful heart. Teach me to see Your blessings in every circumstance, and help me express gratitude in all things. May my heart overflow with thanksgiving, bringing glory to Your name. In Jesus name, we pray. Amen.*

## DAY 14
## Stepping into God's Light

"Your word is a lamp for my feet, a light on my path." - Psalm 119:105 (NIV)

Stepping into God's light is an act of surrender, illuminating the path of faith. In His light, darkness dissipates, and clarity emerges. It's an invitation to trust God's guidance. When you step into His light, you step into truth, hope, and purpose. Embrace this journey with courage, for His light reveals the beauty of His plan for your life.

*Additional Scripture Reference:*

*"Then Jesus spoke to them again, saying, 'I am the light of the world. He who follows Me shall not walk in darkness but have the light of life.'" - John 8:12 (NKJV)*

**Action Plan:**

1. Spend time in prayer and Scripture daily to seek God's guidance.

2. Share God's light with someone in need of encouragement.

**Prayer:**

*Heavenly Father, as I step into Your light, may it guide my path and illuminate my purpose. Help me to trust in Your guidance and share Your light with others. In Jesus name, we pray. Amen.*

## DAY 15
## God's Promises for Your Family

"But as for me and my household, we will serve the Lord." - Joshua 24:15b (NIV)

God's promises for your family are a source of strength and hope. In a world filled with uncertainties, His word stands unwavering. He promises guidance, protection, and a legacy of faith. Hold onto His assurance that as you lead your family in serving Him, you're sowing seeds of eternal significance. Embrace the privilege of nurturing a home where God's love and promises are the foundation.

*Additional Scripture Reference:*

*"The Lord bless you and keep you; the Lord make his face shine on you and be gracious to you; the Lord turn his face toward you and give you peace." - Numbers 6:24-26 (NIV)*

**Action Plan:**

1. Dedicate time for family prayer and Bible study.

2. Encourage each family member to reflect on God's promises for your family.

**Prayer:**

*Heavenly Father, thank You for Your promises for my family. Help us to serve You faithfully and be a testament to Your love and grace. May Your blessings and peace abound in our home. In Jesus name, we pray. Amen.*

## DAY 16
## Growing in Humility

"Humble yourselves before the Lord, and he will lift you up." - James 4:10 (NIV)

Growing in humility is a journey of the heart. It's the art of putting others before oneself, mirroring Christ's servanthood. In humility, we find strength and grace. It's an act of surrender, recognizing our dependency on God. As women of faith, let humility be our garment, embracing the beauty of serving others with love and compassion. Through it, we draw closer to God's heart and experience the transformative power of His exaltation.

*Additional Scripture Reference:*

*"Do nothing out of selfish ambition or vain conceit. Rather, in humility, value others above yourselves." - Philippians 2:3 (NIV)*

**Action Plan:**

1. Practice acts of kindness and service to others daily.

2. Reflect on moments where humility can deepen your relationships.

**Prayer:**

*Dear Lord, help me grow in humility, following the example of Jesus. Teach me to value others above myself and to serve with a humble heart. May Your grace be my guide in this journey. In Jesus name, we pray. Amen.*

## DAY 17
## Finding Freedom in Christ

"So if the Son sets you free, you will be free indeed." - John 8:36 (NIV)

Finding freedom in Christ is a profound liberation of the soul. It's breaking the chains of sin, guilt, and worldly burdens. In Christ, we discover forgiveness, grace, and purpose. The shackles of fear and insecurity fall away as His love envelops us. As women of faith, we're called to embrace this freedom daily, walking confidently in the light of His truth and love.

*Additional Scripture Reference:*

*"It is for freedom that Christ has set us free. Stand firm, then, and do not let yourselves be burdened again by a yoke of slavery." - Galatians 5:1 (NIV)*

## Action Plan:

1. Reflect on areas of your life where you need to experience greater freedom in Christ.

2. Seek His guidance in prayer and meditate on Scriptures that affirm your freedom.

## Prayer:

*Heavenly Father, thank You for the freedom found in Christ. Help me stand firm in this liberty, casting aside burdens that weigh me down. May Your grace empower me to live a life of joy and purpose. In Jesus name, we pray. Amen.*

## DAY 18
## The Power of a Renewed Mind

*"Do not conform to the pattern of this world, but be transformed by the renewing of your mind. Then you will be able to test and approve what God's will is—his good, pleasing, and perfect will." - Romans 12:2 (NIV)*

The power of a renewed mind is a divine transformation. It's shedding the old, worldly ways of thinking and embracing God's truth. When we allow our minds to be renewed by His Word, we gain clarity, wisdom, and discernment. As women of faith, let this renewal be a daily practice, unlocking the potential to align our thoughts with God's will and experience the fullness of His blessings.

*Additional Scripture Reference:*

*"Let this mind be in you which was also in Christ Jesus." - Philippians 2:5 (NKJV)*

## Action Plan:

1. Fast and Pray with Scriptures for renewal of your mind.

2. Talk to God in prayer about your fears and desires.

## Prayer:

Heavenly Father, I seek the power of a renewed mind. Transform my thoughts to align with Your truth and will. May my mind reflect the likeness of Christ, and may my actions follow. In Jesus name, we pray. Amen.

## DAY 19
## The Blessings of Obedience

"Blessed rather are those who hear the word of God and obey it." - Luke 11:28 (NIV)

The blessings of obedience are profound and life-transforming. When we align our lives with God's commands, we open the door to His favour, protection, and guidance. Obedience is a pathway to experiencing His promises in abundance. As women of faith, let us recognize that obedience is not a burden but a source of immeasurable blessings. Embrace God's Word, walk in His ways, and witness the fulfilment of His extraordinary promises.

*Additional Scripture Reference:*

*"The Lord rewards everyone for their righteousness and faithfulness." - 1 Samuel 26:23 (NIV)*

## Action Plan:

1. Identify an area in your life where you can demonstrate obedience to God's Word.

2. Daily meditate on Scriptures that reinforce the blessings of obedience.

**Prayer:**

*Heavenly Father, help us understand the blessings of obedience. Strengthen our resolve to heed Your word and follow Your commands. May Your favour and guidance be our constant companions. In Jesus name, we pray. Amen.*

## DAY 20
### God's Plan for Your Family

"For I know the plans I have for you," declares the Lord, "plans to prosper you and not to harm you, plans to give you hope and a future." - Jeremiah 29:11 (NIV)

God's plan for your family is a masterpiece of divine purpose. It's a tapestry woven with love, guidance, and grace. He desires prosperity, not only in material abundance but also in spiritual richness. Embrace His plan, for in it, you'll find hope and a future filled with His blessings. As women of faith, let us trust in God's sovereign design for our families, seeking His wisdom to nurture a home that reflects His love.

*Additional Scripture Reference:*

*"Unless the Lord builds the house, the builders labour in vain." - Psalm 127:1a (NIV)*

**Action Plan:**

1. Dedicate time for family prayer and Scripture reading.

2. Encourage open communication and spiritual growth within your family.

**Prayer:**

*Heavenly Father, we trust in Your plan for our families. Guide us in building a home rooted in Your love and wisdom. May our lives reflect Your purpose and bring glory to Your name. In Jesus name, we pray. Amen.*

## DAY 21

## Living with Intention

"Teach us to number our days, that we may gain a heart of wisdom." - Psalm 90:12
(NIV)

Living with intention is a call to seize each day with purpose and mindfulness. It's recognizing that our time on earth is a precious gift from God. In intentional living, we find wisdom, fulfilment, and impact. It's a commitment to align our actions with our values and God's will. As women of faith, let us embark on this journey with hearts open to God's guidance, making each day count by loving, serving, and growing in Him.

*Additional Scripture Reference:*

*"So whether you eat or drink or whatever you do, do it all for the glory of God." - 1 Corinthians 10:31 (NIV)*

**Action Plan:**

1. Set daily intentions that reflect your faith and values.

2. Prioritise moments of prayer and reflection throughout your day.

**Prayer:**

*Heavenly Father, teach us to live with intention, honouring You in all we do. Grant us wisdom to prioritise what matters most and make each day a testimony of Your grace. In Jesus name, we pray. Amen.*

## DAY 22
## Focusing on Eternal Values

"Do not store up for yourselves treasures on earth, where moths and vermin destroy, and where thieves break in and steal. But store up for yourselves treasures in heaven, where moths and vermin do not destroy, and where thieves do not break in and steal." - Matthew 6:19-20 (NIV)

Focusing on eternal values is a profound shift in perspective. It's recognizing that the world's fleeting pleasures pale in comparison to the lasting treasures of heaven. As women of faith, let us invest our time, love, and resources in what matters eternally - acts of kindness, faith, and love. Embrace a life that reflects Christ's teachings, for therein lies the promise of imperishable riches and a heart that finds ultimate fulfilment.

*Additional Scripture Reference:*

*"But seek first his kingdom and his righteousness, and all these things will be given to you as well." - Matthew 6:33 (NIV)*

## Action Plan:

1. Reflect on your daily choices and their alignment with eternal values.

2. Seek opportunities to engage in acts of love and service that reflect God's kingdom.

## Prayer:

*Heavenly Father, help us to focus on eternal values and Your kingdom above all else. Guide our choices and priorities, that our lives may bear witness to Your grace. May we store up treasures in heaven and find lasting fulfilment in You. In Jesus name, we pray. Amen.*

## DAY 23
## God's Healing Touch

"He heals the brokenhearted and binds up their wounds." - Psalm 147:3 (NIV)

God's healing touch is a balm for the wounded soul. It's a comforting embrace in times of pain and sorrow. His love brings restoration to our brokenness, renewing our spirits with hope and peace. As women of faith, let us open our hearts to His healing touch, trusting in His perfect timing and unfailing love. In our vulnerability, we find His strength, and in our pain, we discover His comforting presence.

*Additional Scripture Reference:*

*"He himself bore our sins in his body on the cross so that we might die to sins and live for righteousness; 'by his wounds you have been healed.'" - 1 Peter 2:24 (NIV)*

**Action Plan:**

1. Reflect on areas of your life where you need God's healing touch.

2. Spend time in prayer, surrendering your hurts and seeking His healing.

**Prayer:**

*Heavenly Father, we come before you with hearts in need of healing. Touch us with Your love and grace, and bind up our wounds. May we find solace in Your presence and strength in our weakness. In Jesus name, we pray. Amen.*

## DAY 24
## God's Strength in Times of Global Challenges

Isaiah 41:10 (NIV) - "So do not fear, for I am with you; do not be dismayed, for I am your God. I will strengthen you and help you; I will uphold you with my righteous right hand."

In the face of global challenges that can leave us feeling overwhelmed, remember these words from Isaiah. God's strength is our refuge, and His unwavering presence sustains us through every trial. When the world seems uncertain, He is our steadfast anchor.

*Additional Scripture Reference:*

*2 Corinthians 12:9-10*

*' Therefore I will boast all the more gladly about my weaknesses, so that Christ's power may rest on me. That is why, for Christ's sake, I delight in weaknesses, in insults, in hardships, in persecutions, in difficulties. For when I am weak, then I am strong."*

**Action Plan:**

1. Seek His Word daily to find solace and guidance.

2. Reach out to support and uplift those around us.

3. Trust in God's providence, believing that He works all things for good.

**Prayer:**

*Dear Heavenly Father, we thank You for Your unchanging strength during turbulent times. May Your presence empower us to face global challenges with unwavering faith, compassion, and resilience. In Jesus name, we pray. Amen.*

## DAY 25
## The Power of Unity in Achieving Peace

Ephesians 4:3 (NIV) - "Make every effort to keep the unity of the Spirit through the bond of peace."

In the pursuit of peace, unity is our most potent weapon. When women come together, bound by love and understanding, we create a force that can mend brokenness and bring tranquillity to our world. Just as God desires unity among His children, let us join hands and hearts to achieve lasting peace.

*Additional Scripture Reference:*

*Ephesians 4:4-6*

*4 There is one body and one Spirit, just as you were called to one hope when you were called; 5 one Lord, one faith, one baptism; 6 one God and Father of all, who is over all and through all and in all.*

**Action Plan:**

1. Listen and empathise with those different from us.

2. Engage in acts of kindness that bridge divides.

3. Pray for harmony, guided by God's Word.

**Prayer:**

## DAY 26
## The Blessing of Empowering Other

Proverbs 11:25 (NIV) - "A generous person will prosper; whoever refreshes others will be refreshed."

Empowering others is a divine blessing that multiplies blessings. When we lift each other up, we not only enrich their lives but also find enrichment in our own. This act of love mirrors God's heart, who empowers us to empower others.

*Additional Scripture Reference:*

*Ephesians 4 12*

*Their responsibility is to equip God's people to do his work and build up the church, the body of Christ.*

**Action Plan:**

1. Identify opportunities to mentor, support, and encourage.

2. Share your knowledge and resources generously.

3. Pray for guidance to be a source of strength to those in need.

**Prayer:**

*Heavenly Father, help us recognize the joy and fulfilment in empowering others. May our actions reflect Your grace and love, fostering growth and transformation. In Jesus name, we pray. Amen.*

## DAY 27

# Trusting God's Provision for the Needy

Psalm 146:7 (NIV) - "He upholds the cause of the oppressed and gives food to the hungry. The Lord sets prisoners free."

In times of need, God's provision is a testament to His unwavering love. Just as He cares for the lilies of the field, He ensures that the needy are not forgotten. We, as women of faith, are called to trust in God's provision for those less fortunate.

*Additional Scripture Reference:*

*Matthew 25:40*

*'Truly I tell you, whatever you did for one of the least of these brothers and sisters of mine, you did for me. '*

## Action Plan:

1. Seek out opportunities to help the needy in your community.

2. Donate your time, resources, and talents to charitable causes.

3. Pray for God's guidance and provision for those in need.

## Prayer:

*Heavenly Father, grant us the heart to trust in Your provision for the needy. May we be instruments of Your love and compassion in a world that hungers for both. In Jesus name, we pray. Amen.*

## DAY 28
## Trusting God's Guidance in Peacemaking

Matthew 5:9 (NIV) - "Blessed are the peacemakers, for they will be called children of God."

In a world often marred by conflict, women can play a vital role as peacemakers. Trusting in God's guidance, we find strength to sow seeds of reconciliation and unity. Blessed are those who actively pursue peace, for they mirror the character of our Heavenly Father.

*Additional Scripture Reference:*

*Isaiah 26:3 ~ You keep him in perfect peace whose mind is stayed on you, because he trusts in you.*

**Action Plan:**

1. Listen attentively to all perspectives involved.

2. Humbly seek common ground and understanding.

3. Pray fervently for divine wisdom in resolving conflicts.

**Prayer:**

*Lord, grant us the courage to be peacemakers, channelling Your grace and healing in a fractured world. May Your peace reign in our hearts and actions. In Jesus name, we pray. Amen.*

## DAY 29
## The Power of Building Bridges

Colossians 3:14 (NIV) - "And over all these virtues put on love, which binds them all together in perfect unity."

Building bridges is an act of love that unites what may seem divided. As women of faith, we hold the power to mend broken relationships, bridge cultural gaps, and foster unity. Love, as the binding force, reflects God's desire for harmony among His children.

*Additional Scripture Reference:*

*Romans 13 4*

*for he is God's servant for your good. But if you do wrong, be afraid, for he does not bear the sword in vain. For he is the servant of God, an avenger who carries out God's wrath on the wrongdoer.*

**Action Plan:**

1.  Approach differences with empathy, seeking to understand.

2.  Initiate conversations that promote reconciliation and understanding.

3.  Pray for God's guidance in bridging divides, rooted in His love.

**Prayer:**

*Heavenly Father, help us become bridge builders, connecting hearts in a fragmented world. May love be our cornerstone, bringing unity and healing to all. In Jesus name, we pray. Amen.*

## DAY 30
## The Beauty of Restorative Justice

Isaiah 1:17 (NIV) - "Learn to do right; seek justice. Defend the oppressed. Take up the cause of the fatherless; plead the case of the widow."

The beauty of restorative justice lies in its reflection of God's heart for reconciliation and healing. As women of faith, we're called to embrace this divine concept, seeking to mend brokenness, uplift the oppressed, and restore dignity. In the act of restoration, we mirror God's grace and mercy.

*Additional Scripture Reference:*

*Leviticus 19 15*

*"Do not twist justice in legal matters by favouring the poor or being partial to the rich and powerful. Always judge people fairly.*

## Action Plan:

1. Advocate for fair and compassionate solutions in conflicts.

2. Support organisations that aid the marginalised.

3. Pray for the strength and wisdom to bring restoration to broken lives.

## Prayer:

*Heavenly Father, grant us the courage to be instruments of Your restorative justice, bringing healing and hope to a hurting world. In Jesus name, we pray. Amen.*

# DECEMBER

*The Lord your God will put all these curses on your enemies who hate and persecute you. You will again obey the Lord and follow all his commands I am giving you today. Deuteronomy 30:7–8 (NIV)*

## DAY 01
## The Gift of Healing Wounds

Psalm 147:3 (NIV) - "He heals the brokenhearted and binds up their wounds."

God's gift of healing wounds is a testament to His boundless love and compassion. As women of faith, we have the privilege of extending this gift to others by offering love, understanding, and forgiveness. In the process, we witness God's transformative power.

**Action Plan:**

1. Extend forgiveness, releasing the burden of bitterness.

2. Offer a listening ear and a compassionate heart to those hurting.

3. Pray for God's healing touch in the lives of the wounded.

**Prayer:**

Heavenly Father, grant us the grace to be agents of Your healing in a wounded world. May Your love flow through us, bringing restoration and hope to those in need. In Jesus name, we pray. Amen.

## DAY 02
## God's Strength in Times of Hatred

Psalm 18:32 (NIV) - "It is God who arms me with strength and keeps my way secure."

316

In a world sometimes consumed by hatred, God's strength becomes our refuge. As women of faith, we draw upon His unwavering power to combat the darkness of animosity with love and grace. Through Him, we find the strength to persevere, to love our enemies, and to shine as beacons of hope.

**Action Plan:**

1. Pray for a heart filled with compassion.

2. Seek opportunities to build bridges and foster understanding.

3. Remember Jesus example of love and forgiveness.

**Prayer:**

Heavenly Father, empower us to overcome hatred with Your love and strength. May Your grace transform our hearts and inspire reconciliation in a divided world. In Jesus name, we pray. Amen.

## DAY 03
### God's Strength in Times of Injustice

Micah 6:8 (NIV) - "He has shown you, O mortal, what is good. And what does the Lord require of you? To act justly and to love mercy and to walk humbly with your God."

In times of injustice, God's strength emboldens us to champion righteousness. As women of faith, we heed His call to stand against oppression, extending His love and justice to the marginalised. With His strength, we become agents of change, fighting for equality and fairness.

**Action Plan:**

1. Advocate for the voiceless and vulnerable.

2. Engage in peaceful activism for justice.

3. Pray for God's guidance in promoting equity.

**Prayer:**

## DAY 04
### Living a Life of Inclusivity

Galatians 3:28 (NIV) - "There is neither Jew nor Gentile, neither slave nor free, nor is there male and female, for you are all one in Christ Jesus."

Living a life of inclusivity mirrors Christ's all-encompassing love. As women of faith, we're called to break down barriers, embracing diversity, and fostering unity. In Christ, there is no distinction; we are all equal members of His body.

**Action Plan:**

1. Cultivate empathy to understand different perspectives.

2. Actively seek out opportunities to build bridges across divides.

3. Pray for God's guidance in creating an inclusive community.

**Prayer:**

*Dear God, empower us to live inclusively, imitating Christ's love. May our lives reflect Your all-embracing grace and unity, inspiring others to join us on this journey of inclusion. In Jesus name, we pray. Amen.*

## DAY 05
### Trusting God's Wisdom in Environmental Stewardship

Genesis 2:15 (NIV) - "The Lord God took the man and put him in the Garden of Eden to work it and take care of it."

Trusting God's wisdom in environmental stewardship is a testament to our faith in His creation. As women of faith, we're entrusted with the sacred duty of caring for the Earth. God's wisdom, evident in nature, guides us to preserve and protect our environment.

**Action Plan:**

1. Reduce waste and conserve resources in daily life.

2. Support eco-friendly initiatives and advocate for sustainable practices.

3. Pray for God's guidance in responsible stewardship.

**Prayer:**

*Heavenly Father, grant us the wisdom and strength to care for Your creation as faithful stewards. May our actions reflect Your love for the world You've entrusted to our care. In Jesus name, we pray. Amen.*

## DAY 06
### God's Comfort in Times of Discrimination

Isaiah 41:10 (NIV) - "So do not fear, for I am with you; do not be dismayed, for I am your God. I will strengthen you and help you; I will uphold you with my righteous right hand."

In times of discrimination, God's comforting presence is our refuge. As women of faith, we know that His love transcends prejudice, offering solace and strength. We are not alone in our struggles; the Almighty stands by our side.

**Action Plan:**

1. Lean on a supportive community of faith.

2. Educate and raise awareness about discrimination.

3. Pray for God's guidance to promote justice and unity.

**Prayer:**

Heavenly Father, in the face of discrimination, grants us Your comfort and courage to stand against injustice. May Your love prevail, bringing healing and transformation to our world. In Jesus name, we pray. Amen.

## DAY 07
## Finding Joy in Music and Art

Psalm 98:4 (NIV) - "Shout for joy to the Lord, all the earth, burst into jubilant song with music."

In the harmonious realms of music and art, we discover profound joy that resonates with our souls. As women of faith, these creative expressions uplift our spirits and connect us with God's beauty. In the midst of life's challenges, we find solace and inspiration through melodies and brushstrokes.

**Action Plan:**

1. Set aside moments for creative appreciation in daily life.

2. Engage in artistic activities that foster self-expression.

3. Reflect on the spiritual messages conveyed through artistic creations.

**Prayer:**

Lord, thank You for the gift of music and art that brings joy to our hearts. May we find inspiration and draw closer to You through these beautiful forms of expression. In Jesus name, we pray. Amen.

## DAY 08
## Trusting God's Plan in Global Crises

Isaiah 55:8-9 (NIV) - "For my thoughts are not your thoughts, neither are your ways my ways," declares the Lord. "As the heavens are higher than the earth, so are my ways higher than your ways and my thoughts than your thoughts."

In the turbulence of global crises, trusting God's plan can be challenging. As women of faith, we find solace in knowing that God's wisdom surpasses our understanding. Even in the darkest times, His divine purpose unfolds.

**Action Plan:**

1. Anchor yourself in prayer and seek His guidance.

2. Extend compassion to those affected by crises.

3. Act as agents of hope, reflecting His love.

**Prayer:**

*Heavenly Father, grant us the faith to trust Your plan, even in uncertain times. May we be a beacon of hope in a world seeking answers. In Jesus name, we pray. Amen.*

## DAY 09
## Finding Peace in a Hectic World

Philippians 4:7 (NIV) - "And the peace of God, which transcends all understanding, will guard your hearts and your minds in Christ Jesus."

In the chaos of a fast-paced world, finding peace becomes a precious pursuit. As women of faith, we turn to God, the source of unshakable serenity. His peace, surpassing understanding, envelops us in the midst of life's storms.

**Action Plan:**

1. Prioritise daily moments of prayer and reflection.

2. Practice mindfulness to stay present and centred.

3. Share the gift of peace by extending kindness and patience.

**Prayer:**

*Heavenly Father, grant us Your peace that transcends understanding. May it calm our hearts and radiate to those around us, bringing solace to a frenzied world. In Jesus name, we pray. Amen.*

## DAY 10
### Perseverance in Pursuing Dreams

Philippians 3:14 (NIV) - "I press on toward the goal to win the prize for which God has called me heavenward in Christ Jesus."

Perseverance in pursuing dreams is a testament to our faith. As women of purpose, we encounter obstacles but cling to God's promises. Just as Paul pressed on towards his heavenly calling, we persist in our earthly pursuits, trusting God's plan.

**Action Plan:**

1. Keep your vision alive through prayer and vision boards.

2. Seek mentors who can offer guidance and support.

3. Take daily steps, no matter how small, towards your dream.

**Prayer:**

*Heavenly Father, grant us the strength to persevere in our dreams. May our pursuits bring glory to You and fulfil Your divine purpose for our lives. In Jesus name, we pray. Amen.*

## DAY 11
### The Gift of Hospitality

1 Peter 4:9 (NIV) - "Offer hospitality to one another without grumbling."

The gift of hospitality is a radiant expression of love and warmth. As women of faith, we are called to open our hearts and homes to others, mirroring God's grace. In our acts of hospitality, we create spaces where souls find comfort, acceptance, and nourishment.

**Action Plan:**

1. Welcome others with a genuine smile and open arms.

2. Cultivate an atmosphere of love and inclusion.

3. Practice hospitality even in small, everyday gestures.

**Prayer:**

*Heavenly Father, help us embrace the gift of hospitality, reflecting Your boundless love and hospitality towards us. May our homes and hearts be places of refuge and grace. In Jesus name, we pray. Amen.*

## DAY 12
## God's Strength in the Workplace

Philippians 4:13 (NIV) - "I can do all this through him who gives me strength."

In the hustle of the workplace, God's strength becomes our anchor. As women of faith, we draw upon His unwavering power to navigate challenges, exhibit resilience, and spread His light. Our daily toil transforms into an opportunity to glorify Him.

**Action Plan:**

1. Begin each day with prayer, seeking His guidance and peace.

2. Maintain integrity and kindness in all interactions.

3. Inspire others through your work, reflecting God's grace.

**Prayer:**

*Heavenly Father, grant us Your strength in the workplace. May our efforts honour You and inspire others to seek Your strength as well. In Jesus name, we pray. Amen.*

## DAY 13
## Trusting God's Wisdom in Aging

Proverbs 16:31 (NIV) - "Gray hair is a crown of splendor; it is attained in the way of righteousness."

Trusting God's wisdom in aging is embracing the beauty of a life well-lived. As women, growing older can be a journey of grace, filled with lessons and experiences. God's plan for our lives continues to unfold, offering us wisdom, resilience, and opportunities to inspire others.

**Action Plan:**

1. Reflect on your life's journey and the wisdom gained.

2. Share your experiences and insights with younger generations.

3. Seek God's guidance for this new season of life.

**Prayer:**

*Heavenly Father, we thank You for the wisdom that comes with age. Guide us in embracing the richness of this journey, and may our lives shine as a testament to Your faithfulness. In Jesus name, we pray. Amen.*

## DAY 14
## Surrendering Your Desires to God

Proverbs 19:21 (NIV) - "Many are the plans in a person's heart, but it is the Lord's purpose that prevails."

Surrendering your desires to God is an act of faith that unveils His divine plan. As women of faith, we often have dreams and aspirations, but by yielding them to God, we acknowledge His higher purpose. Surrender invites His guidance, transforming our desires into His will.

**Action Plan:**

1. Spend time in prayer, seeking His guidance and peace.

2. Align your desires with His Word and values.

3. Trust in His timing and embrace His plans for your life.

**Prayer:**

*Heavenly Father, we surrender our desires to You, trusting in Your perfect plan. May our lives reflect Your purpose, and may our hearts find contentment in Your will. In Jesus name, we pray. Amen.*

## DAY 15
## God's Comfort in Natural Disasters

Psalm 46:1 (NIV) - "God is our refuge and strength, an ever-present help in trouble."

In the face of natural disasters, God's comfort is our refuge. As women of faith, we find solace in His promise to be with us in times of turmoil. His presence brings strength to endure and reassurance that we are not alone.

**Action Plan:**

1. Seek safety and shelter for yourself and others.

2. Extend a helping hand to those affected.

3. Pray for God's protection and guidance in the midst of the crisis.

**Prayer:**

*Heavenly Father, be our refuge and strength in times of natural disasters. Grant us the courage to assist those in need, and may Your comforting presence bring hope and healing. In Jesus name, we pray. Amen.*

## DAY 16
## Finding Joy in Creativity

Genesis 1:27 (NIV) - "So God created mankind in his own image, in the image of God he created them."

Finding joy in creativity is a divine reflection of our Creator. As women of faith, our creativity is a source of inspiration and fulfilment. When we express ourselves through art, music, or any form of creativity, we tap into the joy of mirroring God's image.

**Action Plan:**

1.  Carve out time for creative pursuits in your daily life.

2.  Share your creative gifts to uplift and inspire others.

3.  Reflect on God's creativity in the world around you.

**Prayer:**

*Heavenly Father, thank You for the gift of creativity. May our creative expressions bring joy to our hearts and glory to Your name. In Jesus name, we pray. Amen.*

## DAY 17
## Hope for a Bright Future

Jeremiah 29:11 (NIV) - "For I know the plans I have for you," declares the Lord, "plans to prosper you and not to harm you, plans to give you hope and a future."

Hope for a bright future springs from God's promise. As women of faith, we anchor our dreams and aspirations in His assurance of a purposeful tomorrow. Even amidst life's uncertainties, His plans for us are filled with hope and promise.

**Action Plan:**

1.  Pray for guidance, entrusting your future to God.

2. Set clear goals and take daily steps towards them.

3. Encourage others with hope-filled words and actions.

**Prayer:**

*Heavenly Father, thank You for the hope of a bright future. Guide us in faith, purpose, and resilience, knowing Your plans for us are filled with promise. In Jesus name, we pray. Amen.*

## DAY 18
## Growing in Spiritual Resilience

Psalm 46:1-2 (NIV) - "God is our refuge and strength, an ever-present help in trouble. Therefore, we will not fear."

Growing in spiritual resilience is a journey of unwavering faith. As women of faith, we face trials that test our endurance, but God remains our refuge. Our resilience blossoms as we lean into His strength, knowing that in every challenge, He is our ever-present help.

**Action Plan:**

1. Deepen your relationship with God through daily prayer and Scripture.

2. Seek community support and share your faith journey.

3. Embrace challenges as opportunities for spiritual growth.

**Prayer:**

*Heavenly Father, grant us the strength to grow in spiritual resilience. May our unwavering faith in You be a beacon of hope to others. In Jesus name, we pray. Amen.*

## DAY 19
## Trusting God's Purpose in Singleness

1 Corinthians 7:17 (NIV) - "Nevertheless, each person should live as a believer in whatever situation the Lord has assigned to them, just as God has called them."

Trusting God's purpose in singleness is an affirmation of His divine plan. As women of faith, we may long for companionship, but in singleness, we discover unique opportunities to serve and grow. Our trust in God's timing empowers us to embrace this season with purpose.

**Action Plan:**

1. Seek His guidance through prayer and discernment.

2. Focus on self-improvement and spiritual growth.

3. Engage in fulfilling activities that serve others and bring joy.

**Prayer:**

*Heavenly Father, grant us the strength to trust Your purpose in singleness. May we find contentment and fulfilment in serving You while we wait for Your perfect timing. In Jesus name, we pray. Amen.*

## DAY 20
### Restoring Trust in Yourself

Proverbs 3:5-6 (NIV) - "Trust in the Lord with all your heart and lean not on your own understanding; in all your ways submit to him, and he will make your paths straight."

Restoring trust in yourself is a profound journey of faith. As women of God, we may face moments of doubt, but God calls us to trust in His wisdom. With His guidance, we can overcome self-doubt, believing in our worth and purpose.

*Additional Scripture Reference:*

*Psalms 56:3–5*

*3 What time I am afraid, I will trust in thee. 4 In God I will praise his word, in God I have put my trust; I will not fear what flesh can do unto me. 5 Every day they wrest my words: all their thoughts are against me for evil.*

## Action Plan:

1. Seek God's counsel through prayer and meditation on His Word.

2. Replace self-criticism with self-compassion.

3. Surround yourself with supportive, faith-filled companions.

## Prayer:

*Heavenly Father, help us restore trust in ourselves through unwavering faith in You. May we find confidence in Your purpose for our lives. In Jesus name, we pray. Amen.*

## DAY 21
## God's Strength in Times of Sickness

Isaiah 41:10 (NIV) - "So do not fear, for I am with you; do not be dismayed, for I am your God. I will strengthen you and help you; I will uphold you with my righteous right hand."

In the depths of sickness, God's strength becomes our rock. As women of faith, we draw on His unwavering presence and healing grace. In our weakness, His power is made perfect.

*Additional Scripture Reference:*

*Isaiah 41:10 - God strengthens you*

*I will strengthen you and help you; I will uphold you with my righteous right hand. God has promised us His strength. He will never give you a trial you are unable to handle. As children of God, we can call upon His power at any time.*

## Action Plan:

1. Lean on Him through prayer and surrender.

2. Seek medical help and support from loved ones.

3. Trust in His plan, knowing that He is our ultimate healer.

## Prayer:

*Heavenly Father, in times of sickness, grant us Your strength, comfort, and healing touch. May our faith grow stronger as we rely on You. In Jesus name, we pray. Amen.*

## DAY 22
## Trusting God's Timing in Career

Ecclesiastes 3:11 (NIV) - "He has made everything beautiful in its time."

Trusting God's timing in our careers is a testament of faith. As women of purpose, we often face moments of impatience or doubt. Yet, God's plan unfolds at precisely the right moment, making our journey beautiful and purposeful.

*Additional Scripture Reference:*

*"He has made everything beautiful in its time. Also, he has put eternity into man's heart, yet so that he cannot find out what God has done from the beginning to the end."*

Ecclesiastes 3:11. From the poetic Ecclesiastes, this Bible verse offers a reminder that God made the entire universe and it is all beautiful.

**Action Plan:**

1. Seek His guidance through prayer and reflection.

2. Be diligent and patient, knowing He prepares you.

3. Embrace opportunities with a heart filled with gratitude.

**Prayer:**

*Heavenly Father, help us trust Your perfect timing in our careers. May we find peace and purpose in every season, knowing You orchestrate our path. In Jesus name, we pray. Amen.*

## DAY 23
## The Blessing of New Beginnings

Isaiah 43:19 (NIV) - "See, I am doing a new thing! Now it springs up; do you not perceive it? I am making a way in the wilderness and streams in the wasteland."

The blessing of new beginnings is a testament to God's grace. As women of faith, we find hope and renewal in His promise of fresh starts. In moments of change, we are reminded of His ability to create beauty from ashes.

*Additional Scripture Reference:*

*2 Corinthians 5:17: "Therefore, if anyone is in Christ, the new creation has come: The old has gone, the new is here!"*

*Psalm 46:10: "Be still, and know that I am God. I will be exalted among the nations, I will be exalted in the earth!"*

*Isaiah 40:31: "But those who hope in the Lord will renew their strength.*

**Action Plan:**

1. Let go of past regrets and embrace forgiveness.

2. Welcome change with faith, knowing God is with you.

3. Seek His guidance in each new step forward.

**Prayer:**

*Heavenly Father, thank You for the blessing of new beginnings. May we walk in faith, confident in Your plans for our future. In Jesus name, we pray. Amen.*

## DAY 24
## God's Comfort in Loneliness

Psalm 34:18 (NIV) - "The Lord is close to the brokenhearted and saves those who are crushed in spirit."

God's comfort in loneliness is a lifeline for our souls. As women of faith, we may experience moments of isolation, but in those times, we find solace in the Lord's presence. He draws near to mend our broken hearts and fill the void.

*Additional Scripture Reference:*

*2 Corinthians 1:3*

*Blessed be the God and Father of our Lord Jesus Christ, the Father of mercies and God of all comfort, who comforts us in all our affliction, so that we may be able to comfort those who are in any affliction, with the comfort with which we ourselves are comforted by God.*

**Action Plan:**

1. Seek His companionship through prayer and meditation.

2. Reach out to a faith community or support group.

3. Use your solitude to deepen your relationship with God.

**Prayer:**

*Heavenly Father, in moments of loneliness, be our refuge and strength. Fill our hearts with Your presence, reminding us that we are never truly alone. In Jesus name, we pray. Amen.*

## DAY 25
## The Gift of Self-Reflection

Psalm 139:23-24 (NIV) - "Search me, God, and know my heart; test me and know my anxious thoughts. See if there is any offensive way in me, and lead me in the way everlasting."

The gift of self-reflection is a divine invitation to draw closer to God. As women of faith, we set aside moments for introspection, allowing God to reveal our hearts. In this quiet communion, we find growth, transformation, and the path to everlasting joy.

*Additional Scripture Reference:*

*1 Corinthians 13:12*

*For now we see only a reflection as in a mirror; then we shall see face to face. Now I know in part; then I shall know fully, even as I am fully known.*

**Action Plan:**

1. Dedicate time each day for prayerful self-examination.

2. Humbly confront areas needing improvement with God's guidance.

3. Cultivate gratitude for the journey of self-discovery.

**Prayer:**

*Heavenly Father, thank You for the gift of self-reflection. May it lead us closer to Your light and grace, making us vessels of Your love. In Jesus name, we pray. Amen.*

## DAY 26
## Growing in Spiritual Maturity

2 Peter 3:18 (NIV) - "But grow in the grace and knowledge of our Lord and Savior Jesus Christ. To him be glory both now and forever! Amen."

Growing in spiritual maturity is a journey of deepening faith. As women of God, we're called to seek wisdom and become more like Christ each day. In this growth, we find strength, grace, and the ability to navigate life's challenges.

*Additional Scripture Reference:*

*Ephesians 4:13*

*until we all reach unity in the faith and in the knowledge of the Son of God and become mature, attaining to the whole measure of the fullness of Christ.*

## Action Plan:

1. Dive into God's Word daily, seeking understanding.

2. Cultivate a heart of gratitude, even in adversity.

3. Serve others selflessly, reflecting Christ's love.

## Prayer:

*Heavenly Father, guide us on the path of spiritual maturity. May we continuously grow in Your grace and knowledge, becoming beacons of Your light. In Jesus name, we pray. Amen.*

## DAY 27
## Hope for a New Beginning

Lamentations 3:22-23 (NIV) - "Because of the Lord's great love we are not consumed, for his compassions never fail. They are new every morning; great is your faithfulness."

Hope for a new beginning emerges from God's unfailing compassion. As women of faith, we find renewal in the promise of each new day. His love and faithfulness, like the dawn, bring light to our darkest moments.

*Additional Scripture Reference:*

*Jeremiah 29:11*

*"'For I know the plans I have for you,' declares the LORD, 'plans to prosper you and not to harm you, plans to give you hope and a future. '" This is one of the most powerful Bible verses about new beginnings.*

**Action Plan:**

1. Let go of past regrets and embrace forgiveness.

2. Start anew with gratitude and faith in God's plan.

3. Seek His guidance in each step forward.

**Prayer:**

*Heavenly Father, thank You for the hope of a fresh start. May Your compassion renew us daily, guiding us toward a brighter future. In Jesus name, we pray. Amen.*

## DAY 28
## Finding Peace in Stillness

Psalm 46:10 (NIV) - "Be still, and know that I am God; I will be exalted among the nations, I will be exalted in the earth."

Finding peace in stillness is a divine invitation. As women of faith, we often rush through life's demands, but God calls us to pause, seeking Him in quietude. In the hush of the moment, we encounter His presence, gaining clarity and tranquillity.

*Additional Scripture Reference:*

*Mark 4:39. "And he awoke and rebuked the wind and said to the sea, 'Peace! Be still!' And the wind ceased, and there was a great calm."*

**Action Plan:**

1. Set aside dedicated moments for silent reflection and prayer.

2. Disconnect from distractions to create an oasis of serenity.

3. Listen attentively for God's whispers in the silence.

**Prayer:**

*Heavenly Father, in stillness, we find Your peace. May we seek Your presence in the quiet moments of life, finding solace and strength in You. In Jesus name, we pray. Amen.*

## DAY 29
### Letting Go and Letting God

Proverbs 3:5-6 (NIV) - "Trust in the Lord with all your heart and lean not on your own understanding; in all your ways submit to him, and he will make your paths straight."

"Letting go and letting God" is an act of surrender rooted in deep trust. As women of faith, we often grasp for control, but God calls us to release our burdens into His capable hands. In this surrender, we find peace, freedom, and the assurance that His divine plan prevails.

*Additional Scripture Reference:*

*Psalm 118:6 The LORD is with me; I will not be afraid. What can mere mortals do to me?*

*Psalm 115:11 You who fear him, trust in the LORD— he is their help and shield.*
*Psalm 34:4 I sought the LORD, and he answered me; he delivered me from all my fears.*

**Action Plan:**

1. Pray for the faith to surrender your worries and anxieties.

2. Replace fear with trust in God's wisdom and timing.

3. Cultivate a heart of gratitude for His guidance.

**Prayer**:

## DAY 30
## Restoring Broken Trust

Proverbs 3:3-4 (NIV) - "Let love and faithfulness never leave you; bind them around your neck, write them on the tablet of your heart. Then you will win favour and a good name in the sight of God and man."

Restoring broken trust is a testament to God's redemptive power. As women of faith, we may face moments of fractured relationships, but through love and faithfulness, we can rebuild what's been lost. Forgiveness and reconciliation become pathways to healing.

*Additional Scripture Reference:*

*1 Peter 5:10. 10 And the God of all grace, who called you to his eternal glory in Christ, after you have suffered a little while, will himself restore you and make you strong, firm and steadfast.*

**Action Plan;**

1. Seek God's wisdom and guidance in humility.

2. Extend forgiveness and open communication.

3. Embrace reconciliation as an opportunity for growth.

**Prayer:**

*Heavenly Father, grant us the strength and wisdom to restore broken trust. May Your love and faithfulness guide us in mending what's been torn and rebuilding with grace. In Jesus name, we pray. Amen.*

Lamentations 3:22-23 (NIV) - "Because of the Lord's great love we are not consumed, for his compassions never fail. They are new every morning; great is your faithfulness."

Renewing faith daily is an embrace of God's boundless grace. As women of faith, each day offers a fresh canvas to deepen our trust in Him. His unwavering love, like the dawn, brings hope, and His mercies are ever new.

*Additional Scripture Reference:*

*2 Corinthians 4:16*

*"So we do not lose heart. Though our outer self is wasting away, our inner self is being renewed day by day."*

## Action Plan:

1. Begin each morning in prayer and gratitude.

2. Meditate on His Word, drawing strength from its wisdom.

3. Share your faith journey with others, inspiring mutual growth.

## Prayer:

*Heavenly Father, renew our faith daily as we bask in Your unending compassion. May Your faithfulness be our guide, filling each day with hope and purpose. In Jesus Name, we pray. Amen.*

## Let's Prayer:

Dear Heavenly Father,

As we conclude this year-long journey of devotion, we are filled with gratitude for the bonds we've formed, the wisdom we've gained, and the strength we've discovered. You've shown us the way, guiding us through each day, and we are humbled by your unwavering love.

Lord, may the seeds of inspiration sown in these pages continue to flourish in our hearts, reminding us of your grace and the incredible power of sisterhood. May we carry the lessons learned here into the world, sharing your light and love with all we meet.

As we step into the next chapter of our lives, we ask for your guidance and protection. Keep us rooted in your word, and may our lives be a testament to your faithfulness.

In your holy name, we pray.

Amen.

# REVIEW

Dear Devotional Readers,

We hope you have found our 365-day journey together in our women's devotional both inspiring and uplifting. Your support and engagement have been a source of immense joy and motivation for us.

We kindly ask you to take a moment to share your thoughts about the book by leaving a review. Your feedback is invaluable in helping others discover the transformative power of these devotionals. Whether it's a few sentences or a more detailed reflection, your review can make a significant impact.

By sharing your insights, you not only contribute to the growth of our community but also help fellow readers connect with the spiritual guidance and encouragement offered within these pages. Your words can be a beacon of hope for someone seeking solace, inspiration, or wisdom.

To leave a review, simply visit the platform where you purchased or borrowed the book. Your feedback will go a long way in spreading the message of faith, unity, and empowerment among women around the world.

Thank you for being a part of this journey, and for helping us shine a light on the path for others.

With heartfelt gratitude,

Ezekiel's Publications

# About the Author

Ezekiel's Publications is a devoted Christian author on a mission to help believers strengthen their relationship with God through his inspirational writing. With a heart aflame with faith, Ezekiel has dedicated his life to guiding others on their spiritual journey. His profound understanding of Scripture and unwavering commitment to the Christian faith shine through his work.

Ezekiel's journey in faith has been marked by a deep desire to share the transformative power of God's love and wisdom. Through the "Daily Devotional 2024," he seeks to offer readers a daily source of encouragement, insight, and spiritual growth. His words are a testament to his belief in the boundless grace and compassion of God.

With each daily entry, Ezekiel's Publications invites readers to draw closer to the divine, providing them with the tools and inspiration needed to build a strong and enduring relationship with the Creator. His devotionals are a beacon of hope, illuminating the path to a deeper faith and a more profound connection with God.

Printed in Great Britain
by Amazon

34155314R00190